Sweet Delights from
a Thousand and One Nights

We dedicate this book to Freda Abu Rizk (Bourzk) Salloum

Wife of Habeeb and mother of Muna and Leila, she was the person who convinced us to write about the history of Arab sweets, one of her favourite subjects. Her love for and pride in her origins inspired her daughters to learn from her and to transcribe what she found best in Arab cuisine. Freda believed in continuing the traditions of old Damascus, for it was she who learned from her mother the continuity of her family's cooking techniques, their secrets and their flavours. Unexpectedly, she left us, but her spirit remains within as we continue what she loved. It was Freda, or 'Sitty', who urged us to dedicate this book to her precious grandchildren, the 'sweets of her life', Laith, Mazin, Jinaan and Shaadi, and to her great-grandsons, Bilal and Tamer, who were to be born after her passing. For it was Freda who said, 'For the love of their heritage and with our past, we give you our future to pass on.'

Sweet Delights

from

a Thousand and

One Nights

The Story of Traditional Arab Sweets

Habeeb Salloum
Muna Salloum
Leila Salloum Elias

I.B. TAURIS

LONDON · NEW YORK

Published in 2013 by I.B.Tauris & Co. Ltd
6 Salem Road, London W2 4BU
175 Fifth Avenue, New York NY 10010
www.ibtauris.com

Distributed in the United States and Canada Exclusively by
Palgrave Macmillan, 175 Fifth Avenue, New York NY 10010

ISBN: 978 1 78076 464 1

A full CIP record for this book is available from the British Library
A full CIP record is available from the Library of Congress

Library of Congress Catalog Card Number: available

Designed and typeset by Dexter Haven Associates Ltd, London
Printed and bound in Great Britain by T.J. International, Padstow, Cornwall

MIX
Paper from
responsible sources
FSC   FSC® C013056
www.fsc.org

Contents

List of plates

كل طعام لا حلوى فيه فهو خداج

Every meal without a sweet is an imperfection.
(al-Raghib al-Asbahani II 620–21)

Acknowledgements

Working on these recipes from the medieval period of Arab history has been an exciting and adventurous challenge. They have been a source of great pleasure and discussion in our household and among friends, family and colleagues.

Our special thanks to Issam for his assistance in explaining certain nuances in specific Arabic phrases; to Laith, Mazin, Jinaan and Shaadi for their patience in taking many of the photographs, their taste-testing and their comments about many of the desserts; and to Yusuf and Aida for spending hours with the authors endlessly re-reading ambiguous passages in classical and medieval Arabic literature. Their interest was worth the effort, done with compassion for and pride in the heritage of their ancestors.

Our gratitude also goes out to Nawal Nasrallah, who clarified some terms from al-Warraq's *Kitab al-Tabikh*, and to Charles Perry for providing us with his unpublished translation of Ibn Jazlah's *Minhaj al-Bayan*, based upon the British Library's manuscript.

Moreover, we acknowledge the University of Toronto and Penn State University library staff for their assistance in obtaining research materials off campus, essential to this study.

And then, of course, there are our friends, colleagues and neighbours who, without hesitation, volunteered to try our adaptations of the medieval sweets. Some even deserve special mention for their readiness to drop by to try a sweet or two or three or to decipher a troublesome old-country mode of preparation.

To all we express our thanks for the tremendous encouragement to complete this project in order to expose the rich culinary history of Arab sweets.

However, most importantly, we thank the writers of these medieval Arabic cookbooks for recording for us what they thought best in their times.

Glossary

Baqlawa	A sweet made of filo pastry sheets with a nut filling and covered with a flavoured sugar-based syrup.
daniq	A measure, equal to one-sixth of a dirham, or approximately half a gram.
dibs rumman	Pomegranate syrup, available in Middle Eastern and Mediterranean grocery outlets.
dinar	A measure, equal to between two-thirds and one teaspoon; also called *mithqal* (in the eastern Arab world between 4¼ and 4½g; in al-Andalus, 5¾g).
dirham	A measure, equal to six *daniq*, or half to three-quarters of a teaspoon (in the eastern Arab world, approximately 3g; in al-Andalus, a little under 4g).
Faludhaj	A sweet and rich pudding or candy.
filo pastry	In the Arab East, filo is called *Baqlawa* dough, a paper-thin dough that originated in the Middle East, where it is a popular base for pastries. Filo pastry is typically sold frozen in one-pound packages in the frozen-food section of supermarkets and Mediterranean and Middle Eastern markets. Before use the box of filo pastry should be defrosted in a refrigerator overnight for about eight hours and then allowed to sit at room temperature for about half an hour. Frozen filo pastry can be kept for up to two months in the freezer. Work quickly with filo, and place a slightly dampened tea towel over any portion of the dough you are not working with to avoid the sheets drying. It is best to assemble all ingredients before beginning a recipe using filo pastry.
Ghurayba	Shortbread-type Arab cookies.
Halwa	Essentially a sweetmeat coming in many forms; the term itself means 'sweet' in Arabic.

Jawadhib	A sweet pudding placed beneath a roasting piece of meat in the *tannur*, to catch the meat drippings.
jubn	Arabic word for cheese.
jullab	A thick rose water sugar-based syrup also used for medicinal purposes.
kataifi	Shredded filo pastry. This can be found in the frozen or refrigerated section of Middle Eastern and Mediterranean groceries and at some of the larger supermarkets. If bought frozen, allow to thaw overnight in the refrigerator before using.
kayl	A measure of dry volume, equal to approximately 1⅕kg, also the name given to the utensil *kalayja* used to measure a *kayl* or *kalayja*.
Khabis	A condensed or jelly-like pudding.
Kunafa	Paper-thin sheets of pastry or a vermicelli type and the name of a specific dessert.
Lawzinaj	Almond-based sweet filo pastry; as a candy, 'the original marzipan', or a very thin pastry dough wrapped around an almond-sugar-based filling.
Ma'mul	Arab cookies with a shortbread-like texture, formed in moulds and stuffed with dates or various types of nuts.
Ma'muniya	A rice-flour pudding, today more popular as a semolina pudding.
mudd	A measure, equal to two *ratl*s, or 812½ g in the eastern Arab world, 4⅓ litres in *al-Maghrib*.
Mushabbak	A deep-fried latticed fritter.
Natif	A type of Arab nougat.
orange blossom water	Called *ma' al-zahr* in Arabic, a distilled water which has been infused with essential oil extracted from the fragrant blossoms of the bitter Seville orange – noted for its fresh citrus scent more than its bitter fruit. It is popularly used in Arab and Iranian desserts, and can be purchased in any Arab, Indian, Iranian or Turkish grocery, or from international food speciality stores. Once opened, it should be stored in the refrigerator.
qashta	A thick custard-like cream used for stuffing a wide variety of sweets.
Qata'if	Pancake-like pockets filled with *qashta* or a nut filling and drenched in a sugar-based syrup. They are also referred to as *qatayif.*
qatr	A sugar-based syrup flavoured with rose water or orange blossom water and used in most Arab sweets.

ratl	A measure, equal to 12 *uqiya*s, or half a kilogram, or two cups of liquid (406g in the eastern Arab world and al-Andalus).
rose water	Called *ma' ward* in Arabic: made from the extract/essence of distilled red and pink rose flowers. The returning Crusaders introduced this extract/essence into European cooking from the Holy Land. In medieval Britain the rose aroma in food flourished, becoming popular in drinks, jams and sweets. It is near essential in the preparation of many Arab desserts and beverages and used sparingly because of its strong aroma and flavour. Like orange blossom water it is available in Arab, Indian, Iranian and Turkish groceries or from international food speciality stores. Store in the refrigerator once opened.
saffron	The dried stigma of the yellow crocus native to the Mediterranean. It is available in threads or as a powder. It is expensive and can be purchased in Middle Eastern and Indian supermarkets and in some western supermarkets. If properly stored in a cool dark place in an airtight container, it can keep for at least three years.
samidh	In medieval recipes, a type of flour, similar to today's semolina.
Sanbusak	When referring to sweets, deep-fried triangular, rectangular or half-moon-shaped pastries stuffed with nuts.
uqiya	A measure, equal to 10 dirhams, or approximately two tablespoons (in the eastern Arab world, $33\frac{4}{5}$g; in al-Andalus, 39 grams).

About this book

This book is not solely a cookbook, nor is it a historical study, rather a combination. It deals with Arab sweets presented in medieval Arabic culinary sources. Working from these original cookbooks, we chose recipes that represented an array of what the elite of medieval Arab society enjoyed. These source recipes show what their authors were saying about their own culture, their own cuisine and their own preferences. This is a reflection of the pleasures of their society and milieu, sitting at the tables of caliphs, kings, emirs, sultans and nobles.

It was not only their works that described the pleasures of desserts. There is ample evidence in Arabic literature to confirm the same. In many cases, anecdotes allude to or give the history of a sweet, or even tell us who enjoyed it. In this sense, we present a blend of cooking and history from the early-medieval Arab world.

Part of this history is Arab influence in the field of sweets. With the Arab conquests, the conquerors' food left an impact on the territories they controlled that remains today.

Each sweet presented in this book includes the original source recipe, the adaptation of it and, in many cases, its modern version. We have attempted to be as faithful as possible to the original. In some instances, however, we were obliged to work with contemporary ingredients or utensils. For example, in some recipes the fat from the sheep's tail must be melted and the liquid retained for use in a dish. We have replaced that ingredient with either shortening or butter.

For a number of the medieval recipes, we present their contemporary versions, and have identified those regions of the world where they are still enjoyed, albeit in most cases under a different name. Although these modern versions retain the original concept of their predecessors, the addition of new ingredients and preparation techniques, over the centuries, testifies that something must have tasted good for it to have lasted.

There are also the times when we simply used our tastebuds in cooking. A case in point is *samidh*, an ingredient called for in a number of the recipes. Nawal Nasrallah's definition of this type of flour is that it is a finely ground flour, while Charles Perry, on the other hand, explains that *samidh* is coarser than flour ('A Critique' 4, 37). For certain recipes, we tried both flour and extra-fine semolina. The extra-fine worked out well taste-wise and texture-wise. This type of semolina is available in Middle Eastern and Mediterranean markets.

We have classified the assortment of sweets by: pastries; cookies; cakes and pies; candies; and puddings and other sweet delights. The name of each recipe is given in transliterated form, followed by its English literal translation in brackets. We found this important because, simply, the names of many of the sweets are interesting and sometimes seemingly bizarre, or allow for a glimpse into the history. We have then given an appropriate descriptive name to each of the sweets for a clearer understanding as to what the sweet actually is.

A NOTE ON THE TRANSLATION OF THE ARABIC SOURCE RECIPES

We decided to translate rather rigidly from the Arabic into the English in order that the reader be alerted to the many instances of difficult interpretation regarding amounts, cooking methods and ambiguous instruction. Many times pronouns proved to be the problem when trying to distinguish the ingredient to which the author was referring. We felt that the reader should share the authors' experience when translating and adapting the recipe. Of course we could have provided a much clearer translation, but this would have taken away from the flavour of the original.

Concerning the recipes from al-Baghdadi's *Kitab al-Tabikh*, although we used the 1934 Arabic text edited by al-Jalabi as the base of our translations, we did incorporate those corrections made by Perry in his *A Baghdad Cookery Book*.

Although it would have been preferable to use the standard method of transliteration for Arabic recipe names and names of authors and other individuals mentioned in this book, we recognise that the exclusion of diacritical marks makes for an easier reading of the text.

HOW TO USE THIS BOOK

The original medieval recipes are referred to as the 'Historical version'. Each recipe is translated from Arabic into English, followed by the name of the source cookbook and/or author. The name(s) of the translator(s) is also indicated. This is then followed by an adaptation of the 'Historical version', referred to as the 'Traditional recipe'. Modern variations of the 'Historical version' are labelled 'Modern recipe'.

ℐ Introduction

If you ask an Arab to name his favourite sweet, responses may vary from *Baqlawa*, a pastry of fine layers of filo pastry with a nut filling, to *Kunafa*, with its hot cheese filling. Others may prefer *Asabi' Zaynab*, *Qata'if* or *Mushabbak* drenched in their syrup. All are rich and tasty, desserts fit to be served to caliph or king.

A medieval Arab might have answered the same. Eleven centuries ago these same sweets with similar names or preparation were present at the tables of caliphs, emirs and society's elite as fashionable, stylish and the *crème de la crème* of Arab cuisine.

We chose the subject of medieval Arab sweets because they fascinate us. Their descriptions, the instructions on how to prepare, decorate and serve them, told us that time and care were taken to create them. Here was sophistication and seriousness in the art of making sweets. Whether a simple fritter or an elaborate nut-filled rolled pastry soaked in syrup, or a brittle nut sweet created from meringue, or even a cookie shaped like the ankle of a gazelle, they were so enjoyed that they – or versions of them – endure. In today's Arab world and in Spain, Portugal, Sicily and Malta, they – or traces of them – remain. The fact that they have gone on being enjoyed means that something about them was just right.

These medieval sweets came to affect the kitchens of almost every region of southern Europe, and some of them came, centuries later, to be the celebrated delicacy of another country. How and why this happened became our subject.

1

WHAT ARE ARAB SWEETS?

Arab sweets can be defined as light and flaky, aromatic and spiced, sweet and savoury, crunchy, crumbly, smooth and creamy, rich and buttery, melt-in-the-mouth, spongy and soft. Deep-fried or baked, or simply prepared and left to cool, Arab sweets are made with filo pastry or *kataifi* (shredded filo pastry), with semolina or flour and sweetened with honey, aromatic syrups or sugar. There are also puddings and candies. Most include nuts, a type of sweet cheese or dates, apricots or other fruits for their fillings or for their garnish.

As the Arab empire expanded, Arab sweets took on many characteristics from regions that had had a long culinary history. The influences of the Far East, India and Persia formed the bases for the development of sweets in the Arab East.

It was the eastern Arabs who moved west, beginning in the seventh century and eventually settling in North Africa and the Iberian Peninsula. Bringing with them the qualities and features of the flourishing civilisations of Damascus and Baghdad, they also brought their food processes, ingredients, manners of presentation and culinary etiquette. In many cases, their eastern sweets retained the same names, *Lawzinaj* (of almonds), or were identified by region, *Qahiriyat* ('of the city of Cairo'), or by an individual, *Ma'muniya* (of the Caliph Ma'mun).

These sweets were transmitted to North Africa, al-Andalus, Sicily and beyond. Making use of ingredients, locally grown and available in their own regions and varying somewhat in taste, these sweets remained basically the same as their eastern counterparts. Syrups, for example, used in many of the medieval Arab sweets were generally rose water-based, even though today's Moroccan desserts are often made with orange blossom water. In the Arab East today, rose water and orange blossom water are almost interchangeable flavourings used in dessert making. With the availability of oranges and rose petals from the Middle East to North Africa, these fragrant ingredients form part of the identity of Arab sweets.

The same can be said about almonds. With the vast cultivation of almonds after the Arab conquest of North Africa and the Iberian Peninsula, almonds became widely available and today are one of the most common types of nuts used in Andalusian and North African cooking. Used quite liberally in sweets in both regions, the almond's status equalled that of the popular pistachio in the preparation of eastern sweets. Today, North African and Spanish sweets continue the heritage of the almond, while the sweets of the eastern Arab countries prefer the pistachio. Thus it is that desserts through the Arab world reflect regional tastes and a continuity of traditional favourites.

THE ROLE OF ARAB SWEETS

Arabs enjoy fruit after a meal, the natural dessert. Sweets, on the other hand, are not part of the normal meal plan. Rather, they are reserved more for special and social occasions, entertaining guests, or as part of the long festive tables during Ramadan, Eid al-Fitr, Eid al-Adha, Christmas and Easter. During these celebrations sweets such as *Qata'if, Ma'mul, Baqlawa, Ghurayba* and *Mushabbak* come out in full force. *Baqlawa* and other varieties of layered filo pastry laden with nuts and drenched in syrup are part of the special-occasion dessert table. Yet this is not to say that these types of sweets are only eaten or made at specific times; rather, they are generally available whenever the sweet tooth dictates.

In Morocco, to break the fast after sunset during Ramadan, *Halwa Shabakiya* is served alongside *Harira* soup. There it is also the norm to serve, at the end of the evening, sweets accompanied with sweetened mint tea. In the Arab East, more particularly Syria, Lebanon, Palestine and Jordan, a type of *Kunafa* served on a sesame-seed bun is eaten for breakfast, while *Zalabiya* dipped in honey is popular for a midday or evening snack. *Yo-yo*s in Tunisia can be purchased from street vendors throughout the day, while the ever-popular North African pancake-like *Beghrir* with honey is a good afternoon snack.

Sweets are part of social culture in the Arab world, where guests are held in high esteem. Food plays its part in this hospitality. The host and hostess offer their best – and the best always includes sweets. Where once these were prepared at home, indicating that the cook had taken the time and gone to the expense to prepare these rich and lavish delicacies, today they are more than usually supplied by the speciality pastry shops that are located in almost all major cities and towns. Whether take-out or eat-in, one can choose from trays and trays of assorted filled filo sweets and all types of semolina cookies. If ninth-century Baghdad could boast over fifty types of sweets available in its souks, today's pastry-sellers in Damascus, Baghdad, Tripoli, Cairo and Marrakesh would put them to shame.

KEY INGREDIENTS IN ARAB SWEETS

The key ingredients in modern Arab sweets are the same as those in medieval times. Almonds, pistachios, pine nuts and walnuts, dates, honey and sugar, clarified butter, custard-like cream, egg whites, rose water and orange blossom water, cinnamon, cardamom, aniseed, ginger, cloves and mahaleb have been important ingredients in the Arabic cookbooks since the tenth century. In addition, fruit has become a prominent ingredient in the production of sweets, leading to the creation of marmalades, jams, candied fruits and a dried-fruit industry.

Despite the introduction and popularity of foreign sweets such as petits fours and gateaux, traditional sweets and their ingredients seem to hold a sacred place in Arab culture. Also, the traditional sweetening agents honey, sugar, dates or sugar- or fruit-based syrups continue to be the basic sweeteners used.

Honey was the main agent for sweetening foods in Europe and, generally, the Middle East before the seventh-century conquest of Persia by the Arabs. Not only a natural sweetener, it was healthy. So embedded was honey in the cuisine of tenth-century Baghdad that one cookbook author includes over ten types of prepared honey for use in cooking (Nasrallah *Annals* 592–93). Although honey continued to be a substantive staple in preparing sweets and even in certain main dishes, it was sugar that revolutionised the dessert table.

When the Arabs invaded Persia, they were introduced to the age-old Persian process of sugar produced from cane. Persia itself had learned the method of crystallising sugar from India, and had its own refineries. Adopting and further developing the techniques of refining sugar, the Arabs planted sugar-cane plantations across their empire, in Syria, Egypt, North Africa and al-Andalus, and by the tenth century the Arabs were growing the crop in Sicily, all the while perfecting the process of refining it in their sugar mills.

Sugar refining became highly developed, and several qualities of sugar were produced and exported to other countries. Good examples of the varieties can be found throughout al-Warraq's culinary manual: *daqiq al-sukkar* (powdered sugar), *sukkar* (generic term), *sukkar abyad* (white, refined and pure cane sugar), *sukkar ahmar* (red sugar, unrefined crystallised brown cane sugar), *sukkar mutayyib* (sugar perfumed with aromatics), *sukkar nabat* (rock-candy sugar), *sukkar qand* or *qand* (cane sugar), *sukkar sulaymani* (hard sugar candy made from white cane sugar), *sukkar ubluj* (a superior white cane sugar) and *tabarzad* (fine quality white and refined sugar) (Nasrallah *Annals* 595, 599–602).

Within this category of sweetening agents, one must not forget *jullab*, a man-made sweetener. This is a thick rose water sugar-based syrup also used for medicinal purposes. The *Anonymous Andalusian Cookbook*, besides including a simple recipe on how to prepare the syrup, advises that two *uqiya*s of it and three of hot water fortifies the stomach and liver and purifies and lightens the body (14).

Jullab served as a base for drinks or could be used as a replacement for syrups in recipes. The English 'julep' is from the Arabic term, which ultimately derives from Persian *gulab*, itself a compound of *gul* ('rose') and *ab* ('water').

Despite the lavishness of the caliph's tables and the influx of new ingredients from across the empire, the Arabs, from whatever strata of society, remained loyal to the original and natural sweet of the desert. The date – never forgotten – kept pace with the development of society, retaining its stature as one of the staples of Arab sweets.

For the medieval tables of the elite, the simple date would transform over time into gourmet desserts. In al-Andalus, one sweet includes thin flatbreads layered with pounded dates; honeyed dates were popular throughout the entire empire; and the age-old Bedouin dish of dates, butter and curds eventually took on an elaborate form with the addition of walnuts, almonds, pistachios and sesame seeds (*Kanz* 130). A well-known condensed pudding made of dates, *Khabis*, popular among the Quraysh, the tribe of the Prophet Muhammad, continued to be a favourite, appearing in al-Warraq's tenth-century manual but in more lavish forms (257).

MEDICINAL/HEALTH FACTORS

The study of medicine contributed to widespread interest in cuisine in the medieval Arab world. Rulers' personal physicians would be present at mealtimes to warn, advise and watch what was being served and what was being eaten. There are anecdotes in Arabic literature warning of indigestion, bloating and abdominal discomfort when certain foods were overeaten or eaten too quickly, and when it was safe to consume particular foods, hot or cold.

With the influx of imported foodstuffs and the expansion of agriculture, physicians had more to work with. Specialist medical treatises dealt with diet, including the benefits and harm of various ingredients, why specific foods or dishes, for example, should be eaten to alleviate an illness. Dietetic manuals could also be read as cookbooks – manuals for good and healthy living. Sweets were part of this new study.

Physicians would recommend, for instance, certain sweets for chest and lung congestion, while other sweets were to be eaten to improve digestion. In fact, one caliph's personal physician advised that sweets should be eaten after the meal for digestive reasons (al-Raghib al-Asbahani II 619).

PREPARATION: UTENSILS AND PRESENTATION

What distinguishes Arab sweets are the techniques involved in their preparation. While some are simple to prepare, others need time and patience. Of course the Arab world has changed a great deal since medieval times. Nearly every city and town has its own pastry shops where, just as in medieval times, sweets can be bought fresh-made or in bulk, especially during holidays and festivities. However, if one chooses to make them at home, specific utensils are required.

In the medieval Arabic culinary treatises, certain types of utensils are specified for making desserts. For example, dough made with yeast rises in a container called the *mi'jana*; the rolling pin, *shawbaq*, is a common feature in the cookbooks; as is the *salaya*, a marble slab onto which hot candy is poured and allowed to cool; the *mihrak*, a stirring poker for cooking; and the *qasaba*, a wooden cane (sometimes made of a metal), used for shaping dough for frying or just for stirring. There are stamp moulds made of wood or other types of materials for baking cookies. These were used to stamp decorative impressions on sweets designed in the form of fish, birds, fruit, cattle and other images (al-Warraq 12–13).

The presentation of the dessert on the table was also an important element in the creative aspect. Appearance was important. The verb *zayyana* ('to adorn or embellish') is found in some cooking instructions as the final step before serving a dish of sweets. For presentation purposes, almonds can be dyed red or yellow when used as a garnish, and in some recipes coloured sugars and nuts added beauty to a dish. While these embellishments sometimes added to the taste of the dish, more than anything they were applied for the pleasure of the eye. Even in al-Andalus, 'the frequency and abundance of information on dish garnishes suggest that this was also a common practice' (Marín 206).

As it was then, so it is today. Appearance remains part of the success of a sweet. *Qalibs*, or moulds used for today's *Ma'mul* cookies, vary in size, shape and design. These shortbread-type cookies stuffed with either dates or nuts present a kaleidoscope of designs and shapes on the sweet table. *Mushabbak*, a deep-fried latticework fritter, is often made rose-coloured as an alternative to its standard golden colour. Some sweets are not complete without a garnish of ground pistachios or a combination of cinnamon and powdered sugar, the latter most popular for North African sweets.

From the Arab East to the Arab West, a book is judged by its cover in the realm of sweets. How a sweet looks, aside from its taste, reflects the skill of the cook, the time taken to prepare it and – just as it did on the tables of the caliphs – presents something rich and luxurious, reflecting the tradition of its history.

REGIONAL INFLUENCE

The greatest influences on the cuisine of al-Andalus came from the constant influx of Arab immigrants from the Arab East, who brought their knowledge to the western peninsula. This occurred especially between the ninth and twelfth centuries. Baghdad, the cultural and political capital of the Arab/Islamic world, epitomised the best there was to offer in the east. And it was from al-Andalus that Europe came to meet this fusion, significantly when Arab culture was defined by those who wished to imitate its luxurious and intellectual life and exotic atmosphere.

One of the most important contributors to the movement of east to west was the ninth-century Ziryab, who emigrated from Baghdad to al-Andalus in AD 822. He brought with him many dishes from his native city, introduced fine tablecloths and glassware, eating utensils and kitchen gadgets, Baghdadi royal court dishes, and developed a new order of serving food for the table. Meals were served in separate courses that included soups, entrées and desserts. This method of serving then spread across the Pyrenees to Europe, becoming the standard meal pattern we still use today.

Iberia's almost eight centuries of Arab culinary heritage is found especially in its sweets. Flavoured with rose water, oranges, aniseed, cinnamon, ginger, nutmeg, cloves, sesame seeds, almonds, pistachios, pine nuts and sweets drenched in honey, or those made or sprinkled with sugar, are the diehard markers identifying their Arab legacy.

Examples of these are *Cabello de Angel*, a type of pumpkin jam; *Huesos de Santo*, marzipan cylinders stuffed with a custard made of egg yolk; *Borrachos* or *Borrachuelos*, cookies sweetened with a honey syrup; and *Turrón*, a soft or crispy candy slab and a favourite Christmas treat in Spain, based exclusively on almonds, eggs and honey or sugar, both legacies of Moorish times. There is also the famous marzipan, made only from almond paste and sugar, for which Spain has gained worldwide fame. Made in Toledo since the eighth century, it comes in various shapes, stuffed with pine nuts or egg yolks crystallised in sugar. In Rioja people add lemon, while in Andalusia it comes in the shape of bars stuffed with crystallised fruits and iced with sugar.

From Valencia's toasted almond cake, Murcia's fig bread and walnut cake, to Medina Sidonia's *Alfajores*, one of the city's most notable sweets made of almonds, hazelnuts, sugar, honey, cloves, cinnamon and coriander, the sweets of southern Spain symbolise the continuity of the Arab influences in that province's culinary tradition.

Following the tradition of Iberia, many of Sicily's desserts hold onto the memories of the Arab presence there (AD 827–1091). The Arabs introduced candied fruits, pistachios, citrus and cinnamon into Sicily's pastry world, along with the art of making confections, combining nuts and fruits with sugar and honey.

The two most famous Sicilian desserts, *Cannoli* and *Cassata*, trace their names and roots back to the Arab period. Other Arab sweets are marzipan, *Cubaita*, a sesame-seed candy, and *Sfinci*, deep-fried balls dipped in honey with a spongy interior. In fact, little appears to have changed between the mention of *Sfingiarius* selling *Sfinci* in a thirteenth-century literary work from Palermo and sellers of the fried fritter in Sicily and Tunisia today (Wright *Mediterranean* 113).

Arab innovations in Sicilian pastry-making included new ingredients that changed the definition of Sicilian sweets. This involved spices such as saffron, cinnamon, aniseed and cloves; almonds, pine nuts and pistachios; sesame seeds; and stuffings made with almonds, sugar and spices like those in today's *Mustazzuoli*. The Arabs also introduced the technique of preserving and candying various fruits. Some new fruits were introduced by the Arabs into Sicily, such as the watermelon in the tenth century. For cooking purposes, its pulp was liquefied and used as an ingredient in puddings such as *Gelo di Melone*, while its seeds were roasted then pounded into a paste or crushed into cakes.

Another European cuisine in which the Arabs left their mark is the Maltese. Many of the island's food and cooking terms still carry their Arabic names: *bajd* ('eggs', from the Arabic *bayd*); *forn* ('oven', from *furn*); *ftira* (a type of bread, from *fatira*); and *gbejniet* ('cheese', from *jubn*). *Imqaret* or *Maqaret* (Maltese date turnovers), which are the *Maqrud* of Tunisia, recall the period of the Arab rule there between AD 870 and 1060.

The dispersal of Arab-inspired sweets went even further. The 'Age of Discovery' brought Spain and Portugal to the New World. With this conquest, not only did the languages and customs of Europe infiltrate the Central and South American regions, but also the culinary practices that eventually left a lasting influence on the cuisine of the Americas. In the area of sweets, the dishes taken to the Americas by the Spanish and Portuguese were hardly altered. Today, few in these countries realise that when they eat their *Buñuelos*, Mexican Wedding Cookies, *Alfajores* and *Arroz con Leche*, they are enjoying sweet dishes inherited from the cooks of Baghdad and Damascus. Equally the chefs of the caliphs in medieval Baghdad would have never dreamt that their creations would one day be eaten in such faraway lands.

Sweets stood at the pinnacle of the countless dishes that the Arabs created. They have delighted the masses, from royalty to rural peasant, for millennia. In the case of medieval Arab cookery these pastries, sweets, puddings and candies became the subject of legend, poetry and gastronomic debates and contests, and most significantly part of our modern world.

♪ The medieval sources

The Arabic culinary treatises which have survived reflect the cooking techniques and tastes of the urban middle class of both the eastern and western Arab world. They include dishes prepared for the royal courts, specifying in many cases those prepared for or by caliphs, sultans, viziers and court physicians. Also included are recipes prepared by the general population. These are not only cooking manuals but also inform the reader about personal hygiene, cleanliness of the kitchen, its utensils and the cook, presentation of the dishes and etiquette of the guest. Nutrition and diet also play a part in these texts.

A culinary historian's dream would be to locate the 'lost' Arabic cookbooks that preceded the earliest tenth-century cookbook from Baghdad by al-Warraq. Although some excerpts from these earlier authors' works are preserved in the medieval Arabic culinary works that we have today, no doubt the originals would have provided an even greater insight into an earlier courtly cuisine enjoyed in Baghdad and other major cities across the Arab/Islamic empire. Many of these works were written by princes, or by high-ranking people at court: the Abbasid Caliph Ibrahim ibn al-Mahdi; the general and prefect al-Harith ibn Bashkhir, who lived during the reign of Harun al-Rashid (r. AD 786–809); and the famous ninth-century poet Ibrahim ibn 'Abbas al-Suli, a poet and civil servant (Rodinson 'Studies in' 98).

However, what we do know is that the Caliphs al-Ma'mun (d. AD 833), al-Mu'tasim (d. AD 842) and al-Wathiq (d. AD 847), the physician Yuhanna ibn Masawayh (d. AD 857), the courtier Yahya ibn Khalid al-Barmaki (d. AD 805), the ninth-century astronomer Yahya ibn Abi Mansur al-Mawsili, and Abu Samin, most probably a professional chef in the service of the Caliph al-Wathiq, all delved into the world of fine cuisine.

History records the stories of individuals, mainly the prominent or significant. However, there are many whose names do not fit into this category and yet have left their imprint on the developing nature of their own society. Such is the case with numerous cooks and chefs who contributed to the medieval Arab kitchen and whose names we come across in Arabic literature, biographical indexes or who are simply referred to by name in a title of a recipe.

Some of these cooks are Hubaysh ibn 'Umar al-Dimashqi, cook of al-Mahdi (*Taj al-'Arus* 4233); Bashir ibn Abi Hazim al-Qasim ibn Dinar, cook of al-Hajjaj ibn Yusuf al-Thaqafi (AD 661–714), Governor of Iraq (Ibn Kathir X 183); Ibrahim, cook of Sultan Qalaj Arslan ibn Saljuq al-Rumi (Yaqut al-Hamawi *Mu'jam al-Buldan* 1590) and Itakh, in AD 814 cook to the Caliph al-Mu'tasim, a cook who rose to high position under this Caliph and later under the Caliphs al-Wathiq and al-Mutawakkil (r. AD 847–861). Itakh would eventually become one of the emirs of Mecca, and responsible for the army (Ibn Kathir X 312).

These few were cooks and bakers, sweet-makers and confectioners. Their dishes graced the tables of caliphs, viziers, notables and the elite of society. The cook, with his knowledge of the rules of cookery, was the unspoken hero, playing an important role in elevating the host's stature.

The works listed below were used as the sources for this study. Our preference was to make use of the edited Arabic texts of these source manuals, edited by established scholars and available in academic institutions near us. We are duly grateful to these scholars, who have devoted their time and effort to facilitate our research venture.

Al-Baghdadi, Muhammad ibn al-Hasan ibn Muhammad ibn al-Karim al-Katib (d. AD 1240) wrote *Kitab al-Tabikh* (*The Book of Cookery*) in Baghdad in AD 1226, during the period of the Abbasids. By virtue of his title (*al-Katib*), al-Baghdadi appears to have been a secretary and a well-cultured man. Yet, he took great pleasure and happiness in food. The book contains approximately 160 of the author's favourite recipes. Al-Baghdadi wrote his culinary treatise almost three decades before the destruction and devastation of Baghdad by the Mongols in 1258 AD and, therefore, his book is one of the most valuable representations of the culinary tradition of the once great capital of the Islamic empire. The book has been translated into English by A.J. Arberry and, more recently, by Charles Perry.

Hereafter referred to as: al-Baghdadi.

Generally, it is Ibn al-'Adim, Kamal al-Din 'Umar ibn Ahmad (AD 1192–1262) who is given credit as the author of *Kitab al-Wusla ilà al-Habib fi Wasf al-Tayyibat wa al-Tib* (*Book of the Bond of Friendship in the Description of Good Dishes and Perfumes*), having written it *c.* AD 1261. Ibn al-'Adim hailed from Aleppo and was one of the great-nephews of Salah al-Din al-Ayyubi (Saladin). He would, then, be someone close to the court because of his many links to the Sultan, the Sultan's cooks and the royal kitchens. He was also a historian who wrote about Aleppo and was appointed as a *qadi* (judge) and as a vizier to Aleppo's Ayyubid rulers, giving him the status of frequent visitor to the courts of the Ayyubid princes. When the Mongols destroyed his native city in AD 1260, he fled to Egypt. The importance of this book is that it details the foods enjoyed in the Syrian courts and the mannerisms of food culture in the thirteenth-century Syrian milieu. The first part of the *Wusla* deals with table manners, the second contains numerous recipes for drinks, omelettes, stews, roasted and fried meat, vegetables, rice, wheat, fruit and yogurt dishes, breads, a good number of pastries, sauces and syrups. There are 74 recipes for cooking chicken, for example, which show the ingenuity and reverence for creativity even in thirteenth-century gastronomy. The book is divided into ten chapters, one of which, titled 'Sweetmeats and Pastries', includes 25 sub-sections for sweets, sweetbreads, puddings and porridges.

Hereafter referred to as: Ibn al-'Adim.

Ibn Jazlah, Yahya ibn 'Isa (d. AD 1100), was a Baghdadi physician and author of the *Minhaj al-Bayan fi ma Yasta'miluhu al-Insan* (*A Systematic Exposition of What is Used by Man*), a medical lexicon in which he included recipes as remedies for specific ailments. He was also author of *Risala fi al-Sukkar (A Treatise on Sugar)*, in which he instructs the reader how, for example, to prepare honey, milk, musk, vinegar, ambergris and camphor (the latter two used for scents) for medical purposes. Both books were dedicated to the Caliph al-Muqtadi (r. AD 1075–1094) and shed light on the period between the earliest existing culinary text of al-Warraq and that of al-Baghdadi (see above). Of great importance is that the author was a physician, and his recipes were written from the perspective of a medical professional. There are over one hundred recipes. The book has been translated by Charles Perry (unpublished manuscript, 2003).

Hereafter referred to as: Ibn Jazlah.

Jamal al-Din Yusuf ibn Hasan ibn 'Abd al-Hadi, more commonly known as Ibn al-Mabrad (or Ibn al-Mubarrad) is the author of the fifteenth-century *Kitab al-Tibakha* (*The Book of Cookery*). Ibn al-Mabrad was a fifteenth-century Damascus legal scholar who also wrote short works on other assorted topics. His work includes 44 recipes, and according to Perry is the only Arabic recipe collection to have survived from the entire period between the fifteenth and the early nineteenth centuries. Although no recipes for desserts appear per se in the book, there is one for rice sweetened with honey. Similar to the modern Arab world's *Aruzz bi-Halib*, a rice pudding made with milk, we chose Ibn al-Mabrad's recipe due to its suitability as a dessert. It has been translated into English by Charles Perry and appears as a chapter in *Medieval Arab Cookery* (Rodinson, Arberry and Perry).

Hereafter referred to as: Ibn al-Mabrad.

The author of *Kanz al-Fawa'id fi Tanwi' al-Mawa'id* (*The Treasure of Useful Lessons in the Varieties of the Dining Table*) and its original date are unknown. However, due to details provided in the text, the editors of the Arabic manuscripts (Manuela

Marín and David Waines) have concluded that it may be Egyptian, written some time in the thirteenth or fourteenth centuries, during the Mamluk period. There are 750 recipes, to which 80 have been added in an appendix. These include recipes from Syria, Baghdad and Mosul, North Africa (al-Maghrib) and al-Andalus, Yemen, Greece, Georgia, Assiut, Nubia, Alexandria, Nablus, Turkey and Cairo, and the cooking habits of the Kurds, laying down for the record the story of the interaction of various cultures in the Arab world at that time. To date there is no English translation of the work.

Hereafter referred to as: *Kanz.*

Kitab Wasf al-At'imah al-Mu'tada (*Book of the Description of Familiar Foods*) was written during the fourteenth century during the Mamluk period, and the author, whose name is unknown, is Egyptian. According to Charles Perry, the cookbook seems to have been written for the author's own use. The book is mainly a compilation of the 160 recipes of al-Baghdadi's thirteenth-century *Kitab al-Tabikh* (see above) and about 260 recipes from various other sources. It has been translated into English by Charles Perry and appears as a chapter in *Medieval Arab Cookery* (Rodinson, Arberry and Perry). Perry's translation is based upon the two existing copies found in the Topkapi Palace in Istanbul, the earliest version dated AD 1373 and originally copied in Cairo.

Hereafter referred to as: *Familiar Foods.*

Ibn Razin al-Tujibi wrote *Fadala al-Khiwan fi Tayyibat al-Ta'am wa al-Alwan* (*The Delights of the Table and the Best Types of Prepared Foods*) some time between AD 1239 and 1269. The author was a native of Murcia. The book contains 441 recipes of Andalusian specialities, with additional ones from the eastern (*mashriqi*) Arab world. The *Fadala* is based upon the cooking techniques of al-Andalus and *al-Maghrib* (North Africa, especially Morocco). The manuscript was translated into Spanish as *La Cocina Arabigoandaluza* by Fernando de la Granja Santamaria in 1960 as a doctoral thesis.

Hereafter referred to as: al-Tujibi.

Al-Warraq's *Kitab al-Tabikh fi Islah al-Aghdhiya al-Ma'kulat wa Tayyib al-At'ima al-Masnu'at* (*The Book of Cookery and Preparing Nutritious Foods and (What is) Tasty of Prepared Foods*, better known in English as *The Book of Dishes*) is a late tenth-century collection of recipes from cookbooks from several centuries which are now lost. It includes 40 recipes from one of the greatest cooks known in Baghdad, Ibrahim ibn al-Mahdi, who was a half-brother to the famous Caliph Harun al-Rashid. It also contains recipes from Abu Samin, a chief cook to the Caliph al-Wathiq. The original work has been edited by Kaj Öhrnberg and Sahban Mroueh and published by The Finnish Oriental Society (Helsinki, January 1987). Nawal Nasrallah has completed an extraordinary English translation of this great work along with a glossary of cooking terms and ingredients, as well as notes about individuals and places to which references are made in the manual (Brill Oriental Society, 2007). Al-Warraq's recipe book not only provides excellent detailed recipes but also samples of *ta'miya* (gastronomic poetry), or rather recipes in poetic form.

Hereafter referred to as: al-Warraq.

The *Anonymous Andalusian Cookbook, Kitab al-Tabikh fi al-Maghrib wa al-Andalus fi 'Asr al-Muwahhidin, li-mu'allif majhul* (*The Book of Cooking in the Maghreb and Andalus in the Era of the Almohads*), is an anonymous Andalusian cookbook written during the early part of the thirteenth century. It contains 543 recipes, some originating in the eastern Arab world, such as excerpts from Ibrahim ibn al-Mahdi's cookbook. There are also recipes from North Africa and even a recipe attributed to Ziryab. Of all the existing medieval Arabic cookbooks, the *Anonymous Andalusian Cookbook* contains more recipes for sweets than for any other food category, about 94 in total. It has been translated by Charles Perry into English and is available at http://italophiles.com/andalusian_cookbook.pdf.

Hereafter referred to as: *Anonymous.*

$\mathcal{J}$ Basic recipes

QATR
SUGAR SYRUP

ᦸ Traditional and modern recipe ᦵ

Makes 2 cups (630 g)
Preparation time: 5 minutes
Cooking time: 15 minutes

Ingredients

2 cups (400 g) sugar
1 cup (250 ml) cold water
2 teaspoons lemon juice
1 tablespoon orange blossom water or rose water

Method

In a medium-sized saucepan, stir together the sugar and the water, then bring to the boil over a medium heat. Continue simmering for ten minutes, then stir in the lemon juice and allow to simmer for one more minute. Stir in the orange blossom water or the rose water. Reduce heat and cook for a further one minute. Set aside and allow to cool.

'ASAL SYRUP
HONEY SYRUP

∽ Traditional and modern recipe ๏

Makes 2 cups (680 g)
Preparation time: 2 minutes
Cooking time: 5 minutes

Ingredients
2 cups (680 g) liquid honey
¼ cup (57 g) unsalted butter

Method

In a medium-sized saucepan, pour in the honey, then add the butter. Over a medium-low heat, bring to the boil, stirring constantly. Reduce heat to very low and keep warm.

QASHTA
A THICK CUSTARD-LIKE CREAM FOR FILLINGS

∽ Traditional and modern recipe ๏

Makes 8 cups
Preparation time: 15 minutes
Cooking time: 35 minutes
Chilling time: 2 hours

Ingredients
1½ cups (180 g) cornstarch/cornflour
6 cups (1½ litres) whole milk
1½ cups (360 ml) whipping cream (double cream)
4 tablespoons granulated sugar
4 tablespoons rose water
4 tablespoons orange blossom water

Method

In a mixing bowl, mix together the cornstarch/cornflour and 1½ cups (360 ml) of the milk. Stir until smooth, making sure there are no lumps in the mixture.

In a large saucepan, stir together the remaining milk along with the cream. Add the sugar and mix well. Then stir in the rose water and the orange blossom water, blending well. Over a medium-low heat, continue to stir the saucepan contents until the liquid is heated through.

Add the cornstarch/cornflour–milk mixture to the heated saucepan contents and continue stirring over a medium-low heat until thick and bubbly.

Remove from the heat and pour into a bowl. Allow to sit until cool, then cover with plastic wrap/cling film and then refrigerate for at least two hours or until ready to use. This mixture will thicken as it cools.

Leftover *qashta* can be kept refrigerated for up to a week, covered with plastic wrap/cling film.

♪ Pastries

AL-SANBUSAK AL-HULU (SWEET SANBUSAK)
CRISPY FILO TRIANGLES STUFFED WITH NUTS

For the experienced cook

❧ *Historical version* ❧

You will need sugar, *qatr* or bee's honey, rose water, hazelnuts, sesame oil and the thin dough of the *Kunafa*. Pound the sugar and toast the hazelnuts and pound them coarsely and knead with the *qatr* of pounded sugar and rose water, or knead with bee's honey. Cut the *Kunafa* dough into the width of four fingers. Place on it a little of the filling on (each) one the amount you want. Roll it over the filling all the way. Cover (the edges) with a little dough. Fry in sesame oil. Put them on dishes and sprinkle the sugar and toasted hazelnuts over them. Serve.

Kanz, p. 49 (#114). Translated by Muna Salloum and Leila Salloum Elias.

Originating in the thirteenth and fourteenth centuries, *al-Sanbusak al-Hulu* can be best described as a fried pastry stuffed with a rich mixture of nuts. The *Kanz* recipe offers a filling of hazelnuts and sugar while in *Familiar Foods* a filling of almonds and pistachios, some spices, aromatics and saffron is used.

Credited as having its origins in the Persian *sambosag*, or 'small pie', the Arabs called it *Sanbusaj* and *Sanbusaq*, even though pronounced *Sunbusak* in the vernacular (al-Safadi *Tashih* 319).

A unique type of *Sanbusak* appears in *Anonymous*, distinctive through its absence of flour. Instead, a spiced and aromatic almond-based paste becomes the 'dough' of the pastry, which is formed into shapes of oranges, pears and apples. It appears that the Almohad Emir Abu Yusuf al-Mansur (d. AD 1199) enjoyed this version, as, according to the recipe, it was prepared for him at his home in Marrakesh.

This recipe follows the original method for creating the sweet, but its filling is a combination of both source recipes.

⤚ Traditional recipe ⤙

Makes 20–24 pieces
Preparation time: 1 hour
Cooking time: 20 minutes

Ingredients

¾ cup (150 g) granulated sugar
½ cup (50 g) finely ground toasted almonds
½ cup (50 g) finely ground toasted hazelnuts
½ cup (50 g) finely ground pistachios
¼ teaspoon cinnamon
⅛ teaspoon ground cloves
⅛ teaspoon saffron, crushed and dissolved in 2 tablespoons light sesame oil
1 pound (454 g) filo pastry, thawed according to package directions
½ cup (170 g) liquid honey
1 egg, beaten
Light sesame or vegetable oil for deep-frying
One basic *'asal* syrup recipe, cooled to room temperature (see 'Basic recipes' section) (optional)

Method

To make the filling, in a mixing bowl, stir in the sugar, almonds, hazelnuts, pistachios, cinnamon, cloves and saffron–sesame oil mixture. Mix well.

Stir in the honey and mix well.

Place the filo pastry horizontally on a flat surface and cut vertically in half. Place the filo sheets in one pile and cover with a slightly dampened tea towel.

Take two filo sheets and lay lengthwise over each other on a flat surface. Place one teaspoon of filling close to the bottom right corner of the filo. Fold the filo over the filling and pat the filling to flatten it slightly. Starting from the bottom right, fold up to the left side, then fold to the right side, forming a triangular shape and continuing right to left until the filo is folded in the shape of a triangle. Brush the opened seam at the end with the beaten egg to seal. Continue the process until all the pieces are made.

Heat the oil in a large saucepan over a medium heat and deep-fry the triangles until golden, turning them over once. Remove with a slotted spoon and place on paper towels to drain any excess oil. If desired, immerse each piece in *'asal* syrup then arrange on a serving platter.

᭥ Modern recipe ᭣

SAMBUSA HILWA (SWEET SANBUSAK)

For the experienced cook

In the Gulf countries, the sweet *al-Sanbusak* has evolved into a simple-to-prepare recipe, locally called *Sambusa Hilwa*. The use of ready-made filo creates a much lighter and crispier pastry than the medieval version. This delicacy is served for weddings and feasts and is usually brought to the table warm. Traditionally, in the Gulf region, the dough of the *Sambusa* was stretched over a wooden stick and baked or fried. They were then stuffed. However, nowadays they are presented in triangular shapes.

Makes 20–24 pieces
Preparation time: 1 hour
Cooking time: 20 minutes

Ingredients

⅔ cup (100 g) ground almonds
½ cup (100 g) granulated sugar
1 teaspoon cinnamon
½ teaspoon ground cardamom
Pinch of saffron diluted in 1 tablespoon of rose water
1 pound (454 g) filo pastry, thawed according to package directions
1 cup (227 g) unsalted butter, melted
1 egg, beaten
Vegetable or canola oil for deep-frying

Method

To make the filling, in a bowl, stir together the almonds, sugar, cinnamon, cardamom and the saffron–rose water. Mix well to form a crumbly mixture.

Lay the filo sheets horizontally on a flat surface and cut into three even sections. Place the three sections in one pile and cover with a slightly dampened towel.

Take one sheet and brush lightly with the butter. Place another sheet over it and brush lightly with the butter. Take the third sheet, place it over the others and brush lightly with the butter.

Place one rounded teaspoon of the filling at the bottom right corner of the sheet. Fold the sheets to the right lengthwise over the filling. Pull up the bottom right corner of the sheet towards the left then to the right, continuing until the filo sheets are folded in the shape of a triangle. Brush the edges with the beaten egg. Continue the process of forming the stuffed triangles until all the filo sheets are used.

Heat the oil in a large saucepan over a medium heat, then deep-fry the *Sambusa* until golden, turning them over once. Remove with a slotted spoon and place on paper towels, then arrange on a serving platter.

AQRAS MUKARRARA (REPEATED PATTIES)
TWICE DIPPED, TWICE FRIED NUT-FILLED FRITTERS

For the experienced cook

✍ *Historical version* ❧

Take fine *samidh* flour and knead into a thin dough. Allow to sit until it rises. Take a *ratl* of sugar and one-third of a *ratl* of almonds, finely pound them and firmly knead with rose water and syrup. Make from this thin patties and coat them with that batter and throw them in sesame oil. Take them out of it and dip in syrup. Dust them in pounded sugar, then return them to the batter in this way three times. Then sprinkle finely pounded scented sugar over them and serve.

al-Baghdadi, p. 80. Translated by Muna Salloum and Leila Salloum Elias. (See also the translation by Charles Perry, *A Baghdad Cookery Book*, p. 104.)

✍ *Historical version* ❧

Samidh flour kneaded into a somewhat thin dough. Allow to rise. Take a *ratl* of sugar and one-third *ratl* of pistachios or almonds. Pound them and knead with rose water and syrup to make a firm paste. Make into patties. Cover them with that dough, fry and remove. Soak them in syrup then dust them with sugar. Then re-cover them with the dough and fry. Remove them and dip into the syrup and dust with sugar three times in this manner. Then sprinkle sugar over them and serve.

Ibn al-'Adim, p. 649 (#41). Translated by Muna Salloum and Leila Salloum Elias.

These patties need patience to make because of the repetitive process of dipping and frying – thus the name *Aqras Mukarrara* (meaning literally 'repeated patties'). Dipped in batter, syrup and confectioner's/icing sugar more than once during the frying process, the procedure may take some time but is well worth the effort. *Aqras Mukarrara* are a type of crispy fritter.

Two similar recipes appear in *Familiar Foods*, differing only slightly, with one using pistachios instead of almonds.

Arab history relates the profound role the almond played in one man's proof of love to his wife. Having witnessed the beauty of a rare snowfall in Cordoba, I'timad al-Rumaykiyya, wife of al-Mu'tamid, poet-king of Seville (AD 1069–91), pleaded with her husband that she be able, once again, to enjoy the beauty of a white landscape. Al-Mu'tamid complied. He ordered that almond trees be planted on the sierra. In this way his wife could relish the trees' white blossoms when they flowered at the end of winter, symbolic of the snow for which she yearned.

✃ Traditional recipe ✃

Makes about 36 pieces
Preparation time: 40 minutes
Standing time: 30 minutes
Cooking time: 40 minutes

Ingredients

Basic *qatr* recipe using rose water (see 'Basic recipes' section)
    4 eggs, beaten
    ⅔ cup (152 g) unsalted margarine or unsalted butter, at room temperature
    2 cups (240 g) plus 2 tablespoons plain flour
    1 cup (250 ml) plus 2 tablespoons warm water
    1¾ cups (200 g) confectioner's/icing sugar
    1 cup (95 g) ground almonds
    2 tablespoons rose water
    2 tablespoons liquid honey
    Light sesame oil for deep-frying
    1 teaspoon cinnamon

Method

In a mixing bowl, add the eggs, margarine or butter, the two cups (240 g) of flour and one cup (250 ml) of water. Beat with an electric mixer until a smooth batter is formed. Cover, and let rest for a half an hour.

While the batter is resting, prepare the filling. In a separate bowl, mix together one cup (115 g) of the confectioner's/icing sugar, almonds, rose water, honey, the remaining two tablespoons of water and the remaining two tablespoons of flour. Form this mixture into patties about 1½–2 inches (3.75 cm to 5 cm) in diameter.

In a large saucepan heat the oil over a medium-high heat. Place half a cup (58 g) of the confectioner's/icing sugar in a bowl and set aside.

Working quickly, dip the patties into the batter and fry until golden on each side. Remove with a slotted spoon and dip into the syrup, then into the half cup (58 g) of confectioner's/icing sugar. Re-dip into the batter, then fry again. Remove with the slotted spoon, then repeat the process by dipping the re-fried patties into the syrup and the confectioner's/icing sugar and then once again into the batter. Fry again, then remove with the slotted spoon, placing the patties on a tray, allowing them to cool.

While the patties are cooling, mix together in a bowl the remaining confectioner's/icing sugar and the cinnamon. Sprinkle the patties with this mixture and place on a serving platter.

ASABI' ZAYNAB (ZENOBIA'S FINGERS)
PISTACHIO-FILLED PASTRY TUBES

Moderately difficult

✑ *Historical version* ✑

Mix together two and a half *uqiya*s of sesame oil for every *ratl* of flour and knead with hot water and a little salt. [To make the *Asabi'*], take for them hollow arrows or pieces of canes. Take the dough and spread it over the tile slab and roll it around the piece of arrow or cane. It should be shorter than a finger. Partly fry in sesame oil. The arrow is removed and [the dough] is fried again on a gentle fire until its interior is cooked through. Immerse in syrup, rose water and musk. Its filling is [made of] peeled pistachio meats that are toasted. They are finely pounded with sugar, rose water and musk. It [the filling] is made into thin rope [shapes]. Stuff them and arrange them in dishes and sprinkle powdered sugar on them.

Kanz, p. 117 (#308). Translated by Muna Salloum and Leila Salloum Elias.

✑ *Historical version* ✑

Two *ratl*s of white flour rubbed with three *uqiya*s of sesame oil then knead it with hot water. It is put on a Persian cane, formed [around it] and fried with the cane. Then take it out and extract the cane from it. They are stuffed with sugar, pistachio meats, musk and rose water. It is thrown in honey and sugar is sprinkled over it.

Ibn al-'Adim, p. 642 (#26). Translated by Muna Salloum and Leila Salloum Elias.

There is a legend in the Middle East that *Asabi' Zaynab* represent the fingers of the heroic third-century Queen Zenobia of Palmyra, known not only for her fight for independence from Rome but also for her intelligence, linguistic abilities and beauty.

For the Baghdadi poet Ibn al-Mutriz, the *Asabi'* were irresistible. One day at a friend's house he was served the sweet. When he went to reach for one 'finger', his friend grabbed his hand. Ibn al-Mutriz responded,

Oh the one who restrained me by the hand
And from the sweets to me forbade
I tried for a finger of Zaynab
And broke five fingers instead
(al-Tha'alibi *Thimar* I 491)

In *Familiar Foods* there are two recipes for this fried sweet, one with sugar in the filling, one without. One version has the fried dough dipped first in honey before stuffing, the other has the dough stuffed first, then dipped into the syrup.

While combining the two source recipes to produce one adaptation, we have also added baking powder to make the dough, after frying, lighter and crispier. The fingers, otherwise, are too hard.

ᴥ Traditional recipe ᴥ

Makes 18–20
Preparation time: 1 hour 10 minutes
Standing time: 1 hour 10 minutes
Cooking time: 20 minutes

Ingredients
1 cup (340 g) liquid honey
1 cup (250 ml) warm water
2 tablespoons rose water
2 cups (240 g) plain flour
¼ teaspoon salt
1 teaspoon baking powder
4 tablespoons light sesame oil
6 *Cannoli* tubes (15 cm)
2 cups (190 g) ground pistachios
1½ cups (300 g) granulated sugar
Light sesame oil for deep-frying
Confectioner's/icing sugar

Method

To make the syrup, in a small saucepan mix together the honey and quarter of a cup (65 ml) of water. Bring to the boil over a medium heat, stirring occasionally. Stir in one tablespoon of the rose water and reduce the heat to very low to keep the honey syrup warm.

In a mixing bowl, add the flour, salt and baking powder, and mix well together. Form a well in the centre and pour in the four tablespoons of sesame oil and the remaining water. Knead into a smooth dough, for three to five minutes, adding more flour or water if necessary. Cover and let rest for an hour.

While the dough is resting, prepare the filling by stirring together in a mixing bowl the pistachios, the sugar and the remaining tablespoon of rose water. Set aside.

Roll the dough out as thinly as possible and cut into 4 inch (10 cm) circles. Wrap each piece around a *Cannoli* tube. Seal the edges where they meet by pinching them tightly. Heat the oil over a medium-low heat and deep-fry the dough-wrapped tubes until golden brown, for about two minutes. Remove and drain on paper towels.

Let the shells cool slightly, then carefully pull out the tubes. Immerse in the honey syrup for about a minute then place on a tray. Continue the process until all the shells have been cooked.

When the shells have cooled, gently stuff each shell with the filling. Place on a serving platter and sprinkle with the confectioner's/icing sugar.

✑ Modern recipe ✒

ASABI' AL-'ARUS (THE BRIDE'S FINGERS), NUT-FILLED FILO ROLLS

Moderately difficult

Continuing with the medieval Arab tradition of naming some sweets after the delicate fingers of women, *Asabi' al-'Arus* mimic the elongated shape of a young bride's fingers. Today there are many more names that allude to the delicacy and finesse of femininity. *Zunud al-Sitt* ('the arms of the young lady') are rolled filo pastries stuffed with *qashta*. *Ghazal al-Banat*, a type of tahini-based candy, similar to candy floss and stuffed with pistachios, literally means 'the girls' spinning' (that is spinning wool). *Aswar al-Sitt* is made from filo pastry rolled around a thin tube then formed into a circle, the centre stuffed with ground pistachios or cashews to represent the 'wrists of a young lady'. *Nuhud al-'Adhra'* (see p.133) are shortbread-type cookies shaped like 'the breasts of the virgins'.

Modern-day *Asabi'* does not involve wrapping dough around tubes, as was done in medieval times. Instead, filo pastry has replaced the tedious process of preparing the dough and deep-frying the tubes before filling them. It is as if the hard work of the past has been simplified to suit the movement of modern society – fast and efficient – but the modernised medieval sweet remains tasty, as does the semblance of a sweet to the delicate beauty of a woman.

Makes 40–44 pieces
Preparation time: 1 hour
Cooking time: 20 minutes

Ingredients

Basic *qatr* recipe using rose water (see 'Basic recipes' section)
2 cups (300g) whole pistachios
²/₃ cup (135g) granulated sugar
½ teaspoon cinnamon
1 pound (454g) filo pastry, thawed according to package directions
½ cup (113g) unsalted butter, melted
1 egg, beaten
Granulated sugar for sprinkling

Method

In a food processor pulverise the pistachios, sugar and cinnamon together for one minute. Set aside.

Cut the filo pastry into quarters and cover with a very lightly dampened tea towel. Preheat the oven to 375°F (190°C).

Lay two sheets of the filo pastry on a flat work surface. Keep the shorter side facing you and brush lightly with the butter.

Place a tablespoon of the filling along the shorter side of the filo closest to you. Fold the longer edges of the filo inward so that the edges of the filling are slightly covered. Roll the filo up from the shorter side forming a thin cigar shape. Place it on a greased baking sheet with the seam down. Repeat this process until all filo sheets are used.

Brush the tops of the 'fingers' lightly with the egg then sprinkle lightly with sugar. Bake for 15–20 minutes or until golden.

Dip the 'fingers' immediately into the *qatr* and arrange on a serving platter.

BAQLAWA
LAYERED FILO PASTRY WITH NUT FILLING

❧ *Historical version* ❧

AL-LAWZINAJ BREAD

Take starch and dissolve into a thick solution and strain. For every *uqiya* add an egg white and beat vigorously and continuously. Then begin by heating the tray and wiping the top of it with a piece of cloth that has wax and walnut meats in it. Spoon out the batter and pour it on it and leave it to the heat [to let it dry]. When it is ready, remove it from it and wipe it [the tray] with the piece of cloth and make another one. Whoever wishes to make thicker *Lawzinaj*, then increase the thickness of the batter and make them look like a disc. Stick it on the tray as I have described it, God willing.

> **al-Warraq, p. 37. Translated by Muna Salloum and Leila Salloum Elias. (See also the translation by Nawal Nasrallah: al-Warraq, *Annals of the Caliphs' Kitchen*, pp. 125–26.)**

❧ *Historical version* ❧

JUDHAB KHUBZ AL-QATA'IF

Take *Qata'if* crepes in the amount needed. Sprinkle a little rose water in the pot and spread the crepes in the pot in layers, between every two layers almonds and sugar or finely pounded pistachios. Sprinkle rose water on it. When the crepes are done in the pot, pour a little fresh sesame oil over them and drown in syrup. Then suspend over it a fatty chicken coloured with saffron. When it is cooked, remove. It can be made with small stuffed *Qata'if* in this fashion.

al-Baghdadi, p. 71. Translated by Muna Salloum and Leila Salloum Elias. (See also the translation by Charles Perry, *A Baghdad Cookery Book*, p. 93.)

❧ Modern recipe ❧

Moderately difficult

Food historians specialising in the history of Arab cuisine are unable to determine how early *Baqlawa* appeared on dessert tables in the Arab world. However, there is ample evidence from Arabic medieval cookbooks of a very thin dough used as a wrap for certain pastries such as *Lawzinaj*. This is why we find a recipe from the tenth century for this type of dough in al-Warraq (37). Later in the thirteenth century in al-Andalus, al-Tujibi instructs how to prepare very thin paper-like sheets made from a pure and fine semolina flour and water to make the dough called *Kunafa* (see p.39) (69).

There is also an interesting recipe in the text of al-Baghdadi that could possibly be the precursor to *Baqlawa*. A filling of almonds or pistachios and sugar spread between every two layers of the *Qata'if* pastry bread could be the starting point of the famous *Baqlawa* of the Middle East. Of course, if al-Baghdadi's *Judhab Khubz al-Qata'if* plays this historical role in the cuisine of Middle Eastern desserts, the dripping from the fatty saffron-coloured chicken hanging above the *Judhab* as they cook together has, of course, been eliminated in the modern cooking process.

Though *Baqlawa*, in name, is not part of the recipe collection of medieval Arab sweets found to date, in a thousand years from now this delicious modern pastry, in its present form, will be spoken of as historically significant. For this reason we have decided to include *Baqlawa* here, offering it as a possible descendant of the two source recipes.

Makes about 35 pieces
Preparation time: 45 minutes
Cooking time: 45 minutes

Ingredients

Basic *qatr* recipe using orange blossom water (see 'Basic recipes' section)
2 cups (300 g) whole walnuts or almonds or pistachios, coarsely chopped
1 cup (200 g) granulated sugar
2 cups (390 g) clarified butter, melted
1 teaspoon cinnamon
1 tablespoon orange blossom water
1 pound (454 g) filo pastry, thawed according to package directions

Method

To make the filling, combine the walnuts or almonds or pistachios, sugar, quarter of a cup (49 g) of the butter, the cinnamon and the orange blossom water, then set aside.

Brush the bottom and sides of a 9 by 13 by 2 inch (23 by 33 by 5 cm) baking pan with two tablespoons of the butter, then set aside.

Remove the filo pastry from the package, unfold and spread out on a towel. Cover the unused filo with a lightly dampened towel or plastic wrap/cling film to prevent it from drying out as you work. Take one sheet and place it in the baking pan, then brush with the butter. Keep repeating the procedure until half of the filo sheets are used. Spread the nut mixture evenly over the buttered layers.

Take one sheet of the filo and place over the nut mixture, brush with butter, then continue this procedure until the remainder of the filo sheets are used.

Preheat the oven to 400° F (200° C).

Heat the remaining butter, then brush evenly over the top of the *Baqlawa*. With a sharp knife, carefully cut into approximately 2 inch (5 cm) squares or diamond shapes. Bake for five minutes, then lower the heat to 300° F (150° C) and bake for 35–40 minutes, or until the sides turn light brown.

After the sides of the *Baqlawa* turn light brown, place the pan under the broiler/grill, then turn the tray around until the top of the *Baqlawa* turns evenly golden. Remove from the oven, then spoon the *qatr* over each square or diamond. Allow to cool before serving. *Baqlawa* can be served directly from the pan or by assembling the pieces in layers on a serving platter. (If a drier and less sweet version of *Baqlawa* is desired, prepare only half the *qatr* recipe.)

ISFUNJ (SPONGES)
SPONGE-LIKE NUT-STUFFED CAKE BALLS

Moderately difficult

❧ *Historical version* ☙

Take semolina and sift it, then take the flour and put it in a dish. Take water and sprinkle it lightly on the semolina. Then knead it into a dough and gather it all up and cover it with a second dish, leaving it until it sweats.

Then uncover it and knead it until it becomes soft. Throw oil in it, and knead it, and put in leavening and eggs, throw in about five eggs and then knead the dough with the eggs.

Then put it in a new pot, after greasing it with oil, and leave it until it rises.

Then take almonds, walnuts, pine nuts and pistachios, all peeled, and pound in a mortar until as fine as salt. Then take pure honey and put it on the fire and boil it until it is on the point of thickening. Then take the almonds, walnuts, pistachios and pine nuts that you have pounded, and throw all this upon the honey and stir it until it is thickened. And if you wish to throw almonds, ground sugar and rose water into the filling, do so and it will come out aromatic and agreeable.

Then take a piece of the semolina dough that was put in the pot, and make a thin, small flat cake of it, and fill it with a morsel of this thickened paste. The dough should be only moderately thin. Make all the dough according to this recipe, until the filling is used up.

Then take a frying pan and put oil in it, and when it starts to boil, throw in a piece of stuffed *Isfunj* and fry it with a gentle fire until it is done. And if you wish to cover with sugar, do so.

Anonymous, p. 190–91. Translated by Charles Perry.

Isfunj means 'sponge', and was so named due to the texture of the finished product, a light cake pastry or fritter with a porous interior, similar to a light bread dough.

The same dough was also used to prepare *Zalabiya Furniya* (oven-baked dough) in the tenth century, and was formed in the shape of a cake and baked (al-Warraq 269). Al-Warraq explains that the dough is also called *zalaqanba'* and *safanj* (also 'sponge') in Baghdad (249).

In the thirteenth century, al-Tujibi provides three different recipes for the fritter. One recipe involves an entirely different process of preparation and presentation using an earthenware bottle as a mould. A cane or reed inserted in the dough remains in the vessel while the yeast dough is being baked. Once done, the cane or reed is removed and honey and butter is poured in the place of the cane. The sweet buttery liquid is absorbed by the *Isfunj*, and when baked, the stoneware vessel is carefully broken to keep the *Isfunj* in one piece, moulded to the shape of the vessel.

In a small saucepan, stir together the honey, cinnamon and orange blossom water and heat over a medium-low heat until soft bubbles appear. Immediately lower the heat to low.

Either arrange the *Sfinci* on a flat serving dish and pour the heated honey over them, or dip the *Sfinci* into the honey one at time and place on a serving platter. Sprinkle the pistachios over the balls and serve immediately while warm.

KHUDUD AL-AGHANI (THE CHEEKS OF THOSE WHO SING)
LIGHT AND FLAKY DOUGHNUT-SHAPED PASTRIES

Moderately difficult

✎ *Historical version* ✎

Knead a *ratl* of flour, one and a half *uqiya*s of crushed starch with four *uqiya*s of sesame oil. Add to it while kneading, a little syrup. Cut with a cup and make a hole in the middle so that it will not break apart. Put them in a frying pan over a gentle fire and turn over. Put them in syrup and bee's honey then take them out. Make for it the sweet *Sabuniya* and layer them and sprinkle sugar over them.

Ibn al-'Adim, p. 637 (#14). Translated by Muna Salloum and Leila Salloum Elias.

Khudud al-Aghani are very simple pastries to make, and take very little time to prepare. They are light and flaky, and look like little doughnuts.

The name seems very strange: 'The cheeks of those who sing'. But then again, Arabic poetry and song are replete with the rich and decorative vocabulary of the language. Arabic verses abound in symbolism, expressive of sensual delight or beauty. Rose petals become 'cheeks' of the flower (*khudud al-ward*); the narcissus has *'uyun* (eyes); the 'lovelock' (*asdagh*) of the myrtle and the 'figure' or 'shape' (*qudud*) of sugar cane all become images of tender beauty, words descriptive of love.

Thus creativity was not reserved only for the invention of new dishes but for the names to go with them. Food was seduction, and certain dishes, through their names, lured the cook or the diner to indulge. Sweet dishes in the medieval Arab culinary texts are to tempt, ready to seduce the connoisseur of good food.

These pastries should be eaten the same day they are made, otherwise they become too hard.

◌ Traditional recipe ◌

Makes 30 pieces
Preparation time: 20 minutes
Standing time: 2 hours
Cooking time: 30 minutes

Ingredients

2 cups (240 g) plain flour
2 tablespoons cornstarch/cornflour
3 tablespoons light sesame oil
3 tablespoons butter, room temperature
2 tablespoons warm water
2 tablespoons any type of sweet syrup, such as date or carob syrup
Half of basic *'asal* syrup recipe (see 'Basic recipes' section)
Vegetable oil for deep-frying
½ cup (100 g) granulated sugar

Method

In a bowl, combine the flour and cornstarch/cornflour, then make a well and add the sesame oil, butter and water. While mixing, add the sweet syrup, then knead to form a slightly sticky dough, adding more flour or water if necessary. Cover the bowl and let sit for two hours.

Roll the dough out to ¼ inch (6 mm) thickness and cut with a cookie cutter into rounds about 2 ¼ inches (5.5 cm) in diameter, making a hole in each circle (like a doughnut).

Heat the oil over a medium-low heat and deep-fry the *Khudud* until golden brown on both sides. Remove from the oil and place in the *'asal* syrup for about 30 seconds, turning them over to cover both sides of the *Khudud*. Place on a serving dish and allow to cool.

Sprinkle with the sugar.

◌ Modern recipe ◌

YO-YO, TUNISIAN DOUGHNUTS

Easy

Tunisia has a very similar deep-fried sweet also in the shape of a doughnut. These are called *Yo-yo*. They are popular throughout the country, and vendors sell them all over as a fast food. They are prepared in a manner similar to that of the *Khudud*, but the ingredients differ. They should be eaten hot.

As for their name, popular lore has it that the *Yo-yo* represents the shape of the woman's mouth when ululating at celebrations to express joy and jubilation.

After having tried *Yo-yo* on his first trip to Tunisia, Habeeb put together the following recipe for his favourite type of 'doughnuts'.

Makes about 24 pieces
Preparation time: 30 minutes
Standing time: 1 hour
Cooking time: 40 minutes

Ingredients

3 eggs
2¼ cups (300 ml) vegetable oil
¼ cup (65 ml) freshly squeezed orange juice
2 tablespoons desiccated coconut
1¼ cups (250 g) granulated sugar
2½ cups (300 g) plain flour
1½ teaspoons baking soda/bicarbonate of soda
2 cups (500 ml) cold water
2 tablespoons lemon juice
1 cup (340 g) liquid honey

Method

Place the eggs, quarter of a cup (60 ml) of the oil, the orange juice, one tablespoon of the coconut, and quarter of a cup (50 g) of the sugar in a food processor. Blend until smooth.

Transfer to a bowl, then sift in the flour and the baking soda/bicarbonate of soda, and knead until the mixture is soft, adding more orange juice or flour if necessary. Cover the bowl with a towel and then set aside to rest for at least an hour.

In the meantime, make a syrup by placing in a pot the remaining sugar, the water and lemon juice, then boil over a high heat until the sugar dissolves, stirring constantly. Reduce the heat to low, and add the honey and the remaining tablespoon of coconut. Simmer for ten minutes, then turn the heat to very low to keep the syrup warm.

Place the remaining oil in a small saucepan, then heat until the oil is moderately hot. In the meantime, divide the dough into walnut-size balls, then flatten the balls slightly.

Hold a ball in the palm of one hand and poke a hole through the centre with the floured index finger of your other hand. Fry, a few at a time, for about five minutes, turning around with a slotted spoon until golden brown on both sides. Then transfer them to paper towels to drain. With tongs, pick up the *Yo-yo*, then dip them into the warm syrup and serve at once.

๙ Alternative modern recipe ๛

ROSCOS, RING-SHAPED FRITTERS

Easy

There are distinctive sweets in Spain, especially in Andalusia, which continue the tradition of Arab sweet ingredients such as almonds, sesame seeds, eggs, flour, spices and honey. Good examples are *Soplillos* (see p. 161) and *Pestiños*, deep-fried fritters dusted with honey or sugar. Others are the plain, spiced or zesty lemon- or orange-flavoured fritters of various shapes and sizes, based upon the popular medieval Arab fritter known as *Mushabbak* or *Zalabiya* (see pp. 62, 92).

This Arab legacy is also to be found in *Roscos*, another type of deep-fried dough. *Roscos* are doughnut cakes or buns, and are popular in various parts of Andalusia.

Makes 24–26 pieces
Preparation time: 30 minutes
Cooking time: 25 minutes

Ingredients

2 eggs, beaten
6 tablespoons light olive oil
4 tablespoons whole milk
1 teaspoon ground aniseed
1 cup (200 g) granulated sugar
1 teaspoon baking powder
2½ cups (300 g) plain flour
Vegetable oil for deep-frying
Confectioner's/icing sugar

Method

In a mixing bowl, combine the eggs, olive oil and milk.

In another large mixing bowl, stir together the dry ingredients except the confectioner's/icing sugar.

Stir the egg mixture into the dry ingredients to make a slightly sticky dough, adding more milk or flour if necessary.

Shape the dough into ropes about 4 inches (10 cm) long and ½ inch (1.25 cm) in diameter, then form each strip into a ring and press the ends together to seal.

Place the vegetable oil in a large saucepan about 2 inches (5 cm) deep and heat over a medium heat. Fry the rings until golden, turning once to brown both sides. Place the fried *Roscos* on paper towels to drain excess oil. Place on a serving platter and, when cool, sprinkle with the confectioner's/icing sugar.

KUNAFA (PAPER-THIN PASTRY)
BAKED FILO WITH MILK SAUCE AND DRIZZLED WITH HONEY

For the experienced cook

❧ *Historical version* ❧

Make a dough by using two *ratl*s of excellent clean *samidh*, then after moistening it with hot water, knead it extremely well. Cover it until it cools. Then pour water over the dough and it is washed in the same manner as you prepare *talbina* [a thick paste] for clothes, until the dough dissolves and it becomes soft. Then squeeze the liquid through a tightly woven cloth until nothing remains except the bare grains, then leave in a receptacle similar to that used for bread. Pour into it a sufficient measurement of water until its texture is between light and heavy. Place a mirror used for it [*Kunafa*] on a charcoal fire with no flame. When it [the mirror] is heated, it is brushed with a clean rag soaked in fresh oil.

Pour enough of the dough on it, as much as it can hold. Leave it [the dough] on for a little time until it becomes very thin bread. Then remove and put it on a platter. Pour on it from the remaining dough and cook it in the same manner as thin bread one after another until it is all finished, [making sure] to brush the mirror with the oiled rag for each one. Remove with a knife so that its edges will not stick to it [the mirror], something that will spoil it.

Then melt the amount of one-quarter pound of butter or clarified butter over the fire with the measurement of two pounds of honey until it is blended. If desired, a little pepper can be added.

Then arrange the thin breads evenly and pour on them the melted butter and honey while it is hot. Clarified butter is better than butter.

He who wishes to use them later and store them, then cut the thin breads with scissors as thin as possible. When ready to use, put a new pot on the fire with enough honey. When it boils and the foam subsides add to it the cut thin bread and cook them in it until fully absorbed. When it is almost cooked, it should be moistened with *tharida* [milky thickened soup] or clarified butter or oil. When it is ready, it should be removed from the fire and from the pot and stored until it is needed. It can be eaten cold or hot. At the time that it is ready to be used, sprinkle sugar or cinnamon on it and eat, God willing.

al-Tujibi, pp. 69–70. Translated by Habeeb Salloum and Muna Salloum.

Kunafa in the medieval Arab period was paper-thin sheets of dough made by pouring the batter thinly onto warmed sheet metal until cooked. These sheets could be rolled with a nut-mixture stuffing or they could be cut into very thin strings similar to *rishta* (noodles) and used for various dishes, especially sweets. *Kunafa* batter was thinner than that of *Qata'if* and *Sanbusak*, the medieval texts clearly recommending one of the three for specific dishes.

Al-Tujibi's account of how to make *Kunafa* from scratch is so detailed that he even explains what should be done with *Kunafa* sheets made ahead of time, so they could be used at a later date (70).

Kunafa was fit for a caliph's table, such as that of the Umayyad Caliph Sulayman ibn 'Abd al-Malik (AD 674–717). According to one source, it was during this Caliph's reign that *Kunafa* made its first appearance (al-'Umari 262). Keeping with his love of food, the Caliph Sulayman consumed 20 *ratls* of it every evening (al-'Umari 262).

A simple dish of *Kunafa* moistened with pistachio oil and sugar syrup is described in a fourteenth-century text as 'outstanding' (al-'Asqalani *Raf'al-Isr* 368). We also find one Abu Hasan al-Jazzar enamoured with *Kunafa*, elaborating on its heavenly taste:

> God has quenched the thirst of the wings of *Kunafa* with syrup
> And made it excellent by putting sugar like continuous pearls upon them.
> (al-Ghazuli 398)

In our adaptation, we have opted to use filo to lessen the hard work involved in creating the specialised *Kunafa* dough from scratch.

The original recipe provides two methods for making this sweet: either stack the layers of cooked thin dough on top of each other, then pour the honey syrup over the top, or cut them into pieces and pour the honey syrup over them. We have combined both methods. When we worked with the first method, we found the sweet too dry; using the second method, the *Kunafa* was too soggy. Merging both gives a crispy result.

So treasured was this sweet that to dream of *Kunafa* meant wisdom, and was a sign of a gift to come (al-Nabulsi 449).

✥ Traditional recipe ✥

Serves 8–12
Preparation time: 25 minutes
Standing time: 10 minutes
Cooking time: 35 minutes

Ingredients

½ pound (227 g) filo pastry, thawed according to package directions
4 tablespoons cornstarch/cornflour
5 cups (1.25 litres) whole milk
²⁄₃ cup (150 g) plus 4 tablespoons caster sugar
⅛ teaspoon salt
1½ cups (510 g) liquid honey
½ cup (113 g) unsalted butter, melted
1½ teaspoons cinnamon

Method

Cut the filo sheets into pieces about 2 inches (5 cm) square. Place on a greased baking tray and bake at 350°F (175°C) until golden, turning them over once to ensure both sides are golden. Distribute evenly onto a large serving platter.

Blend the cornstarch/cornflour in half a cup (120 ml) of the milk until smooth, and set aside.

In a medium-sized saucepan, mix together the remaining milk, two-thirds of a cup (150 g) of the caster sugar and the salt, and bring to the boil over a medium heat. Stirring constantly with a wooden spoon in one direction, add the cornstarch/cornflour paste and cook until thickened, about 15 minutes. Remove from the heat and allow to cool in the saucepan.

While the milk sauce is cooling, in another medium-sized saucepan, mix together the honey and the butter. Over a medium heat, stirring occasionally, bring the honey–butter syrup to a soft rolling boil. Remove from the heat.

Spoon the thickened milk sauce evenly over the filo pieces on the serving platter, then pour the honey–butter syrup evenly over the platter contents.

Mix together the remaining four tablespoons of caster sugar and the cinnamon, then sprinkle evenly over the *Kunafa*. Serve immediately.

⤚ Modern recipe ⤙

KENEFA (OR KTEFA), FROM MOROCCO, LAYERED FILO PASTRY WITH ALMONDS AND CREAM

For the experienced cook

Morocco, even today, retains many dishes that were developed in al-Andalus. The evidence bears witness in Moroccan sweets such as *Kunafa*. The dough which was prepared in medieval times for *Kunafa* was of a very thin texture. Similarly, in Morocco, a dough called *warqa* (spelled more popularly *ouarka*), meaning 'paper', is used especially for the Moroccan *Bastilla* (a pigeon pie) and for that country's many delicious flaky sweets. *Ouarka* dough, with its elastic-like texture, is stretched onto a tray which is heated over charcoal. In fact, there is a delicious pastry called *Kenefa* or *Ktefa* in the Moroccan dialect (also known as *Bastilla*), prepared with milk or custard and almonds using almost the same method as that of our thirteenth-century author.

Ouarka and filo pastry are nowadays used interchangeably in Morocco in traditional cooking.

Serves 8
Preparation time: 40 minutes
Standing time: 10 minutes
Cooking time: 35 minutes

Ingredients

½ pound filo (227 g) pastry, thawed according to package directions
Vegetable oil for frying
1 cup (150 g) blanched whole almonds
4 tablespoons confectioner's/icing sugar
1½ teaspoons cinnamon
4 tablespoons cornstarch/cornflour
5 cups (1.25 litres) whole milk
⅔ cup (150 g) caster sugar
⅛ teaspoon salt
4 tablespoons ground almonds
2 tablespoons orange blossom water

Method

Separate the filo sheets. Cut into 8 inch (20 cm) circles, making 20 circles. Cover the filo that is waiting to be used with a slightly dampened tea towel.

In a large skillet, pour in oil to ½ inch (1.25 cm) depth and heat over a medium heat, then lower the heat to medium-low. Press together two of the filo circles, then fry on both sides until light golden and crisp. (Reduce the heat if the filo browns too quickly.) The two pressed circles will become one. Drain the ten fried circles on paper towels and set aside, being careful not to break them. Keep the oil in the skillet.

Brown the whole almonds in the same oil over a medium heat, stirring constantly. Drain, and when cool, crush with a rolling pin or chop in a processor. Mix the almonds with the confectioner's/icing sugar and the cinnamon and set aside.

Blend the cornstarch/cornflour in half a cup (120 ml) of the milk until smooth, and set aside.

In a medium-sized saucepan, mix together the remaining milk, the castor sugar and the salt, and bring to the boil over a medium heat. Stirring constantly with a wooden spoon, add the cornstarch/cornflour paste and cook until thickened, about 15 minutes. Stir in the ground almonds and the orange blossom water and cook for one minute. Remove from the heat and allow to cool in the saucepan, for about ten minutes.

When ready to serve, assemble the *Kenefa* by first placing two of the ten filo circles on a serving platter. Sprinkle quarter of the almond–sugar–cinnamon mixture evenly over the top. Spoon quarter of the chilled milk sauce evenly on top. Repeat this procedure three times, and then place the last two filo circles on top. Serve immediately.

KUNAFA (ROLLED)
A RECIPE FROM THE ARAB EAST FOR A ROLLED KUNAFA

Moderately difficult

 *Historical version*

KUNAFA MAMLUHA

Oil the *Kunafa* with sesame oil. Cut it very thin like *rishta*. Put it into a plate and moisten it with sesame oil, pounded sugar and toasted pistachio meats.

Ibn al-'Adim, pp. 626–27 (#14). Translated by Muna Salloum and Leila Salloum Elias.

ALTERNATIVE TYPE

If it has been oiled with sesame oil and cut like *rishta*, moisten it while it is in the plate, with butter. Sprinkle over it sugar, pistachio meats and syrup. Indeed it is much tastier than sesame oil in *Kunafa*. In any event, at the time of cutting [the *Kunafa* into *rishta*], sesame oil has to be used.

Ibn al-'Adim, p. 627. Translated by Muna Salloum and Leila Salloum Elias.

ALTERNATIVE TYPE

Fry the *Kunafa* in sesame oil and put it in syrup. Sprinkle sugar and pistachio meats over it.

Ibn al-'Adim, p. 627. Translated by Muna Salloum and Leila Salloum Elias.

ALTERNATIVE TYPE

Toast pistachio meats and pound them with sugar and knead with rose water. Take some *Kunafa* and oil it with sesame oil. Put the pistachios in it. Fold over as is done with *awsat* (sandwich rolls). Moisten it with boiling syrup and fresh sesame oil.

Ibn al-'Adim, p. 627. Translated by Muna Salloum and Leila Salloum Elias.

From thirteenth-century Aleppo, Ibn al-'Adim provides four recipes for *Kunafa*, a thin filo pastry made into sheets of dough or in vermicelli form. Although simple to make, they are rich in flavour.

The first two make use of *Kunafa* dough that has been prepared in vermicelli form. Today, the closest to this type is called *kataifi* – a shredded form of filo pastry.

The third recipe is seemingly made with the *Kunafa* sheets, since the author does not instruct that the dough be prepared like *rishta* (vermicelli). However, the most interesting and slightly more complicated version is the fourth.

The adapted recipe below is based upon that fourth version. In this recipe the *Kunafa* dough is rolled into a log after being filled with a nut mixture. This style of preparation – and in fact recipe – has lasted through the centuries, to become the Arab East's *Burma*, a cylinder of shredded filo pastry stuffed with pistachios or pine nuts and drenched in syrup.

Traditional recipe

Makes 15–18 pieces
Preparation time: 40 minutes
Chilling time: 1 hour
Cooking time: 1 hour

Ingredients

1½ times the basic *qatr* recipe, using either rose water or orange blossom water (see 'Basic recipes' section)
3 cups (350g) coarsely chopped walnuts or pistachios (350g) or cashews (350g) or hazelnuts (350g) or pine nuts (400g)
¾ cup (170g) granulated sugar
1 tablespoon rose water
1 pound (454g) *kataifi* (shredded filo), thawed according to package directions
1 cup (195g) clarified butter, melted

Method

To make the filling, in a bowl, mix together the nuts, sugar, rose water and half a cup (125ml) of the *qatr*. Cover with plastic wrap/cling film and refrigerate for about an hour.

Butter a 17½ by 11½ by 1 inch (44 by 29 by 2.5 cm) baking tray with four tablespoons of the melted butter.

Preheat oven to 300°F (150°C).

Remove the *kataifi* from its package and place on the buttered tray. Spread the *kataifi* evenly, making sure that there are no empty spaces between the strands. Brush four tablespoons of the melted butter evenly over the surface of the *kataifi*.

Distribute the filling evenly along the middle of the length of the buttered *kataifi*.

Starting at the long edge of the *kataifi*, carefully roll it over the filling and continue to roll to the end to form a log-shaped cylinder. Brush the log generously with the remaining butter. Bake for one hour.

Remove from the oven and immediately pour the cooled *qatr* over the hot *Kunafa* log.

Set aside until cool. Slice into 1½ inch (3.75 cm) pieces with a serrated knife, then transfer to a serving platter.

LAWZINAJ (THAT WHICH IS MADE OF ALMONDS)
WRAPPED ALMOND ROLLS

Moderately difficult

≼ Historical version ≽

Take a *ratl* of sugar and pound finely. Take one-third of a *ratl* of shelled, skinned almonds and also finely pound. Mix with the sugar and knead with rose water. Then take thin bread, similar to *sanbusaj* bread – it is better if the bread is thinner – and spread out a loaf of that bread. Spread on it the kneaded almonds and sugar, then roll it up like a belt and cut into small pieces and arrange them. Refine fresh sesame oil as is needed, and put it on them. Then cover them with syrup to which rose water has been added. Sprinkle finely pounded pistachios on them.

al-Baghdadi, p. 76. Translated by Muna Salloum and Leila Salloum Elias. (See also the translation by Charles Perry, in *A Baghdad Cookery Book*, pp. 99–100.)

No cookbook dealing with medieval Arab cookery can be complete without *Lawzinaj*. Interspersed throughout *adab* literature, it appears as the ultimate in sweet luxury. Wrapped in a paper-thin *Lawzinaj* sheet, stuffed with a mixture of sugar and rose-scented almonds, walnuts or pistachios or a combination of nuts, then covered in oil and drenched in syrup, *Lawzinaj* are as lavish as the refined society in which they were cherished. *Lawzinaj* remained one of the most highly regarded sweets through the centuries, so much so that we find a teacher of law advising a student to pursue the career despite the long hours of study, the reward being that future wealth as a jurist would enable him to feast on *Lawzinaj* filled with shelled pistachios (al-Tanukhi I 251).

For the Baghdad poet al-Ma'muni (AD 953–93) especially noted for his poems of *wasf* – descriptive rhyming words,

Lawzinaj heals the one who is ailing as if
It is the hand's tender fingertips not wrinkled
We sent it out embalmed with pure *qatr*
To be buried. However, it was not shrouded.
    (al-Tha'alibi *Yatima* IV 185)

The quintessential *Lawzinaj* was one with a thickened filling, wrapped thinner than the breeze of the east wind (al-Raghib al-Asbahani II 619), the easiest sweet to swallow and the quickest to penetrate the veins (al-Hamadhani p. 63). So idyllic was the sweet that Ibn al-Rumi (AD 836–96) would compare the birth of one patron's newborn son to it, both sweet and splendid. A contest between the favourite sweet of Caliph Harun al-Rashid (d. AD 809) and that of his wife Zubayda pit *Lawzinaj* and *Faludhaj* against each other, the best-tasting one to be decided by the Chief Judge of Baghdad (Ibn Khallikan II 316–17).

Lawzinaj was deemed an esteemed sweet in the court cuisine of ancient Iran. Charles Perry finds it curious, however, that though this sweet was popular in sixth-century Persia, the name itself is derived from *loza*, the Aramaic word for almond, rather than from the native Persian word *badam* (Perry 'What to Order' 222).

A tenth-century recipe creates a type that is placed in a vessel, then drenched with oil as a preservative, this being described as 'taken by kings when travelling' (al-Warraq 265).

Oddly, these recipes do not instruct the cook to fry or bake the cylinders. We took it upon ourselves to do so, since we prefer crispy to soft and syrup-drenched.

⤳ Traditional recipe ⤶

Makes about 54–66 pieces (depending upon number of filo sheets in package)
Preparation time: 1 hour 10 minutes
Cooking time: 30 minutes

Ingredients

Basic *qatr* recipe using rose water (see 'Basic recipes' section)
2 cups (190 g) ground almonds
1¼ cups (250 g) granulated sugar
1 tablespoon plus 1 pound (454 g) unsalted butter, melted
2 teaspoons rose water
1 pound (454 g) filo pastry, thawed according to package directions
1 egg, beaten
Vegetable oil for deep-frying
1 cup (95 g) finely ground pistachios

Method

To make the filling, in a bowl, mix together the almonds, sugar, the tablespoon of butter and the rose water. Set aside.

Placing the filo sheets horizontally, cut the sheets into three equal columns and place on top of each other. Keep the sheets covered with a slightly dampened tea towel.

Take one sheet of the filo and brush lightly with butter on all edges. Place a heaped teaspoon of the filling near the bottom edge of the filo sheet and spread out slightly, not touching the edges of the filo sheet. Fold over the long sides of the sheet, approximately ¼ inch (6 mm) in on both sides, then roll upwards, tucking in the sides to create a log shape. Brush the egg on the seam of the *Lawzinaj* to seal it well. Place the roll, seam-side up, on a floured surface. Continue this process until all the filo sheets are finished.

Heat the oil over a medium heat and deep-fry the *Lawzinaj* for a few minutes until they turn golden. Remove with a slotted spoon and place on paper towels for a few minutes. Dip the *Lawzinaj* into the *qatr*, then place them on a serving tray.

Sprinkle the pistachios over the *Lawzinaj* immediately.

✧ Modern recipe ✧

BRAYWAT, CRISPY ALMOND-FILLED PASTRIES

For the experienced cook

In Morocco, a rich, crispy filled pastry named *Braywat* may well have its origins in the Arab East's medieval *Lawzinaj*. Although other modern eastern Arab pastries in the form of nut-filled filo rolls have evolved from their medieval counterpart, we have chosen this Moroccan pastry as an example of the Arab East's spread west.

Braywat are drenched in honey, unlike the *qatr* of the original *Lawzinaj*. When the expelled Moriscos of Iberia reached the shores of North Africa, they brought with them the tradition of using honey for sweets. *Braywat* are a perfect example of the combination of the two sides of the Arab world.

Makes about 48 pieces
Preparation time: 1 hour
Cooking time: 25 minutes

Ingredients
2 tablespoons orange blossom water
2 cups (680 g) liquid honey
1 cup (150 g) blanched whole almonds
½ cup (100 g) granulated sugar
½ teaspoon cinnamon
1 tablespoon unsalted butter, melted
1 egg, beaten
1 pound (454 g) filo pastry, thawed according to package directions
2 cups (480 g) vegetable oil

Method

To make the syrup, stir together the orange blossom water and the honey in a small saucepan and thoroughly heat over a low heat. Set aside and keep warm.

To make the filling, place the almonds and the sugar in a food processor, then process until the almonds turn semi-fine. Stir in the cinnamon and the butter, then set aside.

Cut the filo sheets into two, lengthwise, then cover with a slightly dampened tea towel. Take one sheet lengthwise and place approximately one tablespoon of the filling near the right-hand bottom corner of the sheet. Fold the sheet in half, lengthwise over the filling, then fold the closed sheet upward into a 3 by 2 inch (7.5 by 5 cm) rectangle or a triangular shape.

Using a pastry brush, paint each open seam of the *Braywat* with the egg to ensure closure.

Heat the oil in a medium-sized saucepan over a medium-high heat, then reduce the heat to medium and place the *Braywat* in the oil. Deep-fry, turning over once, until the *Braywat* turn golden.

Remove the *Braywat* from the oil with a slotted spoon, then place in the syrup for a few minutes. Remove the *Braywat* from the syrup, then place in a strainer until the excess honey drains off.

Arrange the *Braywat* on a platter and serve.

✑ Alternative modern recipe ✑

NASHAB (FIRMLY STUFFED), DEEP-FRIED FILO NUT ROLLS

For the experienced cook

Nashab, popular in the Arab Gulf countries, are similar to the *Braywat* of Morocco, but more akin to what one reads about *Lawzinaj* in medieval Arabic cookbooks and *adab* literature. If the ideal *Lawzinaj* is a thick filling wrapped thinner than 'the breeze of the East wind' then *Nashab* is very close, or a rival, to the medieval *Lawzinaj*.

Makes 72–88 pieces
Preparation time: 1 hour 10 minutes
Cooking time: 40 minutes

Ingredients
Basic *qatr* recipe using rose water (see 'Basic recipes' section)
1¼ cups (190 g) raw whole cashew nuts
1 cup (150 g) whole walnuts
½ cup (75 g) blanched whole almonds
1 teaspoon ground cardamom seeds
1 cup (200 g) granulated sugar
1 pound (454 g) filo pastry, thawed according to package directions
Vegetable oil for deep-frying

Method

To make the filling, place the cashews, walnuts, almonds, cardamom and the sugar in a food processor, then process for a minute. Set aside.

Cut the filo sheets into quarters, then cover with a slightly damp cloth. Take one of the quarter sheets and place one level tablespoon of the filling along the middle of the bottom edge. Fold both sides over the filling. Wet the top edge with fingers, then roll from the bottom up. Repeat until all the filo pieces are finished.

Pour 2 inches (5 cm) of oil into a medium-sized saucepan, then heat over a medium heat. Deep-fry the rolls, turning them over until they turn golden. Remove, then place in the syrup for a few moments. Remove from the syrup with a slotted spoon and place on a tray. Allow to cool, then place on a serving platter.

LUQAYMAT AL-QADI (THE JUDGE'S TIDBITS OR MORSELS)
DEEP-FRIED SYRUP-DRENCHED FRITTERS

Easy

❧ *Historical version* ❧

Prepare an amount of yeast dough as needed, and make it thin. Make [them] like dinars. Fry them in sesame oil and leave them to one side. Then take one *ratl* of syrup, one *uqiya* of starch and three *uqiya*s of shelled and finely pounded pistachios, thickening it with sesame oil. Add to it that which perfumes it, from aromatics such as walnut, cubeb, cloves, saffron, aloewood chips and musk, in the amount needed. Once it is thickened, remove it from the fire. Divide into portions, each portion being two *uqiya*s. Arrange them in dishes and pour over them syrup that has been diluted with rose water and musk, and serve.

Kanz, p. 110 (#286). Translated by Muna Salloum and Leila Salloum Elias.

One of the most popular sweet fritters in the medieval Arab world, *Luqmat al-Qadi* are sweet morsels of yeast dough dipped in syrup, either honey- or sugar-based and, at times, sprinkled with sugar. *Luqmat* are the standard bite-sized fried dough balls. *Luqaymat* are even smaller.

Deep-fried batter was not exclusive to the medieval Arabs. Ibn Battuta in the fourteenth century, during his travels to India, attended a dinner in the city of Multan and was served *Luqaymat al-Qadi* at the same time as the main meal. Ibn Battuta, however, states that though he himself calls the sweets *Luqaymat al-Qadi*, they were called by his hosts '*al-Hashimi*' (406).

In the *Tales from Arabian Nights*, in the tale of 'The Porter and the Three Ladies of Baghdad', we find a porter carrying a platter piled high with open-worked tarts

(*Mushabbak*) and fritters (*Luqmat al-Qadi*) scented with musk, in addition to soap-cakes (*Sabuniya*), lemon loaves and melon preserves. These were purchases made in a souk in Baghdad.

↞ Traditional recipe ↠

Serves 8–10
Preparation time: 1 hour
Standing time: 1 hour 10 minutes
Cooking time: 35 minutes

Ingredients

Twice the basic *qatr* recipe using rose water (see 'Basic recipes' section)
1 tablespoon granulated sugar
1¾ cups (425 ml) warm water
¼ ounce (8 g) active dry yeast
2 cups (240 g) plain flour
½ teaspoon salt
2 cups (190 g) ground pistachios
2 tablespoons light sesame oil
1 tablespoon cornstarch/cornflour
⅛ teaspoon ground cloves
Pinch of powdered saffron
¼ teaspoon cinnamon
Pinch of nutmeg
Light sesame oil for deep-frying

Method

Dissolve the sugar in quarter of a cup (65 g) of the warm water, then stir in the yeast. Cover and allow to rest for ten minutes until frothy.

In a mixing bowl, combine the flour and salt. Make a well and add the dissolved yeast, and the remaining water. Blend together by hand until the mixture resembles the texture of pancake batter, adding more water if necessary and making sure there are no lumps. Cover, then set aside for an hour.

While the batter is standing, prepare the filling by mixing together in a bowl five tablespoons of the *qatr* and the remaining ingredients, except for the sesame oil that will be used for deep-frying. Transfer to a food processor and process for one minute or until the mixture becomes like a thick paste.

Spoon the paste into a frying pan and cook over a low heat until heated through, about eight minutes, stirring constantly. Remove from the heat and form the mixture into walnut-size balls. Set aside.

When the batter is ready, stir through once.

Heat the oil in a medium-sized saucepan over a medium heat.

Using tongs, take a ball and dip it into the batter, gently shaking off any excess. Drop into the hot oil and cook until the *Luqaymat* turns golden. Remove with a slotted spoon and place on paper towels to drain for a few seconds. Immediately dip the *Luqaymat* into the remaining *qatr*, then remove with a slotted spoon and arrange on a serving platter.

(Tip: *Luqaymat* are best served the day they are made, so they are still crispy.)

✍ Modern recipe ➢

LUGAYMAT FROM THE UNITED ARAB EMIRATES,
DEEP-FRIED, SYRUP-DRENCHED CARDAMOM FLAVOURED FRITTERS

Easy

Luqaymat are popular sweet fried balls served all over the United Arab Emirates and are known in the local dialect as *Lugaymat*. Not much has changed from the medieval recipes for this sweet in the Gulf countries. However, over time, the preferred spices of the area have been incorporated, creating a tasty result.

It's always best to serve these the same day they are made; otherwise they lose their crispy outside texture.

In almost every one of the 22 Arab countries, these sweet balls are served for all occasions. Easy to make and delicious to eat, they are one of the most popular desserts in the entire Arab world.

It is especially during Ramadan, the Muslim fasting period, that the greatest variety of sweets is served, at the end of the daily fast. For example, in Saudi Arabia *Luqmat al-Qadi* are part of this group of sweets, sometimes lightly spiced with cardamom and saffron, fried gently in oil and then dipped in syrup. This is Habeeb's version of the recipe, which he developed after his many visits to the Arab Gulf region.

Makes about 36 pieces
Preparation time: 25 minutes
Standing time: 1 hour 10 minutes
Cooking time: 30 minutes

Ingredients

Basic *qatr* recipe using orange blossom water (see 'Basic recipes' section)
1 tablespoon granulated sugar
¼ cup (65 ml) warm water
¼ ounce (8 g) active dry yeast
2½ cups (300 g) plain flour
½ teaspoon salt
¼ teaspoon ground cardamom seeds
⅛ teaspoon saffron
3 eggs, beaten
2 cups (500 ml) cold water
Vegetable oil for frying

Method

Dissolve sugar in the quarter cup (65 ml) of warm water, then stir in yeast. Cover and allow to sit for ten minutes until frothy.

In a mixing bowl, combine flour, salt, cardamom and saffron. Make a well and add dissolved yeast, eggs and water. Blend together until the mixture resembles the texture of pancake batter, adding more water if necessary and making sure there are no lumps. Cover and set aside for an hour.

Heat the oil in a saucepan, then drop one tablespoon of batter into the hot oil. Cook over a medium heat until the *Lugaymat* turn golden, then remove with a slotted spoon and place on paper towels to drain. Dip *Lugaymat* into the syrup, then remove with a slotted spoon and arrange on a serving platter. Continue until all the batter is used.

MUSHASH ZUBAYDA (ZUBAYDA'S SUBSISTENCE)
LIGHT AND CRISPY HONEY-TOPPED FRIED PASTRY

For the experienced cook

Historical version

Grind good-quality *samidh* until it is white and refined. Knead it with yeast into a dough, pressing and rubbing the dough. Take the fat of good tender kidney and extract its fibres and skin. Pound it in the mortar until its consistency is like brains. From the dough form thin round loaves and stretch [roll] them out. Brush the fat on them, placing them one on top of the other one by one. Cut each one into three and pinch their edges. Then roll out with a rolling pin. With a knife, cut into four pieces or as many as possible. They are boiled [deep-fried] in a lot of oil in the earthenware pot (*tinjir*), enough to cover the pieces. When they cook and puff up, remove and drain on wooden rods or in a sieve until they dry out from their oil. Then place in one vessel and sprinkle it well with enough boiled honey after its foam has been removed. Then peel walnuts and almonds and crush lightly. Add to them pepper, ginger, cinnamon, shelled and unshelled sesame seeds. Sprinkle with sugar. Eat it with enjoyment, God willing.

al-Tujibi, p. 79. Translated by Habeeb Salloum and Muna Salloum.

It is obvious from the name of this sweet that it was created by a lady named Zubayda, or created for her, possibly in admiration of her or in honour of something that she did. The most famous Zubayda (d. AD 831) in history is the wife of the Abbasid Caliph Harun al-Rashid and mother of future Caliph Muhammad al-Amin, and daughter of the second Caliph of the Abbasid Dynasty, Ja'far al-Mansur, so it is no surprise that there could be a connection between her and this sweet.

Zubayda gained fame throughout the Islamic world and, as Hitti so adequately explains, 'in tradition shares with her husband the halo of glory and distinction bestowed by later generations' (302). Historians have noted her fashion statements, such as studding her shoes or slippers with precious stones and introducing brocade and embroidery as part of her wardrobe. She insisted that all serving vessels on the dining table be made of gold or silver and be adorned with precious gems. She set the trend when introducing ambergris candles to Baghdad, the most prolific and cultured city of the then known world (al-Mas'udi VIII 298–99).

On one occasion, seeing a gift of silver-coated boxes and dinars and dirhams that Zubayda had sent to one Abu Yusuf, one observer remarked that in the days of the Prophet, dates and milk were considered gifts (Ibn Khallikan VI 386).

Since one meaning of the word *mushash* is 'one who does much service in journeying', it can be assumed that Zubayda's charitable works for the welfare of the pilgrims during the pilgrimage may have played a role in the naming of the sweet. While on the pilgrimage in Mecca some time in AD 859, and realising that there was an acute shortage of water, she decided to have a canal built. When presented with the exorbitant cost of bringing a permanent source of water to the city, she shrugged it off, stating that 'even if each strike of the axe would be at the cost of a dinar', she would continue with the project.

Mushash are light and crispy with a tasty combination of nuts and spices. The original recipe calls for pepper, but we have replaced it with ground cloves, finding pepper too harsh.

The *Mushash* recipe in *Anonymous* is almost identical, but the preparation technique is much simpler. Al-Tujibi's is richer, with its almonds and walnuts, perhaps because it is linked to the splendid Zubayda, while *Anonymous*'s is simply called '*Mishash*'. *Kanz* lists a *Mushash*, but prepared quite differently from the two Andalusian recipes.

✒ Traditional recipe ᷔ

Serves 10–12
Preparation time: 35 minutes
Standing time: 1 hour 15 minutes
Cooking time: 20 minutes

Ingredients

1 tablespoon granulated sugar
¼ ounce (8 g) active dry yeast
¾ cup (185 ml) warm water
2 cups (240 g) plain flour
1 tablespoon vegetable oil
6 tablespoons butter, melted
Vegetable oil for deep-frying
1 cup (340 g) liquid honey
¾ cup (113 g) blanched whole almonds, coarsely chopped
½ cup (60 g) coarsely chopped walnuts
⅛ teaspoon ground ginger
⅛ teaspoon ground cloves
¼ teaspoon ground cinnamon
3 tablespoons sesame seeds
2 tablespoons caster sugar

Method

Dissolve sugar and yeast in quarter of a cup (65 ml) of the warm water, then allow to stand until the yeast begins to froth (about ten minutes).

To make the dough, in a bowl, add the flour, the yeast mixture and the remaining warm water and knead well, adding more water or flour if necessary. Form into a ball and smooth the tablespoon of oil all around the ball. Place the dough in a bowl and cover. Allow to sit for an hour, or until it has doubled in size.

Punch down the dough and divide into six balls. Roll each ball out on a floured surface into a circle of about ⅛ inch (3 mm) thickness. Brush each circle with the butter. Stack the circles on top of each other to form one circle. Pinch the edges, and cut the stack into three equal wedges.

Carefully roll out each wedge as thinly as possible. Cut into 1 inch (2.5 cm) squares.

Heat the vegetable oil over a medium heat, then deep-fry the squares until lightly golden in colour. Drain on paper towels. Place the *Mushash* in a large deep bowl.

Bring the honey to the boil over a medium heat. Remove from the heat and let sit for five minutes.

Mix together the almonds, walnuts, ginger, cloves, cinnamon and sesame seeds. Keep two tablespoons of this mixture aside. Stir the rest of the nut mixture into the honey.

Pour the honey–nut mixture over the *Mushash* and mix thoroughly but gently. Place the *Mushash* on a serving platter and sprinkle with the remaining nut mixture and finally with the caster sugar.

৬ Modern recipe ৶

M'HANSHA (THE SNAKE), AN ALMOND-FILLED COILED FLAKY PASTRY
Moderately difficult

North African sweets, especially Moroccan, are rich and unique confections made mainly with almonds and flavoured with cinnamon and orange blossom water. They represent the best of what was in al-Andalus and what exists today in North Africa.

M'hansha or *M'hancha* is a round type of crispy stuffed pastry, coiled like a snake, which gives it its name. When served to one visitor in Algeria in the mid-1800s, it was described as coils of dough picturesquely presented on a porcelain dish, appearing as if from *A Thousand and One Nights* (Berthoud II 141). It is a baked flaky pastry stuffed with almond paste and sprinkled with confectioner's/icing sugar and cinnamon.

There is no documented evidence, from our research, concerning the origin of this pastry. Andalusian-Arabic has *han(a)sh* as 'snake' in its vocabulary, and the Arabic for snake, serpent or viper is *hanash*.

We decided to include *M'hansha* in our collection of medieval Arab sweets based upon Moroccan oral tradition, which claims that this sweet originated in al-Andalus. The story is that the Andalusian Muslims expelled in the fifteenth century to North Africa brought with them the 'snake' as part of their dessert legacy. Moroccan friends from Fez, Rabat and Casablanca assure us that *M'hansha* is as old as time in the North African kitchen.

Makes two 9 inch (23 cm) rounds
Preparation time: 45 minutes
Standing time: 5 minutes
Cooking time: 45 minutes

Ingredients
4 cups (380 g) ground almonds
1¾ cups (350 g) granulated sugar
1 tablespoon orange blossom water
1 pound (454 g) filo pastry, thawed according to package directions
1 cup (195 g) clarified butter, melted
2 eggs
Confectioner's/icing sugar
1 tablespoon cinnamon

Method

To make the filling, mix the almonds, sugar and orange blossom water in a bowl. Place the mixture in a food processor and process for one minute.

In a large saucepan, add quarter of a cup (50 g) of the butter and add the filling. Over low heat, cook the filling for five minutes, stirring constantly to avoid sticking. Remove from the heat and allow to cool.

Beat one of the eggs and stir into the filling, mixing well.

Place the filling in the processor and process for one minute. Divide the filling into 9, 11 or 12 parts, depending on the total number of filo sheets. (If the package of filo pastry contains 24 sheets, divide the filling into 12 parts; if it contains 22 sheets, then divide the filling into 11 parts; if the package contains 18 sheets, divide the filling into 9 parts.)

Beat the remaining egg and set aside.

Take two filo sheets and lay lengthwise, one on top of the other, on a counter top. Brush the top sheet with the butter.

Take one of the parts of the filling and spread along the bottom of the filo pastry. Starting from the bottom, roll the two sheets of filo upwards, tucking in the sides, to form a long cigar shape. Brush the egg along the seam of the roll.

Place the rolled pastry piece in a greased 9 by 1¼ inch (23 by 3 cm) pie pan by coiling it around the edge of the pan, seam side down. Continue filling and rolling the filo, placing the rolls next to the ones already in the pie in a coil until the pan is filled. Each pan of this size should take five or six rolls. Brush the top of the *M'hansha* with the remaining butter and the beaten egg.

Bake at 325° F (160° C) for 35–40 minutes. If the top is not browned, place under the broiler/grill until golden. Cool completely.

Sprinkle the *M'hansha* generously with the confectioner's/icing sugar and then decorate with cinnamon.

AL-MUJABBANA (THAT WHICH IS MADE OF CHEESE)
CHEESE FRITTERS

Moderately difficult

✧ *Historical version* ✧

Know that *Mujabbana* is not prepared with only one cheese, but of two; that is, of cow's and sheep's milk cheese. Because if you make it with only sheep's cheese, it falls apart and the cheese leaves it and it runs. And if you make it with cow's cheese, it binds, and lets the water run and becomes one solid mass. The principle in making it is that the two cheeses bind together.

Use one-quarter part cow's milk and three-quarters of sheep's. Knead all until some binds and becomes equal and holds together and doesn't run in the frying pan, but without hardening or congealing. If you need to soften it, soften it with fresh milk, recently milked from the cow. And let the cheese not be very fresh, but strong, without it being too dry so that all the moisture has gone out of it. Thus do the people of our land make it in the west of al-Andalus, as in Cordoba and Seville and Jerez, and elsewhere in the land of the *al-Maghrib*.

Knead wheat or semolina flour with some yeast into a well-made dough and moisten it with water little by little until it loosens. If you moisten it with fresh milk instead of water it is better, and easy, inasmuch as you make it with your palm.

Roll it out and let it not have the consistency of *Mushahhada* (a type of pancake) but firmer than that, and lighter than *Musammana* (buttery) dough. When the leaven begins to enter it, put the frying pan on the fire with a lot of oil, so that it drenches what you fry it with.

Then wet your hand in water and tear off a piece of the dough. Bury inside it the same amount of grated cheese. But first squeeze the cheese with your hand, and the extra liquid leaves and drains from the hand. Put it in the frying pan while the oil boils. When it has browned, remove it with an iron dipper and put it in a dripper similar to a sieve held above the frying pan, until its oil drips out.

Then put it on a big platter and sprinkle it with a lot of sugar and ground cinnamon. There are those who eat it with honey or rose syrup, and it is the best you can eat.

Anonymous, pp. 57 and 169. Translated by Charles Perry.

Al-Mujabbana derives its name from *jubn,* meaning cheese. Thus foods made with cheese are 'cheesified' or *mujabban.*

In the sweet version, *al-Mujabbana* was one of the most popular fritters in al-Andalus. There were two types there, sweet dough balls stuffed with cheese soaked in a honey or sugar syrup, or a layered cake filled with layers of cheese (see p. 137).

It is clear that sweet *al-Mujabbana*s were sold in the souks of al-Andalus. In a twelfth-century handbook for *muhtasibs* (market inspectors), the Malagan al-Saqati, describes the correct proportion of ingredients required to make these cheese pastries. Earlier, in the eleventh and twelfth centuries, Ibn 'Abdun notes that the fresh cheese that comes from al-Mada'in, an area south of Seville, should not be sold in the markets of Seville as it is made from the unclean residue of the curds and is of no value (Ibn 'Abdun 97). Flour was not to be mixed with the cheese used when preparing fritters, since this would be 'false representation of a product', another rule that the *muhtasib* would enforce if necessary (Ibn 'Abdun 100).

Even in the east, the fifteenth-century *Kitab al-Hisba* of the *muhtasib* Ibn al-Mubarrad (al-Mabrad) cites regulations for market inspection in Damascus. Number 39 specifies that those who sell and make milk and cheese and other products in this category must produce excellent-quality goods, are accountable for cleanliness, and that all of the containers and vessels used be covered (Zayyat 384).

The Stanford Dictionary of Anglicised Words and Phrases includes the word *almojabana* as a cheese-and-flour cake, derived from the Spanish. This, in turn, is derived from the Arabic *al-mujabbana*. The same reference work notes that Xerex (Jerez) was noted for 'this dainty'. Ben Jonson, in his comedy *The Devil is an Ass*, first performed in 1616, includes the cheese-cake Almoiauana (4.4.143), in a satire of Spanish fashion.

Jubn, in the medieval Arab world, was made by preparing the starter (*al-'aqid*), using the rennet (*al-infaha*) from the stomach of a lamb or goat or from a cow. *Mujabbana* recipes recommend that both sheep and cow's milk cheeses be used for the filling to avoid a runny stuffing. Specific types of cheese are suggested for certain dishes. Al-Tujibi, for instance, begins his chapter on dairy products with a recipe for *'aqid*, providing them various ways to make use of the cheese for various dishes. His recipe for making cheese is long, detailed and gives ideas what to do with it, such as frying it with or without eggs, or eating it with figs or honey by cutting it into long pieces and dipping it into the honey (216).

For the adaptation of the original recipe, we found that a mixture of a creamy cheese mixed with a cheese with a bit of substance, such as ricotta, worked well, providing a subtle creamy taste to the fritter.

❦ Traditional recipe ❦

Makes 25 pieces
Preparation time: 1 hour
Standing time: 2 hours 10 minutes
Cooking time: 25 minutes

Ingredients

1 tablespoon granulated sugar
¼ ounce (8 g) active dry yeast
¼ cup (65 ml) warm water
3 cups (360 g) plain flour
½ teaspoon salt
½ cup (120 ml) warm whole milk
2 tablespoons butter, melted
1 tablespoon olive oil
8 ounce (227 g) cream cheese, softened (at room temperature)
1 pound (454 g) whole milk ricotta cheese
½ cup (100 g) granulated sugar
1¼ teaspoons cinnamon
Vegetable oil for deep-frying

Method

Dissolve the sugar and the yeast in the water, then allow to stand until the yeast begins to froth, about ten minutes.

While the yeast is rising, combine the flour and the salt in a mixing bowl, then make a well in the middle. Add the yeast, milk and butter. Knead into a dough, adding more flour or milk if necessary (do not allow the dough to become sticky). Shape into a ball, then brush the outside with the tablespoon of oil. Place the ball of dough back into the bowl, then cover. Allow to rest in a warm spot for two hours, or until it doubles in size.

In the meantime, prepare the filling by mixing together the cream cheese and the ricotta using a fork. Cover and refrigerate until the dough has risen.

When the dough has risen, punch it down lightly, then break the dough into 25 balls and roll out thinly into 3½ inch (8.75 cm) circles.

Take one circle of dough and place one tablespoon of the filling in the centre of it. Wetting fingertips slightly, pull up the dough evenly, covering the filling, then pinch together and twist to form a small stem. Make sure to pinch the stem tightly to ensure the filling is locked in tightly. Continue the process with all the circles of dough.

Mix the sugar and cinnamon together in a separate bowl.

Heat the oil over a medium heat and deep-fry the *Mujabbana* until golden brown. Drain on paper towels. While still warm, sprinkle the *Mujabbana* with the sugar–cinnamon mixture.

⤜ Modern recipe ⤛

ALMOJÁBANAS FROM ANDALUSIA, FRITTERS

Moderately difficult

Almojábanas (also spelled *Almojávenes*) are part of the typical cuisine of Alicante, Elche and Orihuela. Some continue to be made with the cheese filling, while others are made with flour and eggs and sprinkled with plenty of sugar. At one time, these sweets were made mainly during winter carnivals and festive occasions. Today they are available all year round. They are soft and sweet-flavoured, with lemon zest and soaked in syrup.

Almojábanas reached Central and South America with the Spanish Conquistadors. Though prepared differently there, with, for example, rice or corn flour, the idea of a deep-fried dough mixed with sugar and soaked in syrup, some with cheese, some without, can all be traced back to the kitchens of the Arabs in Spain.

Makes 30–35 pieces
Preparation time: 45 minutes
Standing time: 5 minutes
Cooking time: 40 minutes

Ingredients

2 cups (500 ml) cold water
2 cups (480 ml) vegetable oil
Pinch of salt
4 cups (480 g) plain flour
15 eggs, beaten
2½ cups (500 g) granulated sugar
¾ cup (255 g) liquid honey
¾ cup (185 ml) cold water
1 cup (115 g) confectioner's/icing sugar

Method

In a large saucepan add the water, oil and salt. Bring to the boil, then gradually add the flour and continue to stir over a medium-low heat until a dough is formed. Remove from the heat. Once the dough has cooled, gradually add the eggs, kneading them into a smooth dough.

With oiled hands form the dough into golf-ball-size balls, then, using both forefingers, puncture a hole through the middle of the ball and stretch the dough to expand it into the form of a doughnut. Place these on a lightly greased baking tray.

Bake at 400°F (200°C) for 20 minutes or until golden. Allow to cool.

While they are cooling, prepare the syrup. In a medium-sized saucepan stir together the sugar, honey and water, and bring to the boil. Lower the heat to medium-low and allow to simmer for 15 minutes, stirring occasionally.

Once the syrup is ready, dip each *Almojábana* in the hot syrup and place on a serving platter. Sprinkle generously with confectioner's/icing sugar.

◁ Alternative modern recipe ▷

BRAYWAT, CHEESE PUFFS FROM TUNISIA

For the experienced cook

Tunisia is one of the Arab countries that still retains much of its Arab Andalusian heritage. Iberian exiles brought culinary expertise and Andalusian culture, and Tunisia would come to preserve many of their recipes.

We have, for example, *Braywat*, fried filo pastry stuffed either with meat and spices or, in the sweet version, with a mixture of nuts and sugar or cheese and sugar.

In both cases, they are light and crispy. We consider this recipe for Tunisian *Braywat* a modernised version of *Mujabbana*, and it is just as good.

Makes about 48 pieces
Preparation time: 1 hour
Cooking time: 20 minutes

Ingredients

Basic *'asal* syrup recipe (see 'Basic recipes' section)
1½ pounds (680 g) whole milk ricotta cheese
¾ cup (150 g) granulated sugar
¾ teaspoon cinnamon
1 pound (454 g) filo pastry, thawed according to package directions
1 egg, beaten
Vegetable oil for deep-frying

Method

To make the filling, mix the cheese, sugar and cinnamon together and set aside.

Lay the filo sheets lengthwise on a flat surface and cut in half. Cover filo with a slightly dampened tea towel. Take one sheet of filo, leaving it lengthwise and place a tablespoon of the filling in the bottom right-hand corner. Fold the sheet to the right lengthwise over the filling. To make the triangle shape, pull up the bottom right-hand corner of the sheet towards the left then to the right, continuing until the filo sheets are folded in the shape of a triangle. Using a pastry brush, paint the egg over the openings of the *Braywat* to ensure they are sealed.

Heat the oil in a large saucepan, place the *Braywat* in the oil and deep-fry until golden. Remove from the oil and immerse in syrup for about 30 seconds. Remove and place in a sieve until the excess syrup drains off. Arrange on a serving platter.

(Tip: these pastries will stay fresh for about three days after they have been made, as long as they are refrigerated.)

MUSHABBAK (LATTICE-SHAPED ZALABIYA)
LATTICE-SHAPED LIGHT DEEP-FRIED PASTRIES

Moderately difficult

✍ *Historical version* ✍

A POETIC APPROACH

I have of the sweets *Zalabiya* in form lattice-shaped and round
Yellow, white and coloured, fried in oil of sesame ground
Soft to touch and delicate, drenched in white thinned honey profound
Arranged in rows like pieces of gold, like golden canes woven around
One another intertwined with the other, as embroidered silk cloth
    together bound
In white sugar they are buried, they are veiled from the eyes
    that surround
They are delicate and dainty to the bite and when they are downed.

al-Warraq, p. 270. Translated by Muna Salloum and Leila Salloum Elias. (See also the translation by Nawal Nasrallah: al-Warraq, *Annals of the Caliphs' Kitchen*, p. 417.)

✍ *Historical version* ✍

ZULABIYYA

Knead fine flour and add water little by little until the dough is slack. Let it be lighter than the dough for *Mushahhada*. Leave it in a pot near the fire until it rises. You will know it is done when you tap on the side of the pot with your finger. If you hear a thick, dense sound, it has risen.

And he who wishes it tinted and coloured may add to some of the batter the juice of brazilwood or gum-lac, or juice of madder or saffron, or juice of tender green fennel, or juice of fox grape.

Then put a frying pan on the fire with plenty of oil, and when the oil boils, take this runny batter and put it in a vessel with a pierced bottom. Put your finger over the hole; then raise your hand and the vessel over the frying pan and quickly remove your finger. The batter will run out through the hole into the frying pan while you are turning your hand in circles, forming rings, lattices and so on, according to the custom of making it. Be careful that the oil is not too little or too cool, or the batter will stick to the pan, but let it be abundant and boiling.

When it is done, take it out carefully and throw it in skimmed spiced honey. When the honey has covered it, remove the pastry to a platter to drain. And serve up the *Zulabiyya*.

Anonymous, pp. 168–69. **Translated by Charles Perry.**

Mushabbak, known as *Zalabiya* in North Africa, are a deep-fried, rich and syrup-drenched pastry in lattice forms. The procedure for making them has not changed since medieval times: the batter, as it is released in motion and dropped into the oil in spirals then fried, forms into *Mushabbak*, literally 'that which is lattice-shaped'.

The Andalusian scientist Ibn al-Baytar (d. AD 1248) considered *Zalabiya* (*Mushabbak*) to be light and faster to digest than *Qata'if* and *Lawzinaj* (II 166). As to their form, Ibn al-Rumi compared them to the process of alchemy – silver dough that becomes latticed windows of gold (al-Azdi 158).

Mushabbak are among the sweets carried by the love-crazed porter as he languishes behind his love interest in the story of 'The Porter and the Three Ladies' (*Tales from the Arabian Nights*). They are also described as being presented to 'Ali ibn Abi Bakr ibn Muhammad in the fourteenth century, on a tray under which lay *Qata'if* sweets:

> A dish of varied sweets is a place of piety, this one in it bowing, this one in
>> it prostrate
> Erected in its courtyard a window made of lattice, and birds
> of *Qata'if* beneath them peaceful and placate
>> (al-Safadi *A'yan* III 307–8)

Mushabbak are still popular in the Middle East and across North Africa, the recipe basically remaining the same throughout the centuries. This centuries-old sweet also has a history in North America.

At the St Louis World Fair in 1904, a Syrian immigrant to the US unknowingly introduced the concept of a 'cone' holder for ice cream by using *Mushabbak* or, as the Syrians called it then, *Zalabiya*. Although a number of Syrians have claimed fame for its induction into American culture, a few names stand out: Anas Hamawi (Earnest Hamwi), Abe Doumar and Nick Kabbaz.

At the Fair, Hamawi set up a booth selling his country's traditional *Zalabiya*. Each *Zalabiya* was baked between two waffle iron dinner-plate-size platens, hinged together and held by a handle over a charcoal fire (Marlowe 2–5). The booth next to him was selling ice cream in glass cups or bowls. The scorching heat was so intense that the ice cream was melting too quickly. The vendor had a problem and, according to a letter written by Hamawi to the *Ice Cream Trade Journal* in 1928, Hamawi offered a solution. Why not – as he showed him – roll the ice cream up in one of his wafer-thin crispy pancakes? The deed was done, and it was a hit.

On the other hand, Abe Doumar, another Arab-American at the Fair, rolled his *Zalabiya* in the same way he did to make a sandwich back home in Syria using flatbread. However, instead of filling it with falafel or yogurt spread, he put ice cream in it and called it 'a kind of Syrian ice cream sandwich' (Marlowe 2–5). According to the Doumar family, his idea took off among the other vendors, Hamawi being one of them.

As for Nick Kabbaz, he and his brother Albert both worked for Hamawi in his booth. The Kabbaz family credits the two brothers for the idea.

The International Association of Ice Cream Manufacturers gives credit to Hamawi and his *Zalabiya*, and to the 1904 St Louis World's Fair, for 'inventing' the ice cream cone. Whether it was Hamawi or one of the others, what we know for sure is that a more modern *Zalabiya* reached North America thanks to one quick-thinking and enterprising young Syrian immigrant.

Although *Mushabbak* recipes appear in all the Arabic source cooking manuals, we have opted for one from the Arab East in poetic form and one from the Arab West. Today's *Mushabbak* in both east and west are gold coloured – just like those described in the thirteenth-century source recipe.

✑ Traditional recipe ✐

Makes about 18–20 pieces
Preparation time: 30 minutes
Standing time: 1 hour 10 minutes
Cooking time: 25 minutes

Ingredients
Basic *qatr* recipe using rose water (see 'Basic recipes' section)
1 tablespoon granulated sugar
1¼ cups (300 ml) warm water
¼ ounce (8 g) active dry yeast
1 cup (120 g) plain flour
¾ cup (90 g) cornstarch/cornflour
⅛ teaspoon salt
1 egg white, beaten until stiff
Light olive oil or vegetable oil for deep-frying

Method
Mix the sugar in quarter of a cup (65 ml) of warm water and add the yeast. Cover and keep in a warm spot, allowing the yeast to rise for about ten minutes.

In a deep mixing bowl, add the flour, cornstarch/cornflour and salt, and mix well. Form a well and add the yeast, the remaining water and the egg white. Beat in an electric mixer for one minute to make the batter smooth.

Cover the bowl and let it sit for an hour to allow the batter to rise. After it has risen, stir.

In a deep saucepan, heat the oil over a medium heat.

Using a funnel, place a finger under the opening and spoon three tablespoons of batter into the top of the funnel. Placing the funnel over the saucepan, remove the finger from the opening and dribble the batter quickly into the oil by moving the funnel rapidly over it, creating a lattice form. Fry on both sides until golden.

Remove from the oil, gently shaking to remove excess oil. Immerse in the syrup, making sure to cover both sides. Place on a serving platter.

QAHIRIYAT (OF THE CALIPH AL-QAHIR BI-ALLAH
OR OF THE CITY OF CAIRO)
SPICY ALMOND RINGS

For the experienced cook

❧ *Historical version* ❧

Take sugar and pound sweet almonds well; take equal parts of each in a mortar and mix them and knead them with fragrant rose water, and perfume them with fine spices, like cinnamon, Chinese cinnamon [cassia], lavender, pepper, galingale and nutmeg. Add these in proportion to what the sugar and almonds can bear. Beat all this well, and then kneading will make it stronger. Then make small rings of this the size of cookies. Then take a *ratl* or half a *ratl* of fine flour or as much as the sugar and crushed almonds can bear, knead it with starch and salt and leave it until it rises, then take some starch and put into that starch water. Then take a frying pan and clean it well and put in some fresh oil, and if it is oil of sweet almonds, it is better. Put this on the fire, and when the oil boils, take the rings made before, one after another, and dip them in that batter and throw them in the boiling oil, so that they cook before they are taken out, and they have begun to brown a very little.

Arrange and order them on a dish in an attractive manner. Then pour over them skimmed honey from the comb, or well-thickened julep syrup, and sprinkle with ground sugar and present it, God willing.

Anonymous, pp. 181–82. Translated by Charles Perry.

❧ *Historical version* ❧

AL-QAHIRIYAH

Pound sugar with the same amount of peeled almonds and pound well. Add to it rose water, cassia, cinnamon, ginger, spikenard, pepper, walnuts or galangale and a little camphor. Knead them together until mixed and they stick together, and make small cakes out of them. Then make a dough from good white flour and starch making a light batter made with yeast, enough for them. Leave it [to rest] after having added sugar to it. Then wipe a slab with extracted fat and put them on the slab and pat down by hand and cut into pieces. Sprinkle sugar, pepper, cinnamon and cassia over them. Whoever wants to make it with honey, then cook the honey until it thickens after removing its froth and put crushed walnuts in it until they are mixed in. The process is complete…when it is complete increase the camphor and spices.

Al-Tujibi, p. 248. Translated by Muna Salloum and Leila Salloum Elias.

❧ *Historical version* ❧

QAHIRIYA

Two parts sugar, one part pistachios, both pounded finely. Knead together with rose water and musk. Put in it a third of its (amount) in flour. Make from it rings and small round cakes. Leave overnight on a tray in order to dry. Take two parts flour and one part starch and knead into a dough slightly thicker than the batter of *al-Mushabbak*. Then drench the rings (in this batter). Put musk and rose water over them.

Ibn al-'Adim, p. 630. Translated by Muna Salloum and Leila Salloum Elias.

Perry attributes the name of these pastries to the Abbasid Caliph al-Qahir bi-Allah (r. AD 932–934) (*Familiar Foods* 422). The Abbasid Caliph's brief reign involved a struggle for power with his emirs and other rebels. Eventually he succumbed to the intrigues of a former vizier and was imprisoned and blinded. It was a decade or more before he was freed, and history relates that some saw him in his last days in beggar's clothes and wooden sandals. Naming a rich cookie after one associated with so much drama might seem a little strange.

However, another possibility is that they were simply named after the city of Cairo, founded in AD 969. Cairo's Arabic name, al-Qahira means 'the Victorious' or 'the Triumphant'. Naming a sweet in honour of a city seems somewhat more plausible.

The best way to describe *Qahiriyat* is that they are spicy-sweet filled crunchy pastries. We have added an egg white to ensure that the cookie remains crisp after frying.

We have chosen three source recipes for our adaptation. One recipe is for a flat cookie version, the other two for ring shapes. Ibn al-'Adim's *Qahiriya* uses pistachios for the filling, in contrast to the almond of the other two recipes.

⸜ Traditional recipe ⸝

Makes 40 pieces
Preparation time: 40 minutes
Standing time: about 6 hours
Cooking time: 35 minutes

Ingredients

2 cups (680 g) liquid honey
½ cup (113 g) unsalted butter
2 cups (190 g) ground almonds
1½ cups (175 g) confectioner's/icing sugar
1¾ cups (210 g) flour
2 teaspoons rose water
½ teaspoon cinnamon
¼ teaspoon ground ginger
½ teaspoon ground fennel
¼ teaspoon pepper
½ teaspoon nutmeg
2 eggs, beaten
1 tablespoon granulated sugar
1 cup (250 ml) warm water
¼ ounce (8 g) active dry yeast
¾ cup (95 g) cornstarch/cornflour
⅛ teaspoon salt
1 egg white, beaten until stiff
Vegetable oil for deep-frying
Caster sugar for decoration (optional)

Method

To make the syrup, in a deep saucepan, mix together the honey and the butter over a medium heat, and bring to the boil. Reduce the heat to very low and keep warm.

In a bowl, mix the almonds, the confectioner's/icing sugar and three-quarters of a cup (90 g) of the flour, then add rose water, cinnamon, ginger, fennel, pepper, nutmeg and eggs and mix well by hand.

Form the mixture into 40 ring shapes by taking a heaped teaspoon of the filling and between the palms of both hands carefully roll into a thick rope and form into a ring. Place on a lightly floured cooking sheet. Continue until the mixture is completely used up.

Let the rings sit for four to five hours to allow them to dry.

To make the batter, mix the granulated sugar in quarter of a cup (65 ml) of the water and add the yeast. Cover and keep in a warm place, allowing the yeast to rise, for about ten minutes.

In a deep mixing bowl, add the remaining flour, the cornstarch/cornflour and the salt, and mix well. Form a well and add the remaining water and the egg white. Beat in an electric mixer for one minute to make the batter smooth.

Cover the bowl and allow the batter to sit for an hour to let it rise.

Heat the oil over a medium heat. Stir the risen batter. Take the rings and fully dip into the batter then fry until golden on both sides. Remove with a slotted spoon and place in the syrup for one minute, then place on a serving platter.

If desired, sprinkle with caster sugar.

⤚ Modern recipe ⤝

MUSTAZZUOLI, SWEET SICILIAN ALMOND-FILLED RINGS

For the experienced cook

One of the most favoured pastries of Sicily is *Mustazzuoli* which, according to Sicilians, is either of Arab origin or has been influenced by the cuisine of the Arabs. Evidence of this is the use of pistachios, almonds, cinnamon and honey in its filling, along with, more than anything, couscous.

This pastry was originally made only for Easter celebrations, but its popularity has made it a much-enjoyed favourite all year round. Its shape and taste are very close to the original *Qahiriyat*.

Makes about 45 pieces
Preparation time: 55 minutes
Chilling time: 1 hour 20 minutes
Cooking time: 30 minutes

Ingredients

4 cups (480 g) plain flour
1⅓ cups (265 g) granulated sugar
Pinch of salt
6 tablespoons cold unsalted butter, cut into ½ inch (1.25 cm) cubes
1½ cups (375 ml) warm water
1¼ cups (425 g) liquid honey
¼ cup (65 g) cold water
¾ cup (75 g) ground almonds
½ cup (80 g) toasted sesame seeds
3 tablespoons unsalted butter, melted
2 teaspoons grated lemon peel
1 cup (173 g) dry couscous
2 tablespoons chopped fresh mint leaves
½ teaspoon vanilla extract/essence
½ teaspoon cinnamon
Confectioner's/icing sugar

Method

In a bowl, mix the flour, a third of a cup (65 g) of granulated sugar and the salt. Add the butter cubes and rub by hand until crumbly. Make a well in the centre and slowly add the warm water, working the dough with the fingers until it comes together, adding more flour or warm water if necessary. Cover the bowl with plastic wrap/cling film and refrigerate for an hour.

In a saucepan, combine the honey, cold water, the remaining granulated sugar, almonds, sesame seeds, melted butter and lemon peel. Cook over a medium heat, and bring to the boil. Stir in the couscous. Allow to cook for three minutes, stirring constantly. Remove from the heat and allow to cool for three minutes. Stir in the mint, vanilla and cinnamon. Pour the mixture into a baking tray and allow to cool for 15 minutes. The filling should be cool enough to handle.

Form the filling into a long sausage shape about ½ inch (1.25 cm) thick. Roll the dough into a long rectangle ⅛ inch (3 mm) thick and 2½ inches wide (6.25 cm) wide. Place the filling in the centre of the dough. Bring up the sides and pinch the edges together, then gently roll the filled dough to form ½ inch (1.25 cm) thick rope.

Preheat the oven to 350°F (175°C).

Cut the rope into 5 inch (12.5 cm) lengths and form into rings, either pinching the ends or allowing the ends just to touch each other. With scissors, snip shallow slits on the tops of the rings.

Place the rings on a greased baking sheet and bake for 30 minutes.

When cooled, dust with the confectioner's/icing sugar and place on a serving platter.

HALAQIM (TUBES)
DECORATIVE NUT-STUFFED PASTRY TUBES

For the experienced cook

✌ *Historical version* ✌

HALAQIM WITH WHICH SWEETS ARE DECORATED

Take from dough made of the finest white flour as much as you like and rub very well with olive oil and/or sesame oil. Then take some reed tubes, the length of the full arm, peel the skin off [the canes] and clean them. Wrap the dough around them and cut them into tubes, finger-knuckle-length. Engrave them with a *manaqash* (sculpting chisel), specifically made for them. When you have finished making that which you put on the reeds, colour the fingers with red, yellow, green and blue, as has been mentioned how to do so at the beginning of this book. Then place the reeds in the tanoor bread oven. When they are cooked, take them out of the oven and remove the reeds from inside them, and what remains are hollow tubes. At that time, proceed to stuff the tubes with walnuts and sugar that have been mixed together until these tubes are completely filled. Then dip their tips [ends] into a thickened sugar syrup that has been made from the hard [variety] and it should stick to them. Then, over that, sprinkle on their tips small chips of *sulaymani* sugar that have been dyed with the above-mentioned colours. Indeed, it will look like an orchard, God willing.

> al-Warraq, p. 276. Translated by Muna Salloum and Leila Salloum Elias. (See also the translation by Nawal Nasrallah: al-Warraq, *Annals of the Caliphs' Kitchen*, p. 425.)

✌ *Historical version* ✌

STUFFED QANANIT FRIED CANNOLI

Pound almond and walnut, pine nuts and pistachio very small. Pound fine and mix with the almond, the walnut and the rest. Add to the paste pepper, cinnamon, Chinese cinnamon [cassia] and spikenard. Knead with the necessary amount of skimmed honey and put in the dough whole pine nuts, cut pistachio and almond. Mix it all, and then stuff the *qananit* that you have made of clean wheat flour.

Its preparation. Knead fine white flour with oil and make thin breads with it and fry them in oil. Knead the dough well with oil and a little saffron, and you roll it into thin flatbreads. Stretch them over the tubes of cane, and cut them how you want them, little or big. And throw them, after wrapping them around the reed. [When cooked and cooled] take them out from around the reed.

Stuff them with the stuffing, put in their ends whole pistachios and pine nuts, one at each end, and lay aside. He who wants his stuffing with sugar or chopped almond, it will be better, if God wishes.

Anonymous, p. 175–76. Translated by Charles Perry.

An interesting recipe in al-Warraq's tenth-century cookbook is that of small stuffed tubular pastries, called *Halaqim*, loosely translated as 'in the shape of the oesophagus' or, rather, 'tube-like'. The author states that these pastries should be used as a type of garnish to decorate serving platters filled with sweets. They are small crispy colourful tube-like shells stuffed with a filling of nuts and sugar, dipped in syrup and garnished with coloured sugar. They resemble, in the words of the author, an orchard of colours.

The two Andalusian Arabic cookbooks include recipes for a comparable dessert named *Qananit* (tubes). The similarity lies in the tube-like shells, which are then stuffed, linking the *Halaqim* of the east and the *Qananit* of the west. *Qananit*, however, is a bona fide dessert, whereas the eastern version is used for decoration. These recipes appear to be the origin of what would later become the famous Sicilian pastry *Cannoli*, introduced into Sicily with the Arab conquest. The term *cannoli* itself is a derivative of the Arabic term *qananit*, the plural of the Arabic *qanaah*, 'a tube or pipe; a canal'.

We have included the earlier eastern version of this tubed sweet, *Halaqim*, and the later one from al-Andalus (*Qananit*). Because the recipe for *Qananit* is very similar to the modern *Cannoli*, we felt it important to give credit to the earlier version from the tenth century. Al-Warraq's recipe's directions for the size of the tubes make it clear that they were much smaller than the standard size used for *Qananit*.

If you decide to make the shells in various colours, we suggest dividing the ingredients by the number of colours chosen. We halved the recipe and made one part green, the other red, as a special Arab tray of sweets for Christmas.

◇ Traditional recipe ◇

Makes 24 pieces
Preparation time: 1 hour 10 minutes
Standing time: 1 hour
Cooking time: 30 minutes

Ingredients

3 cups (600 g) plus 3 tablespoons granulated sugar
1 cup (250 ml) cold water
1 tablespoon lemon juice
2 tablespoons rose water
3 cups (360 g) plain flour
6 tablespoons light sesame oil
½ cup (125 ml) warm water
Few drops food colouring
1½ cups (140 g) finely ground walnuts
6 *Cannoli* tubes, 6 inches (15 cm) in length or shorter
Coloured sugar

Method

To prepare the syrup, in a medium-sized saucepan stir together three cups of granulated sugar and the cold water. Bring to the boil over a medium-high heat, stirring occasionally. Reduce the heat to low and add the lemon juice. Simmer for 15 minutes, stirring occasionally. Add the rose water and simmer for one minute, then remove from heat. Set aside.

To prepare the dough, in a bowl, mix the flour and the oil, then gradually add the warm water and the food colouring to form a dough, adding more flour or warm water if necessary. Knead well for five to seven minutes. Cover the dough tightly with plastic wrap/cling film and a tea towel, and allow to sit for an hour.

While the dough is resting, make the filling by mixing together, in another bowl, the walnuts and the remaining granulated sugar. Set aside until ready to use.

Form the dough into 24 balls. Cover the balls with plastic wrap/cling film.

Preheat the oven to 400°F (200°C).

Take one ball and roll into a very thin circle. Place a *Cannoli* tube along the edge of the dough. Lift the dough around the tube and pinch the edges of the dough tightly to seal over the tube. Continue the process until all the *Cannoli* tubes are used. Place the wrapped tubes on a greased baking sheet and bake for ten minutes or until golden brown.

Once the baked shells are cool enough, remove the tubes carefully. Use the tubes again for further batches until all the shells are baked, and allow all to cool completely.

Carefully spoon the filling into both open ends of the shells, and place on a large serving tray, arranging them side by side.

Generously spoon the syrup onto each end of each *Halaqim*. Sprinkle the coloured sugar over them.

(Tip: we baked the *Halaqim* shells according to the source recipe's instructions, but found that when we fried them they were even flakier.)

୶ Modern recipe ୬

SICILIAN CANNOLI

Moderately difficult

Although the Normans invaded the island of Sicily in AD 1091 and ended Arab rule there, Arab influence lasted another hundred and fifty years. Initially, Norman rule was tolerant, in that Arab influences continued to permeate the courts of the rulers, creating an Arab–Norman culture.

The first Norman king of Sicily, Roger I (d. AD 1101) maintained the former system of Muslim governmental administration, surrounded himself with Muslim administrative officials, and used Muslims in his armies. The Normans even issued their official documents in three languages – Latin, Greek and Arabic.

His son and successor, Roger II (r. AD 1130–54), continued his father's tradition of incorporating Arab culture. He wore robes embroidered with Arabic calligraphy and built a chapel, its ceiling covered with Fatimid-influenced paintings and Kufic Arabic inscriptions. He too retained Arab officials in his government and supported scholarly activities, such as those of the famous Arab geographer, al-Idrisi. It was under his rule that the highest office in the realm was that of *ammiratus ammiratorum* – from the Arabic *amir al-umara'*.

Frederick II (r. AD 1215–50) was, over a century after the end of Arab rule in Sicily, proficient in Arabic. He maintained an interest in the Islamic world with commercial and political relations.

The early Norman rulers of Sicily epitomised the link between east and west. And it could also be for this reason that Arab cuisine left an indelible mark on the island's cooking. And it was from Sicily that Arab culture, especially in food, moved into the mainland. This allowed Italy to absorb some of the Arab-introduced agricultural technology and foodstuffs – with the creativity they fostered – such as the use of sugar and its edible by-products.

Cannoli or 'pipes', once a part of this cuisine, are pastry shells formed on metal tubes, fried to a golden-brown colour and extremely crispy. Renowned in Sicily, they are typically filled with creamed ricotta cheese, sugar and pistachio nuts, decorated with chocolate shavings or pieces, or even candied dried fruits.

According to Malzone, a simple version of *Cannoli* existed in pre-Christian Sicily. Later, it was the Arabs who added sugar, candied fruits, pistachios and cinnamon to the original. These were the prototype of *Cannoli*.

There is a popular Sicilian legend that its famous *Cannoli*, synonymous with Sicilian desserts, was invented by the women of a harem in Caltanissetta, which derived its name from the Arabic *qal'at al-nisa'* meaning 'city of women' (Wright *Mediterranean* 177), the term 'city' denoting the fortress and its environs.

As for the origin of the word *cannoli*, the Spanish term *caño* ('pipes, tubes') and *caña* ('cane', i.e. 'tube') derive from the Arabic *qanaah* ('conduit for water, canal;

pipe'), as does the English term 'cane' (Salloum and Peters *Arabic Contributions to the English Vocabulary*). Thus there is a strong possibility that the Sicilian word *cannoli* may have its roots in the Arabic as well.

In the Sicilian dialect, ricotta cheese is called *zammatàru*, meaning 'dairy farmer'. Wright explains that the Sicilian term is derived from the Arabic *za'ama*, meaning 'cow', indicating that ricotta had its origins during the time of the Arabs in Sicily. Further, he states that the first description of making this cheese is a fourteenth-century illustration in the medical text *Tacuinum Sanitatis in Medicina*, a Latin translation of Baghdadi physician Ibn Butlan's (d. circa AD 1063) *Taqwim al-Sihha* (*The Almanac of Health*), a manual of hygiene and dietetics (*Mediterranean* 467).

Makes 24 pieces
Preparation time: 1 hour
Standing time: 2 hours
Cooking time: 20 minutes

Ingredients

3 cups (360 g) plain flour
6 tablespoons cold butter cut into ½ inch (1.25 cm) cubes
3 tablespoons granulated sugar
¾ teaspoon salt
¼ teaspoon cinnamon (optional)
6 tablespoons unsweetened white grape juice
¼ cup (65 ml) cold water
2 pounds (900 g) whole milk ricotta cheese
1 cup (115 g) confectioner's/icing sugar
2 teaspoons orange blossom water
6 tablespoons orange juice
1 egg, beaten
¼ cup (30 g) chopped pistachios
Vegetable oil for deep-frying

Method

In a bowl, add the flour and cut in the butter. Mix in the sugar, salt and cinnamon. Make a well and add the grape juice and the water, bit by bit forming a dough, adding more flour or water if necessary. Knead well for five to seven minutes. Cover the bowl with a tea towel and let sit for two hours.

While the dough is resting, make the filling by mixing together in another bowl, the ricotta, confectioner's/icing sugar, orange blossom water and the orange juice. Refrigerate until the dough is ready.

Form the dough into 24 balls. Roll each ball out into a very thin circle, then place a *Cannoli* tube along the edge of the dough. Lift the dough around the tube and pinch the edges of the dough tightly to seal over the tube. Brush the seam with the egg, making sure that the egg does not touch the tube.

Over a medium-high heat, heat the oil, and then deep-fry the dough-wrapped tubes until golden brown. Remove and place on paper towels to drain off any excess oil. Once the shells are cool enough, remove the tubes carefully. Continue until all the shells are fried and completely cooled.

Place the filling in a pastry bag and squeeze the filling into each end of the shell. Garnish the ends with the pistachios and serve immediately.

(Tip: if there are any *Cannoli* left over, they can be refrigerated, but the shells will be soggy.)

❧ Alternative modern recipe ❧

MUHAJIRIN (MODERN ARAB IMMIGRANTS') CANNOLI, FILO CANNOLI STUFFED WITH CUSTARD-LIKE CREAM

Moderately difficult

It is usually traditional food that is retained by immigrants as a link to their original homeland, and that's exactly what Arab immigrants have done. Many of them re-work their traditional dishes to suit their fast-paced lives. The old ways become simplified. The sometimes complicated and time-consuming recipes practised by their forefathers in the 'old country' become much easier and quicker to prepare.

Such is the case of *Halaqim* and *Qananit*. Using *Cannoli* tubes to form the casing, and replacing the original stuffing of nuts with a type of homemade cheese called *qashta*, this modern Arab immigrant version of the Sicilian *Cannoli* (see recipe above) is one of the hidden treasures of Arab pastries in the big cities of North America.

Makes a large serving platter
Preparation time: 1 hour 10 minutes
Cooking time: 20 minutes

Ingredients

Basic *qashta* recipe for filling (see 'Basic recipes' section)
1 pound (454 g) filo pastry, thawed according to package directions
1 cup (195 g) clarified butter, melted
Cannoli tubes
1 egg, beaten
Vegetable oil for deep-frying
Confectioner's/icing sugar for decoration

Method

Cut the filo pastry into 4 inch (10 cm) squares and cover with a slightly dampened towel.

Place two sheets on top of each other and slightly brush the top sheet with the butter. Place a *Cannoli* tube on the bottom corner of the filo square (at a 45 degree angle) then roll the dough over the tube. Seal to close by brushing with the egg, making sure that the egg does not touch the tube.

Deep-fry the filo tubes over a medium heat for about a minute, until golden. Remove and place on paper towels, allowing to cool slightly. Carefully remove the *Cannoli* tubes from the fried filo. Once all the filo tubes have been fried, set aside.

When ready to serve, fill each tube from both ends with the *qashta*. Place side by side on a large serving tray. Sprinkle with the confectioner's/icing sugar and serve.

(Tip: these should be served the same day they are prepared, otherwise they become soggy.)

QARMUSH (THAT WHICH IS CRUNCHY)
CRUNCHY BITES

Moderately difficult

❧ *Historical version* ❧

Take a pound of flour and knead it with water and milk. You break two eggs in it, their yolks and whites, and knead it well. Spread finely milled starch under it and roll it out with the rolling pin. Splatter it with clarified butter, fold it over two or three times and cut it into triangles and put them [aside]. Put the frying pan on the fire and fry them – let the fire be quiet – until done and not browned. Throw them in honey and sprinkle them with sugar.

Familiar Foods, p. 431. Translated by Charles Perry.

The name of this sweet is derived from the verb *qarmasha*, meaning 'to eat anything dry or crunchy' or 'to crunch', 'to nibble' or 'to grind', and *qarammash* is the term for the individual who eats everything (al-Saghani 179).

This is a very light and delicious pastry, the dough similar to puff pastry. It is rolled out, buttered, folded, cut into small triangles, deep-fried until golden, and dipped in a honey syrup.

✑ Traditional recipe ❧

Serves 8–10
Preparation time: 40 minutes
Cooking time: 15 minutes

Ingredients
Half of basic *'asal* syrup recipe (see 'Basic recipes' section)
2 cups (240 g) plain flour
¼ cup (60 ml) warm whole milk
3 tablespoons warm water
2 eggs, beaten
Cornstarch/cornflour
¼ cup (50 g) clarified butter
Light olive oil for deep-frying

Method

In a mixing bowl, add the flour and make a well in the middle of it. Add the milk, water and eggs, and knead into a dough, adding a little flour or milk if necessary. Continue kneading for about five minutes to make a very smooth dough. Form the dough into a ball and press down lightly to form a disc shape.

Dust a flat working surface with cornstarch/cornflour. Roll the dough out very thinly into a square, to a thickness of ⅛ inch (3 mm) or even less. Lightly brush the dough with the butter.

Fold the dough in half. Pinch the edges to seal, then roll out again to a thickness of ⅛ inch (3 mm) or less. Lightly brush with the butter, then fold again in half and pinch the edges to seal them. Roll out very thinly, and brush again lightly with the butter. Repeat the process one more time, rolling the dough out to a square of about 12 inches (30 cm) square.

With a sharp knife, cut the dough into 2 inch (5 cm) squares, then cut each square diagonally to form triangles. Pinch two of the three edges of the triangle to seal. Cover the triangles with a towel until ready to fry.

Heat the oil over a medium heat, and deep-fry the triangles, turning them in the oil to ensure that both sides are golden. Remove the *Qarmush* with a slotted spoon, and dip into the warm honey syrup. Place on a serving platter. Serve warm or cool.

QATA'IF (THOSE THAT ARE LIKE VELVET)
STUFFED SWEET CREPE-LIKE PANCAKES

Moderately difficult

❧ *Historical version* ❧

QATAYIF, AND IT IS AL-MUSHADDA

Sift *samidh* flour through a fine sieve and pour into it hot water with which yeast and salt have been well dissolved. Stir by hand until it becomes thick. Add fresh milk to it. Mix all together by hand until it reaches the point where it sticks to the hand. Be careful that it is not too light. Put it in a clean pot and bring it near to the cooking fire so as some of the heat from the fire will reach it without touching it. Leave it like that until it rises. Then, take an earthenware saucepan [*tajin*], specially made for it, which is heated from the bottom and unpunctured. Heat it over the fire. Wipe it with a clean cloth into which salt has been tied, and which has been dipped into fresh clarified butter, then pour the batter into the *tajin*, little by little, forming small rounds the size of normal *Qata'if*. When [small] openings form, remove it and make others. You can test the batter: if there is bitterness in it, add more semolina flour, salt and milk, as needed, and stir it up sufficiently. Make enough *Qata'if* as needed. Then arrange in a deep dish and quench them with boiling honey, adding also melted butter or clarified butter. Sprinkle over them pepper, cinnamon and sugar, and make use, God Almighty willing.

al-Tujibi, p. 71 (#15). Translated by Muna Salloum and Leila Salloum Elias.

❧ *Historical version* ❧

This is of various types. There are those that are the stuffed [*Qata'if*] and baked long-wise, in which are put finely pounded almonds and sugar, folded and laid out, and upon which sesame oil, syrup, rose water and finely pounded pistachios are thrown. There are also the fried ones, and they are the ones that are baked into rounds and into which are put finely pounded almonds and sugar kneaded with rose water. Then they are folded and fried in sesame oil, taken out and dipped in syrup and removed. There are those that are plain, which are placed in a dish and over which sesame oil is poured, then syrup, rose water and finely pounded pistachios.

al-Baghdadi, p. 80. Translated by Muna Salloum and Leila Salloum Elias. (See also the translation by Charles Perry, *A Baghdad Cookery Book*, pp. 103–4.)

QATA'IF MAHSHI
STUFFED PANCAKES

✎ *Historical version* ✎

QATA'IF MAHSHI, STUFFED PANCAKES

Take what you want of good almonds, then blanch them and pound them fine with a little flour. Then add a like amount of sugar to them, and pounded walnuts, and crushed pistachio meats. Then stuff and fry them and throw them in sugar. Thicken musk and throw it on them.

Familiar Foods, p. 439. Translated by Charles Perry.

Drinking from its sweetness, until intoxicated
And drowning in the depths of its yellow sea
Like swollen breasts, they come out of heaven
Swimming in the rivers of Paradise for me.
   (al-Taghra'i (al-Azdi 155))

So it is that *Qata'if* – sweet crepe-like stuffed pancakes swimming in a rich and flavourful syrup – were described as the joys of heaven. In verse, they were the objects of love and desire. At times the depiction was almost indistinguishable from that of amorous love, the mere sight making the heart go mad with desire. Seeing and tasting these delicacies caused an elation similar to that of 'Abbas when he became Caliph (al-Mas'udi VIII 238–39). Arranged like precious pearls woven together, *Qata'if* lying along the side of a serving dish appear like a young girl resting (al-Raghib al-Asbahani II 620).

It is little wonder, then, that the medieval Arabic cookbooks include a number of recipes for them.

The Caliph Harun al-Rashid appears to have enjoyed them, as recorded by one cookbook author, who describes a *Qata'if* filling recipe as '*Qata'if* that was made for Harun al-Rashid' (al-Warraq 274). While Harun may have preferred an almond-based stuffing, Ibrahim ibn al-Mahdi's partiality was for 'pretty' *Qata'if*, with a filling made of 'the tender pith of the date palm', its taste similar to that of walnuts (al-Warraq 274). One vizier hosting an elaborate dinner offered his guests a variety of sweets, the *Qata'if* platter alone holding more than thirty *ratl*s (Ibn al-Jawzi XVI 251).

The Arabic word *qata'if* has its roots in the Arabic *qatifa*, meaning 'plush, velvet'. Such is their distinctive texture, soft and delicate. The poet al-Rumi agreed: 'they the palette ease and the throat they please' (al-Mas'udi VIII 240). Not surprisingly, then, *Qata'if* were given the nickname '*Lafa'if al-Na'im*' ('Rolls of Delicacy'), and 'the food of the ones who are patient' (Ibn Hamdun IX 119).

Arabic poetry extols its virtues. During a banquet hosted by the Caliph al-Mustakfi of Baghdad (r. AD 944–946) he asked his guests to recite poetry that had

79

been written about the different types of food enjoyed in his city. One of the visitors recited a poem attributed to the Baghdadi poet Khushajim (d. AD 961), who glorified *Qata'if* like this:

> I have for my friends if their hunger increases
> *Qata'if* like pages of books and their leaves
> As if they shine first from among other sweets near
> Like the bee's flowing honey, white and sheer
> Oozing out is the oil of the almonds that quenched them
> And settled them and they are wetted in that which they swim
> The rose water came with it, the rose water went
> Leaving bubble on bubble on them were set
> Upon seeing them the grief-stricken heart would delight
> Superimposed in layers as a book's pages on which one writes
> More delicious when one sees them wrenched apart
> With every quarrel of its pleasure they are loved more in heart
>   (al-Mas'udi VIII 406)

If to offer *Qata'if* was a part of the stately standard of elite dining, to stuff them fully was a sign of prosperity, an indication of the generosity of a host – the more filling, the higher the cost to prepare them. Yet, beware of their weight! The judge al-Naqqash, when presented with a tray of *Qata'if*, ordered that they be peeled because of their great weight (al-Tanukhi II 59).

Al-Tujibi's recipes for varieties of *Qata'if* include instructions for the actual batter, as does one recipe in al-Warraq's book. Throughout the culinary texts, however, there is an abundance of recipes for the various stuffings. Some *Qata'if* are fried, some are baked, some are folded. Others are presented in the form of a pancake or thick crepe, over which rich syrup is poured, complemented with sugar and various crushed nuts and flavourings.

We have chosen two filling recipes to work with, both almost identical. As for the batter, although al-Warraq provides detailed instructions for a standard batter (274), we decided to work with al-Tujibi, choosing a different type using milk. This – the cooked circle – we will refer to as a *Qata'if* 'pancake' even though the actual 'pancake' is slightly thinner in texture than a pancake, slightly thicker than a crepe.

⤚ Traditional recipe ⤜

Makes 22–24 pieces
Preparation time: 1 hour
Standing time: 1 hour
Cooking time: 50 minutes

Ingredients

2 cups (334 g) extra-fine semolina
½ teaspoon salt
¼ ounce (8 g) active dry yeast dissolved in ¼ cup (65 ml) warm water, allowed
   to stand for 10 minutes
1½ cups (375 ml) warm water
½ cup (120 ml) warm whole milk
3 tablespoons unsalted butter, melted and mixed with ¼ teaspoon salt
6 tablespoons liquid honey, melted with 3 tablespoons water and 3 tablespoons
   unsalted butter, kept hot
2 teaspoons plus ¾ cup (150 g) granulated sugar
⅛ teaspoon cinnamon
⅛ teaspoon pepper
1 cup (95 g) ground almonds
1 cup (95 g) ground walnuts
1 cup (95 g) ground pistachios
2 tablespoons plain flour
4 teaspoons rose water
Basic *qatr* recipe using rose water (see 'Basic recipes' section)
Light sesame oil for deep-frying
Caster sugar for dipping
½ cup (50 g) finely ground pistachios for decorating

Method

In a large mixing bowl, place the semolina, salt, yeast, water and milk, and whisk vigorously until the batter sticks to the fingers, adding more milk if needed but making sure the batter is smooth and creamy. Cover with a tea towel, then leave in a warm place for an hour.

Take a 12 inch (30.5 cm) square piece of cheesecloth, and drench it with the butter–salt mixture and wipe a medium-sized frying pan with it. Heat the frying pan over a medium heat, then ladle the batter into the frying pan, enough to allow it to spread to form roughly a 6 inch (15 cm) circle. Fry until bubbles form and burst. Remove and place on waxed paper, cooked side down. Continue the same process until the batter is finished.

At this point, the *Qata'if* can be served unstuffed, by placing the pancakes evenly on a serving platter then brushing them with the melted honey mixture. Sprinkle them evenly with two teaspoons of the granulated sugar, the cinnamon and pepper, then serve immediately.

The other option is to prepare stuffed *Qata'if*. For the stuffing, in a separate bowl, mix together the ground almonds, walnuts and pistachios, the remaining ³/₄ cup (150g) of granulated sugar, the flour and rose water. Mix well and set aside.

Take one tablespoon of the filling and place in the middle of the circle. Pull up one side of the circle and fold over, pinching the two edges firmly together to form a half-moon shape. Press along the edge again to secure it. Continue the process of forming half-moons until all the rounds are done.

Heat the sesame oil over a medium heat, then place the *Qata'if* in the oil and deep-fry until golden brown, turning over once to ensure both sides are browned. Place the fried *Qata'if* on paper towels to drain for a few seconds, then immerse into the *qatr* for one minute. Then dip into the caster sugar and place on a serving platter. Once all the *Qata'if* have been placed on the platter, sprinkle evenly with the finely ground pistachios.

Serve either warm or cooled.

⤜ Modern recipe ⤛

BEGHRIR (DRENCHED), HONEY-DRENCHED PANCAKES FROM NORTH AFRICA
Easy

Qata'if appears in its pancake form under the Berber name *Beghrir* in Morocco and Algeria, a type of spongy and airy pancake, smooth on one side and full of tiny burst bubbles on the other. *Beghrir* are light and soft, and are served open-faced with butter and honey. These are especially popular during Ramadan.

Makes about 25 pieces
Preparation time: 20 minutes
Standing time: 1 hour 15 minutes
Cooking time: 1 hour 15 minutes

Ingredients

Half basic *'asal* syrup recipe (see 'Basic recipes' section)

2 cups (334 g) extra-fine semolina

1 cup (120 g) plain flour

¼ ounce (8 g) active dry yeast dissolved in ¼ cup (65 ml) warm water and allowed to stand for 10 minutes

½ teaspoon salt

2 teaspoons granulated sugar

2½ teaspoons baking powder

3½ cups (875 ml) warm water

½ cup (50 g) finely ground pistachios or ½ cup (50 g) finely ground almonds (optional)

Method

Place all the ingredients (except the pistachios or almonds if using them) in a large mixing bowl and whisk vigorously by hand for about two minutes, or until smooth and creamy.

Cover, then allow to stand for about an hour until the batter becomes foamy. Stir and allow to rest for 15 additional minutes, stirring a few times.

Heat a non-stick medium-sized frying pan over a medium heat, and then with a ladle pour the batter in the middle of the hot frying pan. The batter should spread evenly into a circle of 6 inches (15 cm). Burst bubbles should soon appear on the surface. Cook for about three minutes – cook only on one side, until slightly coloured on that side and burst-bubble side has dried. (If the cooking process is complete on underside and the top side has not yet dried, flip the pancake over for a couple of seconds, then remove.) Repeat until all the batter is finished. Make sure that the frying pan does not overheat.

Serve *Beghrir* with the *'asal* syrup and, if desired, sprinkle ground pistachios or almonds over them.

↪ Alternative modern recipe ↩

QATA'IF, STUFFED PANCAKES

Moderately difficult

Generation after generation, *Qata'if* have remained a delicacy. Today's Arab world continues to cherish this sweet for its taste and texture. *Qata'if* are especially popular during Ramadan.

The stuffing, consisting of almonds, walnuts, pistachios (or a mixture of them), sugar and rose water or orange blossom water is basically the same as that described in the medieval Arabic cooking texts. However, in addition to the nut filling, today cheese stuffing made of *qashta* (see 'Basic recipes' section) is another popular option.

Although *Qata'if* is centuries old, time has allowed for changes in preparation. Life is easier for the modern cook. Today, batter for *Qata'if* is rarely made at home. Rather, the souk or a sweet shop can now provide the ready-made cooked pancakes, ready to eat as is or to be stuffed with a filling of one's choice.

Qata'if are available in various sizes, and small ones are popularly referred to as *'Asafiri* ('like little birds'), because they are very light. They are stuffed with *qashta*, then some sugar syrup is poured over them. There is no need to bake or fry them – they are ready to serve. There are two other options for the filling – cheese or walnut. Use a much bigger pancake for these.

Makes about 28 pieces or 35 small pieces
Preparation time: 30 minutes
Standing time: 2 hours
Cooking time: 40 minutes for cheese- or walnut-filled, 25 minutes for *qashta*-filled

Ingredients
2 cups (240 g) plain flour
1½ teaspoons baking powder
½ teaspoon salt
2 cups (480 ml) whole milk
2 eggs
1 cup (227 g) unsalted butter, melted

Cheese Filling
2 cups (500 g) whole milk ricotta cheese
¼ cup (50 g) granulated sugar
1 teaspoon cinnamon

Walnut Filling
2 cups (235 g) chopped walnuts
¼ cup (50 g) granulated sugar
1 teaspoon cinnamon
2 teaspoons orange blossom water

Qashta Filling
2 cups prepared *qashta* (see *qashta* recipe in 'Basic recipes' section)
½ cup (50 g) finely ground pistachios

Basic *qatr* recipe using orange blossom water (see 'Basic recipes' section)

Sift together the flour, baking powder and salt. Place with the milk and eggs in a large mixing bowl, then beat until smooth. Add two tablespoons of the melted butter and beat again, then cover with plastic wrap/cling film and let rest for two hours.

In the meantime, prepare one of the above fillings by mixing the ingredients thoroughly.

Heat a griddle, then grease with shortening or butter. Pour about two tablespoons of the batter to make patties about 3 inches (7.5 cm) across (on a griddle, you can make about four pancakes at a time). Cook on one side only, until that side is slightly browned and bubbles appear and burst on the surface. Remove, and place on waxed paper, cooked side down.

For cheese- or walnut-filled *Qata'if*, place about two teaspoons of the filling on each pancake, then fold over to make a half-moon shape. Press the edges firmly together. Transfer to a buttered baking sheet or tray, then repeat the procedure until all the batter is finished.

Preheat the oven to 375°F (190°C).

Pour some of the remaining melted butter over each *Qata'if*, then bake for 10–15 minutes. Remove from the oven and immediately dip into the syrup. Place onto a serving platter, and allow to cool before serving.

For the *Qata'if* filled with *qashta*, pinch the edges of the pancake half way, to close partially. Stuff the open side with the *qashta*, and place on a serving platter. Drizzle with *qatr*.

Sprinkle with the pistachios and serve.

AL-QAYHATA (THAT WHICH IS MADE OF CHEESE)
LAYERED CHEESECAKE PASTRY

Moderately difficult

❧ *Historical version* ❧

MUJABBANA COOKED WITH MILK IN THE OVEN AND CALLED AL-QAYHATAH

Make a dough of white flour with water and salt, kneading firmly. Make loaves as thin as possible after the dough rises somewhat. Bake in the oven, taking heed of the flame. Then wipe away the oven's dust and ashes. Rub fresh cheese well and put in it some mint water, water of fresh coriander, pepper and cloves. If the cheese is too dry, moisten it with milk after softening it by rubbing it a little. Then form good loaves from the dough. Add hazelnuts and bake in the bottom of a *tajin* [round earthenware saucepan] and put over it enough cheese to cover it. Put over the cheese another loaf from the already baked thin loaves and put milk that has been warmed on the fire after it has been heated. Cover all of this with a coarse loaf of the dough and send it to the oven and check it. If the milk dries and the loaves have absorbed it, pour over it more milk in the same fashion and continue to moisten it again and again as you tend to it, with utmost attention to it, until it completely absorbs the milk. Once it has finished baking and the upper loaf begins to brown, take it out of the oven and remove its cover, which is the coarse top loaf. Pour over it hot honey into which was added pepper and Chinese cinnamon after having sliced the cheese cake in slices, and cover them for an hour until it cools down and the honey is absorbed, and use it. Indeed, it is the most delicious thing. Whoever wishes to fry the loaves in oil, do not overcook them. Do it in the same way you did at first. These cheese cakes can be made plain without cheese because these loaves can be baked over one another without placing cheese in between. Then, wet it with milk and cover with a coarse loaf and send it to the oven, and wet it with milk again and again. Once it is finished cooking, remove from the oven and wet with honey, and it is used as previously mentioned.

al-Tujibi, pp. 83–84 (#35). Translated by Muna Salloum and Leila Salloum Elias.

❧ *Historical version* ❧

QAIJATA (MADE IN AL-ANDALUS, AND CALLED 'SEVEN BELLIES')

Take moist, fresh cheese and knead it in the hands. Then take a deep, wide-bellied clay tajine [*tajin min hantam*], and in the bottom of it put a thin flatbread, made like *Kunafa*. Put the cheese over this, and then another crepe, and repeat this until there remains a third to a quarter of the pan.

Pour fresh oil over it, place it in the oven, and leave it a little; then take it out, moisten it with a little fresh milk, and return it to the oven, and take it out and moisten with fresh milk and return to the oven thus, until the milk and the oil disappear.

Leave it until its surface is browned to the colour of musk; then take it out and pour skimmed honey cleaned of its foam, or rose syrup, over it. There are those who sprinkle it with ground sugar and spices, and others who leave it be.

Anonymous, p. 59, 171. **Translated by Charles Perry.**

Al-Qayhata, al-Qayjata or *al-Fayjata* is a layered cake of cheese. Perry and Waines define it as a cake of 'seven bellies'. In the Andalusian Arabic dialect, derived from the root *qyjt, qayjat* is a curd of milk and *qayjata* is a kind of cheese cake made with seven layers of baked waffles and cheese soaked in milk and covered with sugar and honey, the word being derived from the Latin *caseata* (Corriente 450). The recipe for this cake is found only in two Andalusian source cookbooks, demonstrating that it was not known in the eastern Arab world.

Qayjata (also referred to as *Qayshata*) was one of the cities in the district of Jaén in al-Andalus, considered absolutely beautiful and the land extremely fertile (Ibn Sa'id II 63). *Qayjata*, according to *Taj al-'Arus*, was the common Arabic spelling by authors who wrote about or who made reference to this city (4971). Yet it is the Arabic spelling *Qayshata* that prompts one to consider a link to cheese.

In Spanish, the district's name appears as Quesada, derived from the Old Spanish word *queso*, derived in turn from the Vulgar Latin *caseus* ('cheese' or 'pressed curd'). According to the Quesadans, the term *quesada* is used to describe a set of freshly made cheeses. The Arabic *Qayshata*'s base consonants are '*q*', '*sh*', '*t*', which is the root of *qashta*, a rich, thick clotted cream used for fillings, specifically in sweet dishes (see 'Basic recipes' section). Whether the name is from Arabic or Latin, obviously fresh-made cheeses made this locale important.

The adapted recipe is based upon that found in *Anonymous*. Al-Tujibi's version includes cheese flavoured with mint, coriander, pepper and cloves, with hazelnuts added to the bottom layer of the cake.

∽ Traditional recipe ~

Serves 8–12
Preparation time: 40 minutes
Cooking time: 30 minutes

Ingredients

1½ cups (510 g) liquid honey
⅓ cup (76 g) unsalted butter
1½ pounds (680 g) whole milk ricotta cheese
22 sheets filo pastry, thawed according to package directions
¼ cup (60 ml) light olive oil
⅛ cup (30 ml) whole milk

Method

Place the honey and butter in a saucepan, and bring to the boil. Keep warm over a very low heat.

Divide the ricotta into seven portions.

Remove the filo pastry from the package and unroll gently. Cover with plastic wrap/cling film until ready to use.

In a greased 9 by 13 by 2 inch (23 by 33 by 5cm) baking pan, place five sheets of the filo, brushing each layer lightly with the oil, then spread one portion of the ricotta evenly over the dough. Repeat the process using two sheets of filo a further six times, brushing each filo piece with the oil and spreading the ricotta on every two sheets of filo. Finally, place the final five sheets of filo on top, again brushing each piece with the oil.

Preheat the oven to 350°F (175°C).

With a sharp knife, cut the tray of filo into 1½ inch (3.75cm) squares.

Pour the oil evenly over the *Qayhata* and bake for 15 minutes. Remove from the oven and sprinkle one tablespoon of the milk evenly over the top of the *Qayhata*. Cook for a further ten minutes, remove from the oven, and sprinkle with the remaining milk. Return to the oven, and cook for another five minutes.

Immediately pour the honey mixture evenly over the top of the *Qayhata*. Let sit for about five minutes, then serve while warm.

❧ Modern recipe ❧

KUNAFA BI AL-JUBN (SHREDDED FILO WITH CHEESE),
SHREDDED FILO PASTRY CHEESECAKE

Moderately difficult

Kunafa bi al-Jubn is a very popular cake in the eastern Arab world. It is usually served as a breakfast entrée on special occasions or as an after-dinner treat. Light, crispy and sweetened to an individual's taste, it is made with shredded filo pastry (*kataifi*) with a filling of *qashta*, ricotta cheese, or a mixture of both.

Although not necessarily a direct descendant of *al-Qayhata*, it continues the tradition of using cheese as a filling for cakes and other pastries.

Serves 8–10
Preparation time: 35 minutes
Cooking time: 30 minutes

Ingredients

Basic *qatr* recipe using orange blossom water (see 'Basic recipes' section)
1 pound (454g) *kataifi* pastry (shredded filo), thawed according to package
    directions
1 cup (227g) unsalted butter, melted
1 pound (454g) whole milk ricotta cheese, broken down with a fork
1 teaspoon orange blossom water
¼ cup (25g) ground pistachios or ¼ cup (25g) ground almonds

Method

Place *kataifi* in a baking tray and pour the butter evenly over the top. Gently rub the *kataifi* by hand a number of times, ensuring that every part of the *kataifi* is moist with butter and that the strands separate (this could take between 10 and 15 minutes). Divide the *kataifi* into two portions. Take one portion and flatten by hand into a well-buttered 9 by 13 by 2 inch (23 by 33 by 5cm) baking pan.

Preheat the oven to 350°F (175°C).

Combine the cheese and the orange blossom water, then spread evenly over the dough in the pan. Spread the other half of the dough evenly on top.

Bake for 25–30 minutes, or until the edges turn golden brown. If the surface has not turned a golden colour, place the pan under the broiler/grill, and turn it around until the top of the *Kunafa* is evenly golden.

Remove the *Kunafa* from the oven and, while still hot, pour half of the syrup evenly over the top. Garnish with the pistachios or the almonds, then cut and serve while hot. Place the remaining syrup in a serving pitcher, and pour over the cut pieces according to taste.

SANBUSAJ MUKALLAL (CROWNED TURNOVERS)
ALMOND-FILLED TURNOVERS

For the experienced cook

⊱ *Historical version* ⊰

As for *al-Sanbusaj*, it is to take the meat described in the preparation of *al-maqluba*. Cut up the thin bread that is used for that and stuff with the aforementioned meat after having cut it up into strips. Make them triangular. Then stick them [the edges] with a little dough. Drop them in sesame oil, then remove. As for those called *al-mukallal*, put in place of the meat finely pounded sugar and finely pounded almonds made into a paste with rose water, or with *al-halwa' al-sabuniya* and fried in sesame oil. There are some who take it out of the sesame oil and put it in syrup, then remove it from it and leave it in finely pounded sugar scented with musk and camphor, for whoever wants to do so.

al-Baghdadi, p. 58. Translated by Muna Salloum and Leila Salloum Elias. (See also the translation by Charles Perry, *A Baghdad Cookery Book*, pp. 78–79.)

Sanbusaj or *Sanbusaq* were and are popular 'turnovers', or a type of filled pastry made especially in the eastern Arab world and beyond. In medieval times, various forms of *Sanbusaj* appear in triangular, circular, half-moon, crescent, square or rectangular shapes. They are either filled with meat and spices or in the category of sweets, filled with nuts. Both variants are included in al-Baghdadi's source recipe, just as both appear in the recipe for *al-Sanbusak al-Mukallal* in *Familiar Foods* (379).

And it is *Sanbusaj* that proved what good fortune life had bestowed on the thirteenth-century Ibn al-Naqid, Vizier during the reign of the Caliph al-Mustansir (r. AD 1226–42). As a good and honest Vizier, it was only natural that if good things happen to good people, luck will follow. One incident proved this well.

One day before becoming Vizier, Ibn al-Naqid was getting ready for a forthcoming holiday. His kitchen staff was making quite a large number of *Sanbusaj*. In the mood to play a joke on his friends, he ordered that 70 of the *Sanbusaj* be stuffed with cotton seed and bran. This done, he left to visit the Caliph.

While there, the Caliph requested some *Sanbusaj* from Ibn al-Naqid. After all, it was common practice for him to make a very large number for any approaching holiday. Ibn al-Naqid told him that they had just come out of the oven, and thus ordered his servant to bring some to the Caliph.

The servant left not knowing about the ruse of the cotton-seed filling. At Ibn al-Naqid's, he gathered up the *Sanbusaj*, mixed them all together and put them on trays to take back to the Caliph's residence. But before he left, the servants approached him and asked for their share of the filled pastries. They took a hundred of them, and the servant left, continuing on his way back to the royal palace with the remaining trays.

By the time the servant reached the Caliph, Ibn al-Naqid had reached his own house and was already asking about the cotton-seed-filled *Sanbusaj*. He was told that no one knew a thing about them except that a servant had come and gathered them all up together and left with them.

At that moment, Ibn al-Naqid felt the ground fall from beneath him. There was little doubt that he was now doomed. In horror, he felt the strength leave him. His joke was being played on the Caliph. He was very embarrassed.

Were there any left behind?

When he learned that the servants had taken about a hundred of them for themselves, Ibn al-Naqid called for them. They arrived, placing before him the 70 cotton-seed-filled ones, which, it just so happened, had not been among those sent to the Caliph. To Ibn al-Naqid's relief, not one was missing (Ibn al-Tiqtaqà 307). So it was that fate played favourably with Ibn al-Naqid, thanks to servants hungry for *Sanbusaj*.

Clifford Wright includes one theory that *Sanbusaj* is the origin of the Italian *Calzone*. It is said that *Calzone* may have been introduced by the Muslims in the medieval period, and that if this is the case then it is related in some way (*Mediterranean* 563).

Anonymous states that the dough is kneaded with clarified butter or melted fat. Not much has changed. Medieval *Sanbusaj* are much like their modern counterparts, and we have, therefore, given the common dough used in the contemporary eastern Arab world for our adaptation.

We found *Sanbusaj Mukallal* delicious hot out of the oil. However, once we dipped them into the *qatr* and then sprinkled the confectioner's sugar over the top, it was clear that this was the 'crowning' touch.

❖ Traditional recipe ❖

Makes about 25 pieces
Preparation time: 55 minutes
Standing time: 30 minutes
Cooking time: 20 minutes

Ingredients

Basic *qatr* recipe using rose water (see 'Basic recipes' section)
2 cups (240 g) plain flour
1 tablespoon sugar plus 1 cup (200 g) granulated sugar
2 tablespoons unsalted butter, softened
½ cup (125 ml) warm water
1½ cups (145 g) ground almonds
1 tablespoon rose water
Oil for frying (either light sesame or vegetable oil)
Confectioner's/icing sugar (optional)

Method

In a mixing bowl, add the flour and one tablespoon of the sugar, and mix well. Add the butter and water, and knead into a soft dough. Cover and let rest for half an hour.

While the dough is resting, prepare the filling by mixing together in a bowl the almonds, the remaining sugar and the rose water.

Roll the dough to a thickness of ⅛ inch (3 mm), then cut into circles about 3 inches (7.5 cm) in diameter with a pastry cutter. Roll each circle again, and place a level tablespoon of the filling in the centre. Fold, forming either a triangular or a half-moon shape.

Triangular shape: pull up the two opposite sides of the circle over the filling and pinch the edges together, starting from the middle to the end. Lift the bottom open edge up and pinch it to the middle, forming a triangle. Pinch again along the three seams to ensure they are sealed well.

Half-moon shape: pull up one side of the circle and pull over the filling, forming a half-moon, then pinch the edges together to ensure the edges are sealed well.

Over medium heat, fry the *Sanbusaj* in the oil until both sides are golden brown. Dip immediately in the *qatr* for about 30 seconds, then place on a serving platter.

Once the *Sanbusaj* has cooled, you can dip each into confectioner's/icing sugar then arrange on a platter for serving.

ZALABIYA (FRITTERS)
SWEET CRULLERS

Easy

✄ *Historical version* ✄

ZALABIYA PREPARED FOR AL-MA'MUN

Take two *ratl*s of fine *samidh* flour and take a *tinjir* [pot with a rounded bottom] and put half a *ratl* of oil in it. Put it over a gentle fire. When the oil boils, sprinkle that flour over it and stir until toasted. Then pour two *ratl*s of water over it and stir continually until its oil is released. Then remove from the fire. Stir until it reaches a firm consistency and is cooked. Make dough into smooth balls and form into finger-shapes, ring-shapes and round little cakes in the same fashion as *sulaymani* sugar. When all are done take one *ratl* of honey skimmed of its froth, or enough *ratl*s as needed. Sprinkle over it one-half *ratl* of rose water with aromatics. Put it over the coals until it is heated and has boiled once. Remove from the fire. Take a *ratl* of *tabrazad* sugar, pound it and sift it and set aside. Take a new frying pan or *tinjir* and pour into it a *ratl* of fat. Then put it over the fire until it boils. Then throw into it the pieces of dough that have been made into the shapes of *sulaymani* sugar as *Zalabiya* is fried. Even better is to throw them into fresh and good clarified butter. Whenever a *Zalabiya* is taken out of the fryer while it is hot, throw it into the heated honey. Leave them in it for the amount of time needed to soak up the honey. Remove gradually and arrange in layers on a serving vessel. Sprinkle the pounded sugar over them and between them until they are all done. Then serve it.

> **al-Warraq, p. 267. Translated by Muna Salloum and Leila Salloum Elias. (See also the translation by Nawal Nasrallah: al-Warraq, *Annals of the Caliphs' Kitchen*, pp. 413–14.)**

In the tenth century, al-Muqaddasi relates that in *Bilad al-Sham* (Greater Syria) in the winter the people prepare the unlatticed type of *Zalabiya* (183–84). This would be the deep-fried bread fritter *Zalabiya*. Some are elongated in shape, similar to crullers, while the smaller ones, sometimes made into balls, are similar to the shape of dumplings. *Zalabiya* are easy to make, and have remained among the most popular of Arab sweets in Syria, Lebanon, Palestine, Jordan and Iraq to the present day.

Basically, *Zalabiya* are pieces of dough that are deep-fried, then most commonly sprinkled with sugar or dipped in sugar or honey-based syrup.

In North Africa, the name *Zalabiya* is given to *Mushabbak* (see p. 62), a deep-fried lattice-shaped pastry made by looping batter, and drenched in *'asal* syrup or *qatr* (see 'Basic recipes' section).

Zalabiya are one of the 'basic' sweets that reached the dining tables of the caliphs. The source recipe indicates that these were prepared for the Caliph al-Ma'mun, and thus part of medieval Baghdad and its fineries. In the story 'The Rogueries of Dalilah the Crafty and Her Daughter Zaynab' from *Tales from the Arabian Nights*, the Badawi swears he will eat nothing else except *Zalabiya bi 'asal* (*Zalabiya* with honey) once he reaches Baghdad, the fried fritter he had never eaten and the city which he had never entered.

The recipe below is taken from Freda Salloum, who learned the method from her Damascus-born mother, Nabiha. Nabiha learned her culinary skills from the household womenfolk in her traditional home in Syria, cooking methods which seem hardly to have changed over the centuries. Grandmother Nabiha had not met Grandmother Shams – the latter hailing from the Lebanese city of the Qar'awn – until Habeeb and Freda married, but lo and behold, their *Zalabiya* recipes were exactly the same. In Grandmothers Nabiha's and Shams's kitchens, *Zalabiya* was served for either breakfast or as an after-dinner snack, and prepared with love.

Below is the traditional recipe for *Zalabiya*, which is common in the Arab East. *Zalabiya* can also be dipped into *qatr* or honey for a sweeter taste.

(Tip: they are best eaten the day they are made.)

∾ Traditional recipe ∾

Makes about 20
Preparation time: 30 minutes
Standing time: 1 hour 25 minutes
Cooking time: 20 minutes

Ingredients
1 tablespoon granulated sugar
¼ cup (65 ml) warm water
¼ ounce (8 g) active dry yeast
2 cups (240 g) plain flour
½ teaspoon salt
2 tablespoons vegetable oil
½ cup (125 ml) warm water
Vegetable oil for deep-frying
Granulated sugar for dipping

Method

Dilute the sugar in quarter of a cup (65 ml) of warm water, then stir in the yeast. Cover and allow to sit for ten minutes, or until frothy.

In a mixing bowl, stir together the flour and the salt. Form a well in the middle, then add the yeast mixture, oil and half a cup (125ml) of water. Knead into a soft and sticky dough, adding a little water or flour if necessary. Cover, and allow to sit for an hour or until it doubles in size.

Punch the dough down gently. Pinch off a piece of dough the size of an egg and stretch it into an oblong shape, about 6 inches (15cm) long. If necessary, dip your fingers lightly into the flour to make the handling of the dough easier. Cover the pieces with a tea towel, and allow to sit for 15 minutes.

Deep-fry in the oil on medium heat until the *Zalabiya* are a deep golden colour. Drain on paper towels, then, while still warm, dip lightly into the sugar. Place on a serving platter.

⤜ Modern recipe ⤞

HALWA SHABAKIYA (LATTICE-STYLE SWEETS), CRUNCHY SESAME PASTRIES

For the experienced cook

In the contemporary Arab world, from Iraq to Morocco, *Zalabiya* are still popular, with a few changes from the medieval Arabic recipes. Morocco, for example, has added to the original and created a more complicated lattice-fried fritter known as *Halwa Shabakiya*. The same name is also applied to variant forms of this pastry in Tunisia and Algeria.

In Morocco and Algeria, they are colloquially called *Kriyush*, or *Griouches*. They are served during the holy month of Ramadan, and interestingly enough are served as a side dish with the soup which breaks the daily fast.

These crispy sesame-flavoured syrup-soaked pastries take some time to make because of the complicated twisting involved in shaping them. Nevertheless, the result is worth the effort!

Makes about 30 pieces
Preparation time: 45 minutes
Standing time: 2 hours 10 minutes
Cooking time: 25 minutes

Ingredients

¼ cup (65 ml) warm water
1 tablespoon granulated sugar
¼ ounce (8 g) active dry yeast
¼ cup (40 g) sesame seeds, toasted and finely ground
3 cups (360 g) plain flour
1 egg, beaten
2 tablespoons lemon juice or vinegar
2 tablespoons unsalted butter, melted
2 tablespoons vegetable oil
2 tablespoons orange blossom water
1 pinch of saffron, dissolved in 2 tablespoons warm water
2 cups (680 g) liquid honey
Vegetable oil for deep-frying
¼ cup (40 g) sesame seeds, toasted

Method

In a bowl, mix the warm water and sugar, then stir in the yeast. Cover and allow the yeast to rise for about ten minutes.

In a mixing bowl, add the ground sesame seeds, flour, egg, lemon juice or vinegar, butter, two tablespoons of oil, one tablespoon of the orange blossom water and the dissolved saffron. Add the yeast solution and knead into a dough. Cover, and allow to rest for 1½ hours, or until it doubles in size.

Punch down the dough. Roll out the dough as thinly as possible, then cut into 3 inch (7.5 cm) squares. Roll out each square, and score into ½ inch (1.25 cm) strips, leaving the ends attached. Take each square and thread your index finger through alternate strips. Take the top corners and pinch them together. Do the same for the bottom. Gently pull your finger out of the strips. Carefully turn the *Shabakiya* inside out and place each one on a baking tray. Cover and let sit for 30 minutes.

In a medium-sized saucepan, stir in the honey and the remaining orange blossom water, mixing them well, and leave over very low heat.

In a large saucepan, add the vegetable oil for deep-frying, and heat over a medium heat. Deep-fry the pieces until golden, turning over once. Place the hot *Halwa Shabakiya* in the honey, coating the entire piece, then lift with a slotted spoon, allowing any excess honey to drip off. Place the *Halwa Shabakiya* on a serving platter, and sprinkle evenly all over with the toasted sesame seeds.

⸎ Alternative modern recipe ⸎

*LES OREILLETTES MONTPELLIERAINES (MONTPELLIER EARS),
CITRUS-FLAVOURED CRISPY PASTRIES FROM SOUTHERN FRANCE*

Easy

Montpellier in southern France has a connection with the Arabs. In the medieval period, it was famous for its medical school, founded indirectly by the Arabs, because many of the Arabic medical manuals formed the basis of the curriculum. Al-Zahrawi's surgical text, for instance, became the school's manual of surgery (Hitti 577), as was Avicenna's *Qanun fi al-Tibb* (*The Canon of Medicine*), which when translated into Latin in the twelfth century became one of the fundamental texts that students were required to read at the university until the mid-seventeenth century. It was also a trade centre, with links across the Mediterranean, and the city was known for its spices – candied aniseed, for example. By the end of the thirteenth century Europe had adopted much Arab science and philosophy, and Montpellier was one of the chief centres of the transmission of Arab and Muslim thought, and the principal centre of medical and astronomical studies in France (Hitti 589). It is little surprise, then, that there was an edible element to this transmission.

The recipe below is a version of the French *Les Oreillettes Montpellieraines*. Clifford Wright states that these fritters date back to a class of Arab sweets called *qaras* ('patties') because the dough is shaped into a disc then prepared for frying, basically the same concept as *Zalabiya* (*Mediterranean* 164).

Light and delicious, no wonder this pastry, which began in the Arab East and North Africa, spread through the Iberian Peninsula and beyond.

Makes about 30–35 pieces
Preparation time: 30 minutes
Standing time: 2 hours
Cooking time: 20 minutes

Ingredients
3 cups (360 g) plain flour
½ cup (100 g) granulated sugar
3 large eggs, beaten
6 tablespoons unsalted butter, melted
Grated zest of 1 lemon
Grated zest of 1 orange
2 tablespoons whole milk
1 teaspoon orange blossom water
Vegetable oil for deep-frying
Confectioner's/icing sugar

Method

In a mixing bowl, combine the flour and sugar, then make a well in the centre. Into the well pour the eggs, butter, zests, milk and orange blossom water. Begin to work the dough by hand, incorporating all the ingredients, then knead until an elastic ball is formed, adding more flour or water if necessary.

Cover with plastic wrap/cling film and leave to rest at room temperature for two hours.

Dust the work surface with flour.

Cut off a handful of dough. Roll the dough out very thin, to a thickness of about ⅛ inch (3 mm). Cut into rectangular shapes approximately 3 by 2 inches (7.5 by 5 cm).

In a large saucepan, heat the oil over a medium heat. Deep-fry the rectangles until golden, turning once, then drain on paper towels. Allow to cool.

Sprinkle with the confectioner's/icing sugar.

⚛ Alternative modern recipe ⚛

CHURROS, DEEP-FRIED FRITTERS FROM SPAIN

Easy

Churros, and the sweeter version *Pestiños*, are forms of the *Zalabiya* fritter of the medieval Arabs in Spain, another survivor of the Moorish kitchen in today's Spain. However, *Churros* are sprinkled with powdered sugar and served with a piping hot chocolate sauce rather than, as in the past, being dipped in boiling honey. In our household these were the weekend fritters, which we enjoyed almost every Sunday morning as a special treat.

Makes about 30 pieces
Preparation time: 20 minutes
Cooking time: 25 minutes

Ingredients

2½ cups (300 g) plain flour
½ teaspoon salt
2¼ cups (565 ml) cold water
1 tablespoon olive oil
Vegetable or canola oil for deep-frying
½ cup (60 g) confectioner's/icing sugar

Method

In a bowl, mix the flour and salt.

In a medium-sized saucepan, bring the water and the olive oil to the boil over a medium-low heat, then add the flour. Stir quickly over the heat until the flour is completely mixed in with no lumps, forming a stiff, sticky dough.

Allow the dough to cool slightly, but while still warm transfer it to a strong piping bag fitted with a narrow, fluted nozzle.

In another medium-sized saucepan heat the oil for deep-frying to at least ½ inch (1.25 cm) deep, until it is very hot. Reduce heat to medium. Squeeze out the dough to approximately 4 inch (10 cm) lengths. Deep-fry the *Churros*, three or four at a time, turning once, until they just begin to turn golden. Drain on paper towels then dip in the confectioner's/icing sugar to coat lightly.

Serve immediately.

∽ Alternative modern recipe ∾

FARTURAS, LEMON-FLAVOURED FRITTERS FROM PORTUGAL

Easy

The Portuguese language is infused with words of Arabic origin, reflecting the contributions made by the Arabs to the country. The Portuguese 'Age of Discovery' in the early fifteenth century, when the country embarked on exploration and settlement, was instigated in part by the introduction of the lateen sail and the astrolabe by the Arabs, both instrumental for successful sea travel and navigation.

Portugal retains many traces of the almost five hundred years of Arab presence, most evident in the Algarve, the southernmost province of the country. There they introduced new agricultural technologies, thus allowing the expansion of fields of almonds, apricots, carobs, figs, citrus fruits, olives, oranges, pomegranates, rice, sugar cane and various new vegetables and spices. Parts of the Arab diet continued after their defeat, such as cereals, olive oil, butter, mutton, goat, fish, poultry and cheese.

One of the major contributions made by the Arabs to the cuisine of Portugal is the sweetening of desserts with sugar instead of honey. The technique of marinating and combining ingredients to produce a sweet-and-sour taste, and the method of frying a flour-and-egg-based batter, are other contributions that survive.

The mixture of almonds, sugar and honey from the days of the Arabs gave Portugal its nougats and marzipans. Among fried sweet doughs, the popular *Fartura* is a development of the original Arab *Zalabiya* (Sobral 73).

Makes about 12–15 pieces
Preparation time: 20 minutes
Cooking time: 25 minutes

Ingredients

1 cup (250 ml) cold water
½ cup (113 g) unsalted butter
Grated peel of 1 lemon
2 tablespoons granulated sugar
1 cup (120 g) plain flour
4 eggs
Vegetable oil for deep-frying
1 cup (200 g) granulated sugar mixed with 1 teaspoon cinnamon

Method

In a medium-sized saucepan, combine the water, butter, grated peel and the 2 tablespoons of sugar. Cover, and bring to the boil over a medium-high heat. As soon as the water mixture begins to boil, pour in the flour while stirring quickly with a wooden spoon, until the batter pulls away from the sides of the pot and begins to form into a ball of batter. Remove the saucepan from the heat and allow the batter to cool for one minute while still in the saucepan.

Beat eggs one at a time into the dough, making sure to mix them in well.

In a large saucepan, add the oil for deep-frying, and heat over a medium heat.

Using a pastry bag with a serrated nozzle, half fill the bag with some of the batter. Squeeze some of the batter into the oil in the shape of the letter 'S'. Fry until golden. Remove with tongs, and place on paper towels to drain off any excess oil.

Sprinkle each *Fartura* on both sides with the sugar–cinnamon mixture, and arrange on a serving plate.

◅ Alternative modern recipe ▻

BORRACHUELOS, HONEY-DRENCHED COOKIES FROM SPAIN

Easy

Also of Arab origin in Andalusia are the fritters called *Borrachuelos*, served traditionally during Easter, especially in Malaga. They are immersed in a honey syrup, inspired by the honey-drenched sweets of the Arabs. Today, however, for those with a less sweet tooth, honey is dribbled over them. In addition, in some parts of the country, confectioner's/icing sugar and cinnamon are sprinkled on each fritter once they have cooled. The following recipe is the version from Malaga.

Makes about 30 pieces
Preparation time: 30 minutes
Cooking time: 20 minutes

Ingredients

4 tablespoons olive oil
Peel of half an orange
2 tablespoons sesame seeds
2 teaspoons fennel seeds
½ cup (125 cm) red grape juice
⅛ cup (32 ml) cold water
2 tablespoons lemon juice
3 cups (360 g) plain flour
Vegetable oil for deep-frying
1 cup (340 g) liquid honey mixed with 4 tablespoons water
Confectioner's/icing sugar

Method

In a medium-sized saucepan, heat the olive oil over a medium-low heat, then fry the orange peel for about three minutes. Remove from the heat and set aside to cool. Discard the orange peel.

In a mixing bowl, add the cooled olive oil, sesame seeds, fennel seeds, grape juice, water and lemon juice, and mix well. Gradually add the flour, and knead into a dough, adding more flour or water if needed.

Roll the dough out to a thickness of ⅛ inch (3 mm), and cut into circles 3 inches (7.5 cm) in diameter using the top of a drinking glass.

In a medium-sized saucepan, heat the vegetable oil over a medium heat and deep-fry the *Borrachuelos* until golden. Remove with a slotted spoon and place on paper towels to drain any excess oil. Allow to cool completely.

Heat the honey–water mixture until it comes to the boil. Remove from the heat and immediately dip the *Borrachuelos* completely into the hot honey. Remove and place on a tray and allow to cool.

When the honey-dipped *Borrachuelos* have cooled, dust with confectioner's/icing sugar and place on a serving platter.

∽ **Alternative modern recipe** ∾

BUÑUELOS, CINNAMON-SUGAR FRITTERS FROM MEXICO

Easy

These fritters from Mexico, are the offspring of Spain's *Buñuelos*. Most of the Spanish sweets of Arab origin were brought over to the Americas by the Conquistadors and adopted into the Latin American kitchen, evolving somewhat. This descendant of the *Zalabiya* is a fine example of a typically Arab Andalusian sweet.

Makes about 22 pieces
Preparation time: 25 minutes
Standing time: 1 hour
Cooking time: 25 minutes

Ingredients
½ cup (125 ml) cold water
½ cup (100 g) granulated sugar
3 cups (360 g) plain flour
1 teaspoon baking powder
½ teaspoon salt
1 egg, beaten
4 tablespoons unsalted butter, melted
Vegetable oil for frying
Caster sugar
Cinnamon

Method

Place the water and sugar in a small saucepan, then bring to the boil and cook for two minutes, stirring a number of times. Remove from the heat, and allow to cool.

Place the flour, baking powder and salt in a mixing bowl and combine well, then make a well in the middle. Stir in the saucepan contents and the egg and butter, then knead into a dough, adding a little flour or water if necessary. Cover and let rest for an hour.

Divide the dough into 22 balls the size of walnuts, then roll as thinly as possible into circles about 5–6 inches (12.5–15 cm) in diameter. Place the oil in a frying pan to a depth of about 1 inch (2.5 cm), and heat over a medium-low heat. Fry the circles until golden, turning once. Drain on paper towels, sprinkle with the caster sugar and cinnamon, and place on a serving platter.

❧ Alternative modern recipe ❧

ZEPPOLE, HONEY BALLS FROM SICILY

Easy

Sicily's modern version of *Zalabiya* is *Zeppole*, a deep-fried fritter ball. Some are plain, then dipped into a honey-based syrup or covered with sugar. Other, more festive types are sprinkled with ground almonds and candied orange peel. They are served hot, and are always available at fast-food stands in Sicily, just as *Zalabiya* are in the Arab world.

A look at the ingredients and method of preparing *Zeppole* gives a very strong indication that its origins lie in *Zalabiya*. Felice Cùnsolo believes that there is an evolutionary parallel to the Arab fritter, and goes further to suggest that the term *Zeppole* is derived from the Arabic *Zalabiya* (*Manoscritto Lucano* 211). According to Clifford Wright, *Zeppole* are called *Zippula* in Sicilian, from the Arabic name for the fried dough ('Zeppole').

Makes 20–22 pieces
Preparation time: 20 minutes
Standing time: 2 hours
Cooking time: 25 minutes

Ingredients
1½ cups (180 g) plain flour
⅛ teaspoon salt
1 ounce (8 g) active dry yeast
¾ cup (185 ml) plus 2 tablespoons warm water
Vegetable oil for deep-frying
⅓ cup liquid honey
½ cup (50 g) ground toasted almonds
Candied orange peel, diced

Method

In a bowl, combine the flour, salt and yeast. Form a well and add three-quarters of a cup of warm water, then mix well to make a sticky dough. Cover with plastic wrap/cling film, and allow to rest for two hours.

In a large saucepan, heat the oil over a medium heat. Pull off small balls of dough about the size of walnuts, and deep-fry until golden. Remove with a slotted spoon and place on paper towels to absorb any excess oil.

Arrange the *Zeppole* on a serving platter.

Stir together the remaining water with the honey. Drizzle the honey over the *Zeppole*, then decorate with the almonds and the candied orange peel.

ZALABIYA MAHSHUWA (STUFFED FRITTERS)
SAVOURY ALMOND-STUFFED FRITTERS

For the experienced cook

✒ *Historical version* ✒

Knead flour with yeast into a stiff dough. Spread it out and fill it with almonds and sugar and flavour with rose water, musk and camphor. Shape in any kind of mould you like. Leave them for an hour or so until they become dry. Immerse in *Zalabiya* dough, then throw them in fresh sesame oil and fry. Place them in syrup then remove. Sprinkle sugar on them.

Ibn al-'Adim, p. 646. Translated by Habeeb Salloum and Muna Salloum.

By the thirteenth century, the simple *Zalabiya* (see pp. 62, 92) had evolved into a more complex fritter. Rather than a basic fried dough, we find a version in which the dough is stuffed with a nut filling and then allowed to dry out. It is then dipped into a runny batter, deep-fried, immersed in syrup, and finally sprinkled with sugar.

Not only made at home, *Zalabiya* were sold in the medieval souks of the Arab world, just as they are today. Then and now, there were rules to follow when selling them. Agents who represented the *muhtasib* (market inspector) made on-site visits to these public markets, making sure that food sellers such as *Zalabiya* makers were following market regulations for cooking utensils, weights, measures and hygiene. For example, *ratl* weights used for frying fritters could only be made of iron in Seville; the copper frying cauldrons used by fritter sellers were to be tinned to stop the oil used for frying from spoiling (Ibn 'Abdun 100).

Ibn al-Ukhuwa (d. AD 1329) of Egypt, in the *Kitab Ma'alim al-Qurbà fi Ahkam al-Hisba*, a guide for the *muhtasib*, provides regulations for preparing *Zalabiya*, 'a tart filled with almonds and sugar, flavoured with rose water'. For instance, the pan in which the *Zalabiya* was fried must be made of a good-quality red copper. To make the pan ready for frying, it must first be cleaned with chard leaves after having burned bran in it. Once the pan has cooled, a little honey should be added to it, then heated until the honey burns. It should then be polished with crushed pottery fragments and washed out (180). The quality of the flour for the dough was also important. *Zalabiya* was to be made with the best quality of flour, and neither salt nor *natron* (hydrated sodium carbonate) should be used, because when 'eaten with sweet edibles... would nauseate if it contained salt' (180).

Even though this recipe is relatively simple to prepare, the dough's rising and drying time is lengthy. The original recipe adds musk and camphor to the stuffing, but we have replaced them with cinnamon and cloves, common flavourings in contemporary Arab pastries, and more easily available.

☙ Traditional recipe ☙

Makes 20 pieces
Preparation time: 1 hour
Standing time: 4 hours 20 minutes
Cooking time: 20 minutes

Ingredients

Basic *qatr* recipe using rose water (see 'Basic recipes' section)
¼ cup (50 g) plus 2 tablespoons granulated sugar
1½ cup (375 ml) warm water
½ ounce (16 g) active dry yeast
2 cups (240 g) plain flour
3 tablespoons clarified butter
½ cup (50 g) finely ground almonds
¼ teaspoon cinnamon
⅛ teaspoon ground cloves
1 tablespoon rose water
¾ cup (90 g) cornstarch/cornflour
1 egg white, beaten until stiff
Light sesame oil for deep-frying
Caster sugar or confectioner's/icing sugar for sprinkling

Method

To make the first dough, mix one tablespoon of the granulated sugar in quarter of a cup (65 ml) of the water and add a quarter of an ounce (8 g) of the yeast.

Cover and keep in a warm place, allowing the yeast to rise for about ten minutes.

In a mixing bowl, add one cup (120 g) of the flour, the butter, yeast mixture and quarter of a cup (65 ml) of water and knead into a dough, adding more flour if necessary. Continue kneading for five minutes. Cover the dough with a tea towel and allow to rest for an hour, or until it doubles in size.

To make the filling, combine the almonds, the quarter cup (50 g) of sugar, the cinnamon, cloves and rose water. Set aside.

When the first dough has risen, punch down, then form into 20 balls. Carefully roll the balls out into rounds to a thickness of ⅛ inch (3 mm). Place one teaspoon of the filling in the centre of the round. Fold the dough over, then pinch closed. Shape the stuffed dough in any shape you want. Continue the process until all the dough is stuffed and shaped. Leave to sit uncovered for three hours, to dry out. Turn over every half hour to allow the dough to dry out evenly.

One hour before the drying process has ended for the first dough, prepare the second dough, or *Zalabiya* batter.

Mix the remaining sugar in a quarter cup (65 ml) of the warm water and add the remaining yeast. Cover and keep in a warm place, allowing the yeast to rise for about ten minutes.

In a mixing bowl, add the remaining flour, cornstarch/cornflour and salt, and mix well. Form a well, and add the yeast mixture, the remaining water and the egg white. Beat with an electric mixer for one minute to make the batter smooth. Cover the bowl and allow to sit for an hour to allow the batter to rise. After it has risen, stir the batter well. The batter should be very thin (thinner than pancake batter). If necessary, add a little water to thin the batter, since it will be used as a coating for the first dough.

Heat the oil in a medium-sized saucepan over medium heat.

Take the stuffed first dough and dip completely into the *Zalabiya* batter (the second dough). Remove with tongs, making sure to shake off any excess batter. Deep-fry until the *Zalabiya Mahshuwa* begins to brown. Remove with tongs, and immerse in the *qatr* for three minutes. Remove and place on a serving platter.

Sprinkle with caster sugar or confectioner's/icing sugar.

Cookies

IRNIN (ISHTAR'S COOKIE)
COOKIES STUFFED WITH ROSE-SCENTED GROUND ALMONDS

Moderately difficult

✺ *Historical version* ✺

Take good-quality white flour, for each *ratl* put four *uqiya*s of sesame oil and one *uqiya* of sesame seeds and a handful of pistachios and almonds. Once it rests, make pattie-loaves out of it. Bake until browned. This is *khubz al-abazir*. If one wants to make *Irnin* from this, once it rests, take a round cookie mould and make the delicate patties in the shape of the mould. Fill with sugar and pounded pistachios or almonds. The sugar should be two parts, and the pistachios or the almonds one part. This will have been scented with rose water, musk and camphor. Close the tops tightly then put in the oven and remove when golden brown. There are those who make a paste from dates and sesame oil. The pits are removed [from the dates], and aromatic spices are added to become a filling for these rounds.

Ibn al-'Adim, p. 652. Translated by Muna Salloum and Leila Salloum Elias.

Irnin is made with the same dough as *Khubz al-Abazir* (a dry and brittle type of cookie mixed with sesame seeds and at times with nuts), except that it is stuffed with almonds and spices or dates. In the medieval Arabic cooking manuals, recipes for *Irnin* are included in the recipe instructions for *Khubz al-Abazir*. While *Khubz al-Abazir* is a dry-tasting cookie, *Irnin* is sweeter.

Nawal Nasrallah offers an interesting theory on the origin of the name *Irnin*. In the Sumerian language, one of the names of the goddess Ishtar is Irnini. A type of moon-shaped cookies, *Qullupu*, were made and offered to her during religious festivals. Added to this, *Irnini* in Sumerian means 'a sweet-smelling lady', making the link between goddess and cookie very feasible.

Familiar Foods (461) and al-Baghdadi's text (79) also include a similar recipe.

The recipe calls for a *qalib* to make the patties. This is a mould used for shaping a cookie, usually a cookie with a filling. Wooden moulds would have a design etched into them, and this would be imprinted on the cookie.

❦ Traditional recipe ❧

Makes 20 pieces
Preparation time: 45 minutes
Standing time: 2 hours
Cooking time: 40 minutes

Ingredients

2 cups (240 g) plain flour
2 teaspoons sesame seeds
2 tablespoons chopped pistachios
6 tablespoons ground almonds
4 tablespoons unsalted butter, melted
4 tablespoons light sesame oil
6 tablespoons water
6 tablespoons sugar
½ teaspoon cinnamon
¼ teaspoon ground cloves
2 tablespoons rose water
Confectioner's/icing sugar (optional)

Method

In a bowl, mix together the flour, sesame seeds, pistachios and two tablespoons of the almonds. Form a well and add the butter, sesame oil and water. Knead to form a dough. Cover and let rest for two hours.

While the dough is resting, make the filling by mixing together the four remaining tablespoons of almonds, the sugar, cinnamon, cloves and rose water. Set aside.

Form the dough into 20 balls. Take one ball and form a hole in the middle with the forefinger. Place one teaspoon of the filling inside the dough, then seal it. Place the stuffed ball into a mould, press slightly, then turn the mould and tap lightly to release the *Irnin*. If no mould is available, slightly press the stuffed ball between the palms of the hands to form a disc. Place on a greased baking tray.

Bake in a 350°F (175°C) preheated oven for 35–40 minutes or until lightly browned underneath and on top. Cool, then place carefully on a serving plate.

If you prefer a sweeter version of this cookie, dip the *Irnin* in confectioner's/icing sugar once the cookies have cooled.

≪ Modern recipe ≫

MA'MUL (MADE), NUT-STUFFED COOKIES

Moderately difficult

One way we always knew the holidays had arrived in our house was hearing in the very early morning the tapping of the *qalib* or cookie mould for *Ma'mul*. Freda would have already prepared the nut and date fillings the night before. But it was the aroma of the rose water emanating from the kitchen along with the fresh percolating coffee that will always be a reminder of what is good about *Ma'mul*.

To make the cookie you will need the special mould (*qalib*) used for *Irnin* (see above). These moulds can be purchased in most Middle Eastern grocery outlets, and usually you will have a choice of designs. The round deeper moulds are usually reserved for walnut fillings, the long oval ones for pistachios. The larger round ones are for the date-stuffed variety. There are no rules as to which moulds to pick or use – it is the baker's choice. Don't be surprised by the moulds that are about 1 inch (2.5 cm) round – those we've learned are for the patient and tolerant cook willing to take hours to prepare miniature *Ma'mul*s.

It is best to dust the inside of the mould lightly with flour for every few balls of dough that are pressed. The trick to removing the uncooked *Ma'mul* from the mould is to tap the *qalib* lightly at the tip on the work surface. That work surface should have a clean tea cloth on it to dampen the sound, a technique Leila learned one Palm Sunday morning when her husband Issam came into the kitchen, informed her that he had counted 68 taps in the previous hour and asked whether there were more coming!

We suspect that there is a connection between *Irnin* and *Ma'mul*, both being made with flour and stuffed with nuts and formed in a *qalib*. Just like *Irnin*, *Ma'mul* are basically a shortbread cookie filled with nuts or dates.

Makes 24 pieces, dependent on the size of the cookie mould
Preparation time: 1 hour
Cooking time: 20 minutes

Ingredients

2 cups (190 g) ground walnuts or 2 cups (190 g) ground pistachios
¼ cup (50 g) and 2 tablespoons granulated sugar
1 tablespoon rose water
1 tablespoon unsalted butter, melted
2 cups (240 g) plain flour
1 cup (195 g) clarified butter
1 tablespoon whole milk
Icing sugar

Method

In a bowl, combine the nuts, the quarter cup (50 g) of granulated sugar, rose water and melted butter. Set aside.

In a mixing bowl, combine the flour, the remaining sugar and the clarified butter. Add the milk and knead well.

Form the dough into 24 balls.

Take one ball and make a hollow as wide as possible in it with your forefinger, without tearing the ball.

Take one tablespoon of the filling and gently place it into the hollow. Close the ball with your fingertips, so that the filling is completely covered. Roll the ball between the palms of your hand until the seam is smooth.

Lightly dust the mould with flour, and insert the stuffed ball. Press lightly with the palm of your hand, then flip the mould over and lightly tap the upper portion of the mould on the edge of the working surface, catching the cookie with your hand. Place on a baking tray. Continue the process until all the balls are used.

Bake in a preheated 400° F (200° C) oven for 15 minutes, or until the bottoms are light brown. Place under the broiler/grill until the tops are very light brown.

Allow to cool, then sprinkle with icing sugar.

⤙ Alternative modern recipe ⤚

KLAYCHA, DATE-STUFFED COOKIES

Moderately difficult

Iraq's most popular cookie is the *Klaycha*, a crumbly dry cookie considered a national food. *Klaycha* come in various shapes, with fillings such as nuts and sugar or dates, the latter being the most popular. They are round cookies which Ibn al-'Adim alludes to in one of his recipes for *Ka'k*. His recipe gives the option of forming the *Ka'k* in the traditional manner or 'choose to form them like *Kalija*' (658), in other words, into a round shape.

The name of this cookie, according to Nasrallah, is derived from a dry measure used for the flour when making the cookies. The measure itself, and the measuring utensil, were called *kayl* or *kaylachah* (in the Iraqi dialect) or *kalayja* (classical Arabic) (Nasrallah *Delights* 528).

There is a type of cookie called *Nasiriya* in Ibn al-'Adim's work, for which a *Kalija* mould is used (625). Similarly, in *Kanz* we find in the recipe for *Khudud al-Aghani* instructions for the use of a round cookie cutter like that used for *Kalija* (105).

These round cookies were one of the foodstuffs served to Ibn Battuta at the dining table of Qutludumur, Emir of Khawarizm in his travels. Ibn Battuta's description of *Kalija* is of a type of bread made with clarified butter (361–62).

Makes about 24 pieces
Preparation time: 40 minutes
Cooking time: 35 minutes

Ingredients

1 pound (454 g) soft dried dates, pitted and finely chopped
1 cup (227 g) unsalted butter, cut into ½ inch (1.5 cm) cubes
½ teaspoon ground cardamom
¼ teaspoon ground cloves
2 cups (240 g) plain flour
⅓ cup (70 g) granulated sugar
1 teaspoon baking powder
½ teaspoon salt
⅓ cup (80 ml) whole milk

Method

Place the dates, half a cup (113 g) of the butter, the cardamom and cloves in a saucepan, then cook over a low heat, stirring occasionally until the dates become a paste, about ten minutes. Remove from the heat and allow to cool thoroughly.

In a mixing bowl, combine the flour, sugar, baking powder and salt. Add the remaining butter, and mix by hand until coarse and crumbly. Add the milk, and work into a dough similar to pie dough, adding more milk if necessary. Divide into four parts. Roll one at a time to a thickness of about ⅛ inch (3 mm).

Preheat the oven to 325° F (160° C).

Divide the date paste into four parts, then roll out between two sheets of plastic wrap/cling film or waxed paper, the same size as the dough. Remove the plastic, then place the date layer on the dough, then roll into a cylinder shape, jelly roll (Swiss roll) style. Continue the process with the remaining three parts of the dough. Cut into pieces ¾ inch (2 cm) long, then place on a greased baking tray.

Bake for 20–25 minutes, or until *Klaycha* begin to turn golden.

✑ Alternative modern recipe ✑

KARABIJ HALAB (WHIPS OF ALEPPO), PISTACHIO-STUFFED COOKIES

Easy

Irnin was one of the many stuffed cookies that developed over time. The availability of new spices and ingredients, and contacts with new cultures allowed for more adventure in gastronomy. It appears that people enjoyed their stuffed cookies. One such example is *Karabij Halab*, a cookie speciality in the northern Syrian city of Aleppo. Made with a very fine semolina flour, they are stuffed with ground pistachios, almonds, pine nuts or walnuts.

They may have been named *Karabij* because of the whipping process used to make the meringue-like mousse that is served with them. Called *Natif*, this whipped, sticky mousse is made from the roots of the *Quillaja Saponaria* tree. The traditional method, still practised in Syria and Lebanon, is to boil the roots with water. Once the water has boiled for a certain time, sugar is added bit by bit, and the mixture is then whipped with branches of the pomegranate tree, forming a white thick marshmallow-like sticky paste. The pomegranate branch carries an enzyme which naturally thickens the mixture. The term *Natif* appears in medieval Arabic cookbooks as well, and was used as an ingredient for making candies and cookies or, as in the tenth century, a candy nougat or brittle (see *Natif*, p.157). However, as the times change and the modern cook looks for shortcuts, *Karabij* are served in many homes with ready-made marshmallow topping or with whipped cream.

Mahaleb is the aromatic spice used in this recipe. It is called *mahlab* in Arabic, and is the pit of the sour cherry (*Prunus mahaleb*). Used for centuries in Syria and other parts of the Middle East and the Mediterranean region, mahaleb gives a unique flavouring to breads and cookies. It can be purchased from any grocery outlet that specialises in Middle Eastern goods, and is sold in small packets either in its seed form or ground.

Makes 30–35 pieces
Preparation time: 40 minutes
Chilling time: 30 minutes
Cooking time: 20 minutes

Ingredients

½ cup (50g) finely ground pistachios

¼ cup (60g) caster sugar

1½ tablespoons cold water

1 teaspoon rose water

1 pound (454g) extra-fine semolina

½ cup (113g) unsalted butter, softened

½ cup (100g) granulated sugar

1 teaspoon ground mahaleb

¼ cup (60ml) warm whole milk

¼ ounce (8g) active dry yeast dissolved with one tablespoon sugar in ¼ cup
    (65ml) warm water, allowed to sit for 10 minutes until frothy

Whipped marshmallow fluff or whipped cream (optional)

Method

Combine the pistachios, caster sugar, cold water and rose water to make a filling, then set aside.

In another bowl, mix together by hand the semolina, butter, sugar and mahaleb, making sure that the butter is mixed in well. Form a well, then pour in the milk and the yeast mixture. Knead into a dough. Cover with plastic wrap/cling film and refrigerate for half an hour.

Form the dough into walnut-sized balls. Take one ball, and form a hollow with the index finger. Place a teaspoon of the filling in the hollow, pinch to close, then shape into a cylinder. Place on a greased baking tray. Continue the process until all balls are done.

Bake in a 300°F (150°C) oven for 20 minutes, or until golden. Allow to cool, then place on a serving dish.

If desired, serve with whipped marshmallow fluff or whipped cream, allowing each person to dip the cookie into the marshmallow or cream.

KA'B AL-GHAZAL (THE GAZELLE'S HEEL)
CRESCENT-SHAPED ALMOND-FILLED COOKIES

Moderately difficult

Historical version

Moisten flour with a little oil and knead well with slightly salted warm water without yeast. Add to it enough aniseed, pepper and ginger. Then pound almonds and sugar well together until they stick together and can be put into a bowl, adding rose water and the familiar spices [that is a mixture of spices commonly used in pastries] and combine together until well mixed.

Grease both palms with oil, then take pieces of stuffing, and between palms, roll [each piece] into very thin ropes. Roll pieces of the dough out on a table, then place a roll of stuffing [on each] and fold the edges [of the dough] over and roll [dough] by hand into ropes, as one does for *Ka'k*, making sure that the rope is straight and not curled. Then place these ropes in the *malla* [a pit in which dough and meat is baked in the heat created from ashes and stones] after having cut them into near equal widths with a knife. Then bake on a low flame in the oven of the *malla* into which they were placed. Then separate them from each other. Place them in a clean container until ready to use. And this type mentioned is new. And those, which are more elegant, are those to which is added to the stuffing ground pine nuts, and when the rolls are cut, one peeled pine nut is inserted into each end. And this can only happen with patience and perseverance. And he who wants it without stuffing, should not add the familiar spice mixture in the dough at the time of its kneading. Then prepare the ropes as mentioned before and understand this.

al-Tujibi, p. 65. Translated by Habeeb Salloum and Muna Salloum.

Because *Ka'b al-Ghazal* are not mentioned in the extant medieval eastern Arabic cookbooks, it seems they were unique to the western Arabic-speaking countries of North Africa. However, from the east, the Baghdadi poet Abu Talib al-Ma'muni (AD 953–993) composed verses about a number of sweets, one of which was named *Ki'ab al-Ghazal*, and presented to him in a glazed earthenware vessel:

Possessor of delicateness like syrup embracing cotton
As if the coolness of spring caused it to turn white
Stamped with translucency from the gardens of the white sparrowhawk
And in it the white flowers of the white poplar tree
      (al-Tha'alibi *Yatima* IV 178)

And in tenth-century Egypt, the Fatimid Caliph al-'Aziz bi-Allah included *Ka'b al-Ghazal* among the sweets distributed for the celebrations for Eid al-Fitr (al-Maqrizi *Al-Mawa'iz* II 401).

The contemporary *Ka'b al-Ghazal* served throughout North Africa are very similar to the source recipe, but are usually dipped in *qatr*, while their medieval counterparts were not. Also, it is more common that orange blossom water replaces the medieval use of rose water. Though some of the ingredients differ, the basic components and method of preparation have remained the same. In some regions, the name of the cookie has changed. In Algeria, they are called *Cherek/Tcherek*, in Libya *Ka'k Halkum* and in France *Cornes de gazelles*. When Algerians choose not to sprinkle the cookies with confectioner's/icing sugar, the name of the sweet is thus *Cherek/Tcherek al-'Aryan* (naked *Tcherek*).

Even though *Ka'b* is translated commonly as 'horn' because of its shape, the Arabic actually means 'heel'.

While adhering as close as possible to the medieval recipe, we decided to go a little bit further by fusing the historical with the modern. We have added an extra step, as is done today, by dipping the baked cookies in *qatr* for an extra-sweet touch.

⟨ Traditional recipe ⟩

Makes about 36 pieces
Preparation time: 40 minutes
Standing time: 30 minutes
Cooking time: 20 minutes

Ingredients

Half the basic *qatr* recipe using rose water (see 'Basic recipes' section)
2 cups (240g) plain flour
¼ teaspoon ground aniseed
¼ teaspoon ground ginger
Pinch of black pepper (optional, see 'Tip')
½ cup (113g) unsalted butter, melted
¼ cup (60ml) vegetable oil
½ cup (125ml) cold water
2 teaspoons rose water
½ cup (50g) finely ground almonds
¼ cup (50g) granulated sugar
½ teaspoon cinnamon
⅛ teaspoon ground cloves
½ cup (60g) confectioner's/icing sugar

Method

Place the flour, aniseed, ginger, black pepper (optional), butter and oil in a mixing bowl, and rub together until crumbly, then add the water and one teaspoon of the rose water, and knead to form a smooth dough, adding a little water or flour if necessary. Cover with a cloth and set aside for half an hour.

In the meantime, prepare the filling by mixing the almonds, sugar, cinnamon, cloves and the remaining rose water.

Form the dough into walnut-size balls, and place on a cloth, then remove one ball at a time and roll into a very thin circle. Place a heaped teaspoon of the filling on the centre, and fold over to make a half-moon shape, then close by pinching the edges. Trim the edges with a pastry wheel, then form into a crescent shape once more.

Continue the same process until all the balls are used, then place on an ungreased baking tray. Bake in the middle rack of a 350°F (175°C) oven for 15–20 minutes or until golden brown.

Place the *Ka'b al-Ghazal* in the *qatr* for a few moments while they are still hot, then remove and place in a serving dish. Allow to cool, and sprinkle with the confectioner's/icing sugar.

(Tip: one of the interesting ingredients is *fulful*, which in Arabic means 'pepper'. We included it as an option only after making the *Ka'b* with it. However, the second batch, without the pepper, was much tastier. But then again, taste is in the tastebuds of the taster.)

⟪ Modern recipe ⟫

KA'B GHAZAL FROM MOROCCO

Easy

The following contemporary version, also from Morocco, takes less time to make, since the stuffing is the cookie itself. There is no dough to cover the filling.

Makes 30–35 pieces
Preparation time: 30 minutes
Cooking time: 55 minutes

Ingredients

1¼ cups (190 g) blanched whole almonds
1 cup (200 g) granulated sugar
4 tablespoons unsalted butter
¾ cup (90 g) plain flour
2 teaspoons vanilla extract/essence
½ teaspoon cinnamon
2 eggs, beaten and placed on a plate
1 cup (155 g) sesame seeds, placed on a plate

Method

Put the almonds in a medium-sized saucepan and cover with water, then bring to the boil and cook over a medium heat for 20 minutes. Drain and allow to cool.

In a food processor, mix the almonds with the remaining ingredients except the eggs and the sesame seeds, and process into a dough. (If too soft, add a little more flour.)

Form into balls about 1 inch (2.5 cm) in diameter, then roll in the palm of the hands into ropes about 2 inches (5 cm) in length, with tapered ends. (Be careful, as the balls tend to crumble.)

Roll each rope into the beaten eggs, and then in the sesame seeds. Form the rope into a crescent shape.

Preheat the oven to 350°F (175°C).

Place on a greased cookie tray, then bake for 35 minutes, or until the *Ka'b* just begin to turn brown. Allow to cool, then place on a serving platter.

KA'K
A DRY COOKIE OR BISCOTTI

Easy

✑ *Historical version* ✑

Take for each pound of flour, 4 ounces of sesame oil. Or, if you like, you can use sheep tail fat but then you will not need the sesame oil because you have used fat. Then add the flour until it is mixed well. Pound artemisia and mix it with water, then squeeze out the liquid from it. Then pound it until it is a paste. If you soak it, it is easier to pound. Also add a little bit of fenugreek and mastic, as much as you want and pound together [with the artemisia]. Add to the flour toasted aniseed, black caraway, dried coriander seed and peeled sesame seed. Form into a dough by adding milk and yeast and knead it very well, then let it rest until it has risen well. Make from it delicate *Ka'k*s. Sprinkle on top of each *Ka'k* the same spices which were kneaded into the dough. Bake. Allow the baker to put on top [of each *Ka'k*] egg white, honey and poppy seeds. [Return to oven] and toast very well and eat it. If you want them to be yellow, add ground saffron to the milk before kneading.

Ibn al-'Adim, pp. 657–58. Translated by Habeeb Salloum and Muna Salloum.

Based upon the sources, *Ka'k* is generally regarded as a dried cookie or dried bread, one of the most ancient baked products in the Middle East. It can be made with or without sugar, thus allowing it to be served as a sweet or as a simple snack.

From the medieval Arabic culinary texts we learn that one version of the cookie was prepared by al-Qadi al-Fadil (AD 1131–99), chancellor and advisor to Salah al-Din, to present to heads of state (*Kanz* 266). We also learn from *Taj al-'Arus* (6773) that the popularity of the cookie created an actual vocation, *al-Ka'ki* (the specialist baker who makes them). From ancient through medieval times they were available in souks, and were often given as gifts, and in one case at least as a form of medicine.

At the time when Harun al-Rashid appointed 'Ubayd Allah ibn al-Mahdi as Governor of Egypt, the new Governor, in appreciation, sent the Caliph an exceptionally beautiful maiden. The Caliph fell in love with her. But she fell ill, very ill, and no doctor in Iraq could cure her. The Caliph contacted 'Ubayd, asking him to find the most skillful Egyptian physician to treat the girl.

'Ubayd called upon Balitiyan (Balatian), the Melkite Patriarch of Alexandria renowned throughout Egypt for his skills as a physician. Balitiyan agreed to help, and left for Baghdad, carrying with him some Egyptian *Ka'k* of the coarse type and *al-Sir*, a type of small salted fish. When he reached the Caliph's residence and saw the patient, Balitiyan fed her the *Ka'k* and the small fish. She recovered. The Caliph rewarded the Patriarch-physician with a large sum of money, and restored to him the churches that the Jacobites had confiscated from the Melkites. After this incident, *Ka'k* and *al-Sir* began to be exported to the storehouse of the Sultans (Ibn Abi Usayba'a 540).

Reading through the various culinary sources, we find that *Ka'k* were shaped in different forms such as rings, rounded cookies or even in the shape of fruits and birds. The author of *Anonymous*, for example, suggests that in the preparation of *Ka'k*, when the time comes to shape the *Ka'k* dough before baking, the *qursa*s [patties] can be made into the forms of 'birds, gazelles and the like' similar to the various shapes of a another type made in the Tunisian city of Bougie (181).

Their texture is crispy on the outside and flaky inside. The dough contains an interesting combination of spices, forming a bread-like biscotti not-too-sweet dessert. Perry compares *Ka'k* to biscotti since both the biscotti and *Ka'k* are baked then returned to the oven for a final baking.

Ibn al-'Adim lists three recipes for *Ka'k*, and the one we have chosen is very similar to a modern version made in Syria today. Though simple to prepare, these *Ka'k*, because of their variety of spices, make them unique in this collection of medieval cookies. Although there are dozens of recipes for *Ka'k* in the medieval sources, we chose the one that used the most interesting mixture of spices.

The artemisia called for in the historical recipe is most likely sagebrush.

◅ Traditional recipe ᐅ

Makes 18 pieces
Preparation time: 40 minutes
Standing time: 2 hours 10 minutes
Cooking time: 20 minutes

Ingredients

1 tablespoon granulated sugar
¼ cup (65 ml) warm water
¼ ounce (8 g) active dry yeast
2 cups (240 g) plain flour
⅛ teaspoon ground sage
¼ teaspoon ground fenugreek
Pinch of ground mastic
¼ teaspoon ground black caraway seeds
¼ teaspoon ground coriander seeds
1 tablespoon sesame seeds
4 tablespoons light sesame oil
¼ cup (60 ml) warm whole milk
1 egg white, beaten lightly
Extra ground sage, ground fenugreek, ground black caraway seeds, ground
    coriander seeds and sesame seeds for topping
½ cup (170 g) liquid honey
1 tablespoon poppy seeds

Method

In a bowl, dissolve the sugar in the warm water, then stir in the yeast. Cover and allow the yeast to sit for ten minutes until frothy.

In another bowl, mix together the flour, sage, fenugreek, mastic, caraway, coriander and sesame seeds. Make a well, and add the yeast mixture, oil and milk, then knead well, forming a soft dough, adding more flour or water as necessary. Form into a ball, and cover. Let rest for two hours, or until the dough has doubled in size.

Preheat the oven to 350°F (175°C).

Divide the dough into 18 balls. Flatten each ball by hand, forming a disc. Lightly brush the egg white on top of each disc. Sprinkle the topping ingredients: ground sage, ground fenugreek, ground black caraway, ground coriander and the sesame seeds on top of each *Ka'k*, and place on a greased baking sheet.

Bake for 15 minutes. Remove from the oven, and carefully brush each *Ka'k* with the honey then sprinkle with the poppy seeds. Return to the oven, and cook for a further five minutes, or until the *Ka'k* are slightly browned. When slightly cooled, remove from the baking sheet and place on a serving platter.

(Tip: this adapted version is a non-sweet *Ka'k*, and we recommend a good hot cup of sweet mint tea to go with them.)

⤺ Modern recipe ⤻

KA'K SURI (SYRIAN COOKIES), RINGED SPICED SESAME-SEED COOKIES

Easy

This type of *Ka'k* is popular all over Syria, and is a simplified version of the medieval *Ka'k*. They can be described more as a type of spicy seed bread, but are not sweet. However, they can be dipped in any type of syrup for that added touch. In the Arab world, these *Ka'k* are most commonly served as a snack with coffee, tea or a cup of warm milk.

Makes about 22 pieces
Preparation time: 35 minutes
Standing time: 40 minutes
Cooking time: 30 minutes

Ingredients

1 tablespoon granulated sugar
½ cup (125 ml) warm water
¼ ounce (8 g) active dry yeast
2 cups (240 g) plain flour
½ teaspoon salt
¼ teaspoon ground cumin
¼ teaspoon ground coriander seeds
½ teaspoon ground aniseed
¼ teaspoon ground caraway seeds
½ teaspoon ground mahaleb
4 tablespoons unsalted butter, at room temperature
1 egg, beaten
½ cup (80 g) sesame seeds

Method

In a bowl, dissolve the sugar in quarter of a cup (65 ml) of warm water, then stir in the yeast. Cover, and let the yeast sit for ten minutes until frothy.

In a bowl, mix together the flour, salt, cumin, coriander, aniseed, caraway and the mahaleb, then form a well. Pour the yeast mixture, the remaining water and the butter into the well. Knead into a soft dough (for about five minutes), adding more water or flour if necessary. Form into a ball, and cover. Allow to rest for half an hour.

Preheat the oven to 325°F (160°C).

Divide the dough into 22 balls. Take a ball and roll it between the palms of your hands, stretching it into a cylinder 6 inches (15 cm) long. Bend the cylinder into a ring, and connect the ends. Place on a greased baking tray.

Bake for 15 minutes. Remove from the oven, then dip each *Ka'k* into the beaten egg, then into the sesame seeds. Return the rings to the baking tray, and continue baking for a further 15 minutes, or until the *Ka'k* is lightly browned all over. If necessary, place under the broiler/grill until browned on top. Immediately but carefully place the rings on a platter, and allow to cool.

◈ Alternative modern recipe ◈

KA'K BI HALIB (MILK COOKIES), ANISEED MILK COOKIES

Moderately difficult

Ka'k bi Halib is a festive traditional and popular treat served throughout the Arab East. Very similar to the medieval *Ka'k* cited by Ibn al-'Adim, the modern *Ka'k* uses fewer spices. It is best described as a sweet bread fit for kings. Or rather it is pretty much the same as a medieval (late twelfth or early thirteenth century) *Ka'k* made with milk and almond oil by the concubine al-Hafiziya for the Ayyubid Sultan of Egypt, al-Malik al-'Adil I (Ibn al-'Adim 658).

Our modern recipe of *Ka'k bi Halib* comes from Freda Salloum, who learned how to make them from her mother, handing down a recipe that had come from her own great-aunt in Damascus.

Never a holiday has passed in our house without *Ka'k bi Halib*. The aroma of the mahaleb and aniseed as the *Ka'k bi Halib* baked was a signal that a special occasion was on the horizon. Unfortunately, the tradition of making this sweet bread at home is slowly dying out. With the multitude of Middle Eastern bakeries in both the Arab world and wherever the emigrants have settled, it seems that *Ka'k bi Halib* has lost its once famous status as the holiday sweet bread, being replaced by fancier filo-based desserts.

An interesting tradition in our family is adding salt to the dough, which Freda explains is called the *baraka*, or 'blessing'.

You have the option of using ground or whole aniseed for this recipe, the latter being the most commonly used when making *Ka'k* in the Middle East.

For the Arabs, *Ka'k bi Halib* are a favourite when preparing sweets for Easter.

Makes about 50 pieces
Preparation time: 30 minutes
Standing time: 3 hours 10 minutes
Cooking time: 50 minutes

Ingredients

2½ cups (500g) granulated sugar plus 2 tablespoons granulated sugar
½ ounce (16g) active dry yeast
½ cup (125ml) warm water
8¾ cups (1.05kg) plain flour
1 teaspoon salt
3 tablespoons ground mahaleb
3 tablespoons ground or whole aniseed
2½ cups (600ml) whole milk
1½ cups (300g) granulated sugar
1 cup (195g) clarified butter, melted
½ cup (120ml) vegetable oil
½ cup (113g) unsalted butter
2 teaspoons rose water

Method

In a bowl, dissolve two tablespoons of sugar in the water, then stir in the yeast. Cover, and allow to sit for ten minutes until frothy.

Thoroughly mix the flour, salt, mahaleb and aniseed in a large bowl. Set aside.

In a saucepan, heat two cups (484ml) of milk a over medium heat until heated through. Remove from the heat, and quickly stir in one and a half cups (300g) of the sugar, the clarified butter and oil, mixing thoroughly.

Make a well in the centre of the flour mixture, and pour into it the yeast mixture and warm milk mixture, then knead until the dough is smooth and elastic. Form into a ball and cover, allowing to rise for 2½ hours, or until the dough has doubled in size.

When the dough has risen, break off into walnut-sized balls. Cover and let rest for 15 minutes.

Roll out each ball into a circle ¼ inch (6mm) thick. Place each circle on an ungreased baking tray. Cover with a tea towel and let rest for 15 minutes.

Bake in a preheated 350°F (175°C) oven for 25 minutes, or until bottoms are browned. Place under the broiler/grill until evenly light brown on top. Remove from the oven and allow to cool.

While the *Ka'k* is cooling, prepare the glaze by combining the unsalted butter, the remaining milk, remaining sugar and the rose water in a saucepan. Cook over a medium heat, stirring constantly until the glaze is heated through.

Once the *Ka'k* has cooled, dip each piece in the warm glaze and place on a serving tray.

∽ Alternative modern recipe ∾

MOROCCAN FAKKAS (THOSE THAT BREAK APART),
TWICE-BAKED CRUNCHY BISCOTTI

Easy

Morocco seems to have continued the tradition of the original twice-baked *Ka'k* in their *Fakkas*. The traditional *Fakkas* require two bakings, just like the medieval *Ka'k*, but are also made with almonds, raisins and/or sesame seeds. The dough is rolled into approximately foot-long cylinders, then left to rise for about an hour. They are baked half-way then left to dry out for at least an hour, while some prefer to leave them to dry overnight. The logs are then sliced into thin pieces. These are then baked again, the same baking process as biscotti, and producing the same texture.

Makes 40 pieces
Preparation time: 30 minutes
Standing time: 30 minutes
Cooking time: 45 minutes

Ingredients
2½ cups (300 g) plain flour
1 teaspoon cinnamon
1 tablespoon baking powder
3 eggs, beaten
⅛ teaspoon salt
1 teaspoon vanilla extract/essence
1 cup (200 g) granulated sugar
½ cup (113 g) unsalted butter, melted
1 cup (117 g) coarsely chopped blanched almonds
¾ cup (115 g) seedless raisins
2 tablespoons sesame seeds
Extra flour for shaping dough

Method
Preheat oven to 350° F (175° C).

In a mixing bowl, stir together the flour and the cinnamon, then stir in the baking powder and set aside.

In a large mixing bowl, mix together the eggs with the salt, then stir in the vanilla. Slowly stir in the sugar, then the butter. Once well blended, stir in the almonds, raisins and sesame seeds. Fold in the flour–cinnamon mixture making sure that all the ingredients are well blended. The mixture should be soft and sticky.

Place the mixture on a floured surface and generously sprinkle flour over it. Pat the mixture gently all around to form a dough. Divide the dough in half and form into two equal-sized logs, the length of a standard baking tray. Cover the baking tray with parchment paper, then carefully place the logs on the tray. Pat the logs down to about 2½–3 inches (6.25–7.5cm) wide. Bake for 30 minutes, or until golden and firm to the touch. Allow to cool for 30 minutes.

Carefully slice each log into 20 pieces, and place on baking trays covered with parchment paper. Bake for 15 minutes. Remove and allow to cool. Place the *Fakka*s on a serving platter.

*Fakka*s can be stored in an airtight covered container for up to a month.

(Tip: they are best served with Moroccan mint tea.)

KA'K MAHSHI (STUFFED DRY COOKIES)
COOKIE RINGS STUFFED WITH SUGAR AND ALMONDS

Moderately difficult

✑ *Historical version* ✑

AL-KA'K AL-MAHSHU BI-AL-SUKKAR WA AL-LAWZ

Moisten good white flour with oil and rub well together with both hands. Then knead into a firm dough with water and salt and a little yeast. Do not put too much water in it but rather put the water in little by little until it becomes a proper [dough], and the sign of that is when you take a piece of it and stretch it and it does not break off, after soundly smashing sugar with the same amount of shelled almonds in a copper mortar. Then mix them together – if it is too sweet then add some almonds, enough to even out the taste. Then add to them rose water, ginger, spikenard, cinnamon, cloves, pepper and a little camphor, and knead them together by hand until they stick together. Then, with both hands, form into tightly twisted pieces resembling fingers, thin and long. They should be a little longer than fingers and even thinner than that, according to preference in making *Ka'k* thin, large or small. Stretch out a piece of dough on a clean table or board. Place the rope-shaped filling lengthwise in its fold until it is spread all along it. Fasten the edges of the dough over the filling and twist it on the table with both hands until it is twisted in the measure chosen for length and thinness. Then make this twisted dough into *Ka'k*, firmly sticking the ends together [forming rings]. Etch impressions with a copper *minqash* [decorating tweezers to make etching designs on pastries] made for it. Then take another piece of dough and form it as the first one. Continue the process like that one after another until all the dough and filling are finished. Layer them out on a board after having dusted it with a little of the flour.

Bake in the oven, keeping a watchful eye on them while they bake and being careful transferring them from the board one by one. Then wipe with a clean piece of cloth and sprinkle them with rose water and a little mastic, and perfume a container into which has been put aromatic *'ud hindi* [a type of aloe wood (chips)] after sprinkling it with rose water. Place the *Ka'k* [in the container] and fill it up with them while [the container] is still moist [with the rose water]. Leave them in it until ready to use, God Almighty willing.

al-Tujibi, pp. 63–64 (#1). Translated by Muna Salloum and Leila Salloum Elias.

These rings are made in the same shape as the unstuffed *Ka'k* (see p. 120) but are filled with a delicious sweet-spiced filling.

Plain *Ka'k* may have been popular among the general public, and even among the elite, but it was the *Ka'k Mahshi* that were reserved for special occasions and festive celebrations, as they are today in the Arab world.

Although *Anonymous* has a recipe for *Ka'k* stuffed with sugar, al-Tujibi's version is much more detailed in its instructions and ingredients.

✧ Traditional recipe ✧

Makes 24 pieces
Preparation time: 55 minutes
Standing time: 1 hour 30 minutes
Cooking time: 20 minutes

Ingredients

¼ ounce (8 g) active dry yeast mixed with 1 tablespoon granulated sugar, dissolved in ¼ cup (65 ml) warm water, covered and allowed to sit for 10 minutes until frothy
2 cups (240 g) plain flour
½ teaspoon salt
4 tablespoons olive oil
⅓ cup (85 ml) warm water
½ cup (50 g) ground almonds
½ cup (100 g) granulated sugar
1 tablespoon rose water
½ teaspoon cinnamon
⅛ teaspoon ground cloves
½ cup (60 g) confectioner's/icing sugar

Method

In a bowl, mix together the flour and salt. Form a well, and add the yeast mixture, the oil and one-third of a cup of water. Knead for five minutes, forming a soft dough, adding more flour or water if necessary. Shape into a ball and cover, allowing to rest for one and a half hours, or until it has doubled in size.

In the meantime, in a separate bowl, prepare the filling by thoroughly mixing together the remaining ingredients except the confectioner's/icing sugar.

When the dough is ready, punch down, then form into 24 balls. Take a ball and roll it between the palms of your hands into a cylinder 4 inches (10 cm) long. Place on a flat surface, then roll until 6 inches (15 cm) in length. Flatten out to ¼ inch (6 mm) thick, then place one heaped teaspoon of the filling along the centre of the dough, lengthwise. Pull up the sides, and pinch dough together, ensuring the seam is tightly sealed. Bend the cylinder into a ring so that the edges of each end almost touch. Place the ring on a greased baking sheet. Continue the process until all the balls are done.

Bake at 350°F (175°C) for 20 minutes. Remove from the oven, and immediately but carefully place the rings on a tray and allow to cool.

Sprinkle each ring with the confectioner's/icing sugar, covering all sides lightly, then place on a serving platter.

KHUSHKANANAJ (DRY BREAD)
DRY SHORTBREAD COOKIE

Easy

❧ *Historical version* ❧

It is to take a top quality *samidh* flour and to put with every *ratl* three *uqiya*s of sesame oil and knead to make a firm dough. Leave it to rise. Then make into long cakes and put in the middle of each an appropriate amount of pounded almonds and sugar kneaded with fragrant rose water (the almonds should be half the sugar). Then put them together in the usual way and bake in the oven and serve.

al-Baghdadi, p. 78. Translated by Muna Salloum and Leila Salloum Elias. (See also the translation by Charles Perry, *A Baghdad Cookery Book*, p. 102.)

This cookie, called in Arabic *Khushkananaj*, is derived from the Persian *khushk* ('dry') and *nan* ('bread').

From the number of recipes appearing in the eastern and Andalusian cookbooks *Khushkananaj* (sing. *Khushkananajah*) (al-Safadi *Tashih* 245) seem to have been a real favourite. Some were plain, such as *Khushkananaj Gharib* (al-Warraq 271), some were filled with nuts, both similar in texture to shortbread. In fact, al-Warraq decided not to include the plain version in his text simply because they were so well known and easy to prepare that everyone knew how to make them (273).

Interestingly, it was this cookie that brought about the downfall of the famous poet Ibn al-Rumi. Ibn al-Rumi, caught up in the intrigue of palace politics, died after eating *Khushkananaj*. Qasim ibn 'Ubayd, Vizier to the Abbasid Caliph al-Mu'tadid (r. AD 892–902) lived in fear of the poet's satire. The Vizier arranged with someone named Ibn Firas to slip some poison into some *Khushkananaj*, and these were served to Ibn al-Rumi (al-Safadi *Tashih* 21)

Realising the *Khushkananaj* he had just eaten were poisoned, the poet stood up to leave. At that point the Vizier asked him where he was going, to which Ibn al-Rumi responded, 'To the place where you are sending me.' The Vizier replied, 'Give greetings to my father!' The poet departed with the words, 'I'm not headed towards hell.' A few days later he died (Ibn Kathir XI 75).

The original recipe does not call for water. In our attempts to re-create the original, the end result was a very dry dough, so we added a little water to make the dough more pliable. Also, for some, sesame oil might be a little too pungent, and if this is the case, you can replace it with vegetable oil.

⤳ Traditional recipe ⤝

Makes about 36 pieces
Preparation time: 50 minutes
Standing time: 30 minutes
Cooking time: 20 minutes

Ingredients

2 cups (240 g) plain flour
½ cup (109 ml) light sesame oil
¼ cup (65 ml) cold water
½ cup (50 g) ground almonds
1 cup (200 g) granulated sugar
¼ teaspoon ground cloves
¼ teaspoon nutmeg
½ teaspoon cinnamon
2 tablespoons rose water

Method

To prepare the dough, in a mixing bowl, add the flour and make a well. Pour into the well the oil and the water. Knead well until a smooth ball of dough is formed, adding more flour or water if necessary. Cover the dough, and allow to sit for half an hour.

For the filling, in another bowl, mix together the almonds, sugar, cloves, nutmeg, cinnamon and rose water. Mix well. To ensure enough filling for each cookie, divide the mixture into 36 sections.

Working with the dough, form into 36 walnut-sized balls, then roll each piece thinly into an oval form.

Preheat the oven to 350°F (175°C).

Place the filling in the centre of each oval. Pull one side of the dough up over the filling to meet the pastry on the other side, pinching it along the seam, and roll slightly to form a smooth edge. Place the *Khushkananaj* on a greased baking tray, seam-side down.

Bake for 20 minutes, then broil/grill until they begin to brown on top.

Remove from the oven and place on a serving tray.

✍ Modern recipe ↬

GHURAYBA (LITTLE MARVELS), ARAB SHORTBREAD

Easy

The dough used for *Khushkananaj* is very similar to the modern cookie *Ghurayba*, very popular in the eastern Arab world, especially during holidays. One could best describe these cookies as a type of shortbread that melts in the mouth.

As for the name *Ghurayba*, there may be a possible connection to *Khushkananaj Gharib*. *Ghurayba* is a diminutive of *gharib*, and both are a type of shortbread.

This is Habeeb's version of his favourite cookie.

Makes 40 pieces
Preparation time: 30 minutes
Cooking time: 20 minutes

Ingredients

1½ cups (340 g) unsalted butter, at room temperature
1¾ cups (200 g) confectioner's/icing sugar
1 teaspoon orange blossom water
1 egg yolk, slightly beaten
3 cups (360 g) plain flour
40 blanched whole almonds

Method

In a mixing bowl, place the butter, 1½ cups (173 g) of confectioner's/icing sugar, the orange blossom water and egg yolk, then gradually add the flour, mixing by hand, until a smooth dough is formed.

Preheat the oven to 300°F (150°C).

Form the dough into balls a little smaller than a walnut, then place on an ungreased cookie sheet and flatten slightly to a thickness of about ½ inch (1.25 cm). Press an almond onto each piece, then bake for 20 minutes, or until the bottoms turn light brown. Remove from the oven and allow to cool, then sprinkle with the remaining confectioner's/icing sugar.

✋ Alternative modern recipe ✌

POLVORONES A LA ANDALUZA, POWDERED OR
DUST SUGAR COOKIES FROM ANDALUSIA

Easy

Creative cooks in the medieval Arab world lightened and enriched their dough mixtures with egg yolks, egg whites, butter and milk, and sweetened them with syrups made of honey or sugar. Myriad cookies and cakes appear in the literature and culinary texts of the time. The tasty cookies, rich in sugar and butter, travelled with the Arabs wherever they settled.

Polvorones fall into this realm. These are a common Spanish holiday cookie, made especially at Christmas. Seville and especially the town of Estepa are famous for these cookies, but they are also found throughout the rest of Andalusia.

When Spain conquered the New World in the sixteenth century, many of these cookies, including *Polvorones*, were introduced there.

Makes about 36 pieces
Preparation time: 25 minutes
Cooking time: 25 minutes

Ingredients

1¼ cups (285 g) unsalted butter, melted
2 egg yolks
1½ tablespoons rose water
2½ cups (300 g) plain flour
1 cup (200 g) granulated sugar
½ teaspoon salt
½ teaspoon cinnamon
⅓ cup (40 g) confectioner's/icing sugar

Method

In a mixing bowl, thoroughly combine the butter, egg yolks and rose water. Add the flour, granulated sugar, salt and cinnamon, and knead into a dough.
Preheat the oven to 300°F (150°C).

Form the dough into balls the size of walnuts. Place balls on an ungreased cookie tray, and pat down to a thickness of about ½ inch (1.25 cm).

Bake for 25 minutes, or until the cookies begin to brown lightly. Remove from the oven and allow to cool.

Sprinkle with the confectioner's/icing sugar, and serve or store in an airtight container.

MAQRUD (THAT WHICH IS CUT)
SEMOLINA DATE COOKIES

Moderately difficult

✺ *Historical version* ✺

It is made with *samidh*, as mentioned before, and kneaded with yeast and a little water to make a firm dough. Then make a filling with sugar and almonds in the manner made previously. Then stretch the dough out in a square form on a table. Place the filling, fold over it, and twist it with both hands the same way as twisting *Ka'k*. Then pat it down gently until it flattens out. Cut into pieces with a sharp knife, each piece being the length of a finger and the width of two fingers. Then fry them evenly for a little while in oil in a frying pan until brown. Then put them in a vessel until their oil dries off. Put them in a glass tray and sprinkle over them sugar and use them, God willing.

Whoever wants them filled with dates, then they are made exactly in the same manner as has been mentioned as in the filling for *Ka'k*, and fry them in the same way as mentioned above. Take note of that.

al-Tujibi, p. 79. Translated by Muna Salloum and Leila Salloum Elias.

✺ Traditional and Modern recipe ✺

MAQRUD, TUNISIAN DATE COOKIES

Moderately difficult

Maqrud, a semolina pastry stuffed with dates, became popular during the time of the Aghlabid Dynasty (AD 800–909) in Tunisia (Abedi 30). Kairouan, the Dynasty's capital, is now the home of the best variety, and they are available year-long in speciality pastry shops and public markets, and of course continue to be made at home.

The cookies are also referred to as semolina honey-cakes because they are drenched, after being fried, in a honey syrup. Today, *Maqrud* are prepared especially for Eid al-Fitr.

Al-Tujibi's recipe for *Maqrud* is basically the same as the contemporary Tunisian version, the difference being that baking soda/bicarbonate of soda has replaced the yeast. Down the centuries, *Maqrud* has remained the perfect cookie, with no need for change.

For many of their desserts, the Tunisians prefer to use olive oil. Although the dough is saturated with butter, its added rich flavour comes from it being fried in olive oil, although some prefer to use a lighter cooking oil.

Makes 20–25 pieces
Preparation time: 50 minutes
Standing time: 15 minutes
Cooking time: 25 minutes

Ingredients

1 cup (340 g) liquid honey
½ cup (125 ml) cold water
1 tablespoon orange blossom water
3 cups (500 g) medium semolina
¼ teaspoon salt
Pinch of baking soda/bicarbonate of soda
1 cup (227 g) unsalted butter, melted and slightly cooled
1 teaspoon ¼–½ cup (65 ml) water at room temperature
2 cups (350 g) finely chopped dates
¼ teaspoon cinnamon
1 tablespoon finely grated orange peel
1 tablespoon vegetable oil
Olive or vegetable oil for deep-frying
¼ cup (30 g) confectioner's/icing sugar (optional)

Method

To prepare the syrup, in a small saucepan, add the honey, cold water and the orange blossom water, and stir well. Over medium heat, bring to a soft boil then immediately lower heat to low and keep warm over a very low heat until ready to use.

To make the dough, in a large mixing bowl, combine semolina, salt and soda. Slowly stir in melted butter by hand, forming a dough. If too crumbly, add another teaspoon or so of melted butter. Place the dough on a floured surface. Sprinkle dough with one teaspoon of the water, and knead lightly adding more water if necessary until the dough is soft and smooth, with a slight stretchy texture. If the dough is too dry and does not hold together, add a little more water.

Return the dough to the bowl and cover with a dampened tea towel. Allow to rest for 15 minutes.

While the dough is resting, prepare the filling.

To prepare the filling, in a food processor, pulse together the dates, cinnamon, orange peel and the one tablespoon of vegetable oil for about 15 seconds to make a paste. Set aside.

On a floured surface, divide the dough into two equal portions. Take one portion of the dough and form it into a log about 3 inches (7.5 cm) in depth. Along the centre of the log, from one end to the other, form a trough about 1½ inches (3.75 cm) deep with the end of a wooden spoon. Take half of the filling and fill right along the trough. Fold the sides of the loaf lengthwise over the filling, ensuring the seam is pinched tightly and smooth. Cut the loaf at a diagonal into 1½ inches (3.75 cm) widths. Repeat the process with the second portion of the dough.

In a medium-sized saucepan, heat the deep-frying oil over a medium heat. Drop the *Maqrud*, a few at a time, into the heated oil, and deep-fry for two to three minutes, or until golden on both sides. Remove and place on paper towels to drain off any excess oil.

Dip the *Maqrud* in the warmed honey, and place on a serving platter. If desired, sprinkle with confectioner's/icing sugar, then serve.

⤌ Alternative modern recipe ⤍

IMQARET, DATE TURNOVERS FROM MALTA

Moderately difficult

The Maltese *Imqaret* most likely came from Tunisia when the Arabs called the island home, or was introduced at a later date. The Maltese describe them as date-filled, deep-fried pastries, and they are served piping hot from takeaway stands or from the fryer at home.

Serves 6–8
Preparation time: 50 minutes
Chilling time: 45 minutes
Cooking time: 25 minutes

Ingredients

- 2 cups (240 g) plain flour
- 2 tablespoons granulated sugar
- 4 tablespoons unsalted butter, chilled and cut into ½ inch (1.25 cm) cubes
- 4 tablespoons anisette liqueur
- 4 tablespoons orange blossom water
- 2 pounds (900 g) pitted dates, chopped and soaked in small amount of water for about 25 minutes, then drained
- 1 teaspoon ground cloves
- 2 tablespoons orange zest
- 2 tablespoons lemon zest
- Vegetable oil for deep-frying

Method

In a bowl, mix together the flour and sugar. Cut in the butter with a pastry cutter or with two table knives. Add two tablespoons of the anisette and two tablespoons of the orange blossom water to make a soft dough, and form into two balls. Wrap each ball in plastic wrap/cling film and refrigerate for 45 minutes. While the dough is resting, prepare the filling.

Mash the dates, and mix them with the cloves, orange zest, lemon zest, the remaining anisette and the remaining orange blossom water. Divide the mixture in half and set aside.

Roll each ball of dough out on a well-floured surface into a long wide strip. Spread the filling lengthwise along the middle of each strip. Moisten the edges of the rectangles with a little water, and fold one panel of the strip to cover the filling and the other panel to cover the first folded panel. Press all edges well together to seal. Cut the sealed strips into diamond shapes, pressing the edges of each diamond closed.

Heat the oil over a medium-high heat and deep-fry the *Imqaret* until golden-brown. Remove and drain on paper towels for a few seconds, then serve immediately.

NUHUD AL-'ADHRA' (BREASTS OF THE VIRGIN)
DELICATE SHORTBREAD-TYPE COOKIES

Easy

✑ *Historical version* ✑

FIRST VERSION

One part flour, one part clarified butter, 15 of ground sugar. Everything is mixed and made well. Then it is made like breasts and baked in a tray [*tabaq*] in the bread oven. It emerges nice.

Familiar Foods, p. 416. Translated by Charles Perry.

SECOND VERSION

Knead sugar, almonds, *samid* and clarified butter, equal parts, and make them like breasts, and arrange them in a brass tray. Put into the bread oven until done, and take it out. It comes out excellently.

***Familiar Foods*, p. 422. Translated by Charles Perry.**

In Arabic literature, the breasts of a young woman were compared to pomegranates, pears and apples, the ultimate in perfection, or in the words of one Cordovan poet of the tenth/eleventh century, 'as if their roundness was poured into moulds brimming' (Ibn al-Kattani 136).

The beauty of a woman's body exemplified in a cookie even dates back to ancient Mesopotamia, where one of the shapes of the three hundred varieties of bread was the shape of a woman's breast (Bottéro 'The Cuisine' 38). These buttery shortbread-type cookies are simple to make, and delicious.

Traditional recipe (based upon the first version)

Makes 24 pieces
Preparation time: 35 minutes
Cooking time: 30 minutes

Ingredients

2¼ cups (270 g) plain flour
¾ cup (150 g) clarified butter
1 cup (115 g) confectioner's/icing sugar

Method

In a bowl, mix all the ingredients together by hand, and form into a dough. Divide the dough into 24 balls.

Preheat the oven to 300° F (150° C).

Shape each ball into a patty, forming a point in the middle.

Bake on an ungreased tray for 30 minutes, or until the cookies begin to brown underneath.

Remove the tray from the oven and allow to cool, then place the cookies on a serving platter.

◅ Traditional recipe (based upon the second version) ▻

Makes 24 pieces
Preparation time: 35 minutes
Cooking time: 20 minutes

Ingredients

1 cup (115 g) confectioner's/icing sugar
1 cup (95 g) ground almonds
1½ cups (250 g) extra-fine semolina
1 cup (195 g) clarified butter

Method

In a bowl, mix the dry ingredients together, then add the butter and form into a dough. Divide the dough into 24 balls.

Preheat the oven to 325°F (160°C).

Shape each ball into the form of a patty, forming a point in the middle.

Bake on an ungreased tray for 20 minutes, or until the cookies begin to brown underneath.

Remove the tray from the oven and allow to cool completely, then place the cookies on a serving platter.

◅ Modern recipe ▻

BISCOCHITOS, SUGAR BUTTER COOKIES

Easy

Biscochitos are better known as 'New World' cookies coming from the 'Old World', and are a cross between shortbread and a sugar cookie. They were introduced to Mexico in the sixteenth century by the Conquistadors.

However, although connected to Spain, these cookies have their true origin in medieval Arab desserts, which were rich in sugar, spiced cinnamon or aniseed, and flavoured with orange zest or orange blossom water.

The bitter orange had found a new home in the Iberian Peninsula after it was introduced there by the Arabs, so it is not surprising that Iberia's sweet industry would undergo a dynamic change. After the Arab conquest, citrus fruits such as the Seville bitter orange would play a major role in flavourings and aromas, based on their use in traditional Arab sweets, which would form the basis of the sweets that would later be known as Spanish. *Biscochitos* fall into this category.

In Mexico, they are served mainly at Christmas and sometimes on other festive holidays.

135

Makes 24 pieces
Preparation time: 40 minutes
Cooking time: 15 minutes

Ingredients

¾ pound (340 g) unsalted butter
¾ cup (150 g) granulated sugar
1 teaspoon ground aniseed
1 egg
4 tablespoons orange juice
3 tablespoons chopped orange peel
4 cups (480 g) plain flour
1 teaspoon baking powder
½ teaspoon salt
3 tablespoons granulated sugar, mixed with 2 teaspoons cinnamon

Method

Cream the butter, the three-quarters of a cup (150 g) of sugar and the aniseed in a mixing bowl. Add the egg, orange juice and orange peel, and beat well.

Mix together the flour, baking powder and salt, and stir into the creamed mixture. Knead slightly, forming into a stiff dough, adding more flour if necessary.

On a slightly floured surface, roll the dough out to a thickness of ¼ inch (6 mm), then with a cookie cutter, cut into circles 3 inches (7.5 cm) in diameter.

Preheat the oven to 350°F (175°C).

Dust the top of each cookie with the sugar and cinnamon mixture.

Place on a greased baking tray, and bake for 15 minutes, or until the cookies are lightly browned underneath.

Allow to cool for a few minutes, then remove carefully from the tray and place on a serving platter. Store in a cookie jar or an airtight container.

Cakes and pies

MUJABBANA (MADE OF CHEESE)
A SWEETBREAD CAKE MADE WITH CHEESE

Moderately difficult

✤ *Historical version* ✤

SAN'A MUJABBANA UKHRÀ

Knead the necessary quantity of flour, one time with water, another
with oil, and to it add yeast and milk until it has the same consistency as
the dough of *Isfunj*, and leave it until it has risen. Then grease a large tajine
with oil, stretch into it a piece of dough, in this way, layer over layer until
the dough and cheese are finished. Then, cover it with a final layer of cheese
as was done previously, and bake in the oven as previously mentioned.
Afterwards, drizzle it with honey, sprinkle it with sugar, cinnamon and
pepper and make use of it, God Almighty willing.

al-Tujibi, p. 84. Translated by Habeeb Salloum and Muna Salloum.

The Andalusian scientist al-Arbuli defines in his study on food that *Mujabbana* is
any type of food made mainly of cheese. These can be cheese puffs, cakes and even
breads. In his treatise, written some time between AD 1414 and 1424, he advises that
after eating any type of *Mujabbana*, a drink made of oxymel and ginger paste should
be taken to alleviate the difficulty of digestion (Diaz Garcia 128).

Those who sold any variety of *Mujabbana* in the souks of the medieval Arab
world had strict rules to follow, in that cheese and any foodstuffs made with it were
perishables. The souk or market inspectors enforced these regulations. According

to Ibn 'Abdun's twelfth-century manual for market inspectors, cheese should only be sold in small leather-skinned containers that could be washed and cleaned daily, other pots being susceptible to contamination (Ibn-'Abdun 97). In fifteenth-century Damascus, cheese was only to be of the best quality when sold (Zayyat 388). Egyptian Ibn al-Ukhuwa's (d. AD 1329) market inspector's manual gives regulations for 'small traders', which includes friers of cheese. To purify the cheese, it must be washed twice in hot water, otherwise it could cause leprosy. All hot water used to purify the cheese had to be drained, and cheese friers were only permitted to use fresh sesame oil for cooking (207).

In re-creating the traditional recipe, we encountered some problems with the ingredients. First, the author does not name the type of cheese that should be used in the recipe, other than explaining that the cheese needs to be spread over the bread. We therefore decided to use ricotta cheese, a good spreadable. Also, by spreading cheese on the top as the final layer, it made the cake too dry. What worked instead was to cover the cake with a final layer of dough. As for *fulful*, we preferred the milder taste of white pepper over the black variety. Al-Tujibi's *Mujabbana* is a sweetbread cake made with cheese and a 'spongy' dough. The cake is light and slightly sweet. It is best to eat this *Mujabbana* immediately after the honey has been drizzled over the top. If left too long, the cake will become soft and soggy.

∽ Traditional recipe ≈

Serves 8
Preparation time: 45 minutes
Standing time: 2 hours 10 minutes
Cooking time: 1 hour 10 minutes

Ingredients

3 tablespoons granulated sugar
¼ ounce (8 g) active dry yeast
½ cup (125 ml) warm water
3 cups (360 g) plain flour
½ teaspoon salt
¾ cup (180 ml) warm whole milk
3 tablespoons unsalted butter, melted
1 tablespoon olive oil
1 pound (454 g) whole milk ricotta cheese
½ cup (170 g) liquid honey
½ teaspoon cinnamon
Pinch of white pepper

Method

Dissolve one tablespoon of the sugar and the yeast in the water, then allow to stand until the yeast begins to froth (about ten minutes).

In the meantime, combine the flour and salt in a mixing bowl, then make a well in the middle. Add the yeast mixture, milk and two tablespoons of the butter. Knead into a dough, adding more milk or flour if necessary. Shape into a ball, and then brush the outside with the oil. Place in a bowl, then cover. Allow to rest in a warm spot for two hours, or until the dough doubles in size. Once the dough is ready, punch down and divide into ten balls.

Divide the cheese into nine sections.

Roll one ball of dough very thin to fit into a 9 inch (22 cm) square and 2 inch (5 cm) deep greased baking pan, and stretch until it touches all sides. Spread evenly one section of the cheese over the dough. Take the next ball of dough and roll out thinly, then place over the ricotta, stretching it to touch each side of the baking pan. Spread another section of the cheese over the dough. Repeat the process until the dough and the cheese are finished, with the dough as the final layer. With the fingertips, press and pinch along each side to seal.

Bake in a 350°F (175°C) preheated oven for one hour, or until the cake is evenly browned. Broil/grill slightly for a few minutes to ensure the top is golden brown. Remove and allow to cool.

In a small saucepan, mix the honey and the remaining butter, and bring to a soft boil over a medium-low heat.

Drizzle the honey–butter mixture evenly over the cake, then sprinkle the remaining sugar, cinnamon and the pepper evenly over the top, and serve immediately.

✐ Modern recipe ✎

CASSATA ALLA SICILIANA, SICILIAN CHEESECAKE

For the experienced cook

It is generally accepted throughout Sicily that *Cassata*, the island's famous cake made with cheese, is one of the many Arab culinary bequests to the island, claimed to have been first made in Palermo under Arab rule. We believe that *Mujabbana* may be the forerunner to *Cassata*. Ironically, Sicily's two most famous desserts, *Cassata* and *Cannoli*, have their origins in the sweet kitchen of the Arabs.

Cassata appears in the tenth century as a basic cake of flour and eggs in the story concerning Ibn al-Fadl, the orthodox Muslim jurist. While in Sousse (present day Tunisia) some time during the period of the Aghlabid Dynasty (AD 800–909), a certain Ibn Mu'tib gave as a present to the jurist a sweet cake made with sugar. Ibn al-Fadl returned the gift, refusing to eat it on the grounds that it was made with sugar from Sicily – then under the rule of the non-orthodox Shi'ite Fatimids (al-Qadi 'Ayyad III–IV 315).

The name *Cassata* derives from the Arabic *qas'a*, a big wide earthenware or wooden bowl, a standard cooking utensil in al-Warraq's culinary manual. This round pan with sloping sides is still used in Sicily for *Cassata*. One legend concerning its origin is that an Arab peasant in Sicily mixed together some fresh cheese and cane sugar, and when asked what it was responded that it was '*qas'a*', referring to the bowl it was in. This may have been the first *Cassata*, in its rudimentary tenth-century form.

Cassata is the official Easter cake today in Sicily.

This is a simplified version of the medieval *Cassata*. Buying prepared sponge cake saves the time of making the sponge-cake portion of this recipe from scratch.

Serves 8
Preparation time: 30 minutes
Chilling time: 3 hours

Ingredients

1½ cups (300 g) granulated sugar
¼ cup (65 ml) water
2 cups (454 g) whole milk ricotta cheese
1 teaspoon cinnamon
3 tablespoons powdered sweet chocolate or melted sweet chocolate
1½ cups (340 g) chopped candied fruits
½ cup (60 g) pistachio nuts, chopped
1 tablespoon rose water
1–2 pounds (454–900 g) sponge cake, sliced into ½–1 inch (1.25–2.5 cm) thick layers*
1 16.6 ounce (470 g) container chocolate frosting*

* for those who prefer to make the sponge cake and the frosting from scratch, we recommend the recipes below)

Method

In a medium-sized saucepan, place the sugar and water, then, stirring, bring to the boil over a medium heat. Remove from the heat, then allow to cool.

Place the dissolved sugar, cheese, cinnamon and chocolate in a food processor, then process into a smooth paste. Transfer into a mixing bowl, then stir in the candied fruits, pistachio and the rose water to make a filling.

On a serving platter, place a portion of the filling between each slice of cake, and press together, then cover and chill for an hour.

Frost the cake, then return to the refrigerator and chill for a further two hours.

Cut and serve while the cake is still chilled.

Sponge cake ingredients

1½ cups (180 g) plain flour
1 teaspoon baking powder
½ teaspoon salt
6 large eggs, separated
1½ cups (300 g) granulated sugar
½ cup (125 ml) cold water
2 teaspoons vanilla extract/essence
½ teaspoon cream of tartar

Sponge cake method

Preheat oven to 325° F (160° C).
In a bowl, mix together the flour, baking powder and salt.

With a mixer, beat the egg yolks until foamy. Gradually beat in the sugar until pale and thickened, about eight to ten minutes. On low speed, beat in the flour mixture, water and vanilla alternately. Set aside.

In a large bowl, beat the egg whites and cream of tartar until stiff peaks form.

Gradually fold the egg yolk mixture into the beaten egg whites, and pour into an ungreased 10 by 4.5 inch (25 by 11 cm) tube pan (a ring-shaped pan with a tube in the centre).

Bake for 55 minutes. Increase the oven temperature to 350° F (175° C) and bake for ten minutes more. The cake is done when the sides pull away from the pan. Remove from the oven and allow to cool for ten minutes.

Invert the pan, placing the tube over a bottle so that the pan does not touch the surface. Loosen the sides of the cake with a spatula to remove the cake.

Chocolate frosting ingredients

¼ cup (65 ml) cold water
2 tablespoons unsalted butter
½ teaspoon vanilla extract/essence
2 1 ounce (30 g) squares unsweetened chocolate, melted
2 cups (230 g) confectioner's/icing sugar

Chocolate frosting method

In a medium-sized saucepan, heat together the water and butter, then add the vanilla and chocolate. Stir in the sugar, and vigorously whisk until smooth and of spreading consistency.

MUQAWWARA (SCOOPED OUT)
A STUFFED CAKE WITH ALMONDS AND WALNUTS

For the experienced cook

⊷ *Historical version* ↣

STUFFED MUQAWWARA

Knead an amount of one and one-half *ratl*s of fine white flour with the egg yolks of 15 eggs and a little yeast and enough milk to make a firm dough, not a thin one. Make them into thin patties and leave them to rise. Then place a frying pan with sweet oil over the fire. When the oil is heated, the patties are put into it and turned again and again until they are slightly browned. Keep an eye on them. Then remove from the frying pan and hollow it out as *Muqawwara* is hollowed. Then take out its crumbs and rub them with your hands, crumbling them extremely well. Then sprinkle sugar, shelled walnut meats and shelled almonds and mix that. Inside the hollow, take turns [layering] with a little of it and a little of the rubbed crumbs until it is filled. Sprinkle over every two layers pounded sugar, in the meantime sprinkling rose water. Then boil clarified butter and honey and pour over the *Muqawwara*s until it soaks through them. Sprinkle them with sugar and use them, God Almighty willing.

al-Tujibi, p. 67 (#9). Translated by Muna Salloum and Leila Salloum Elias.

⊷ *Historical version* ↣

STUFFED MUQAWWARA

Sift a *ratl* and a half of wheat flour well, knead it with the yolks of 15 eggs and as much fresh milk as they will bear. Put in a little leavening and let the dough be stiff, make a *qursa* [patty] like a *raghif* loaf of this, and leave it to rise.

Then fill a frying pan with fresh oil and put it on the fire, and when it has heated, put in the *raghif*, turn it little by little, and watch that it not break apart. Then turn it over, and when it has browned a little, take it out and put it in a dish and hollow it out as a *Muqawwara*. Take out all the crumbs that are in it and crumble it by hand until they are pounded fine. Then take sufficient peeled walnuts and almonds and sugar, pound them well and put a layer in the loaf, then a layer of crumbs, until it is full; and sprinkle sugar between every two layers and sprinkle during that with rose water. Then boil fresh clarified butter and good honey, pour it on the loaf, and when it makes a boiling sound, put the lid back on top and seal it, and pour the rest of the honey and butter over the top, sprinkle with sugar, and present it.

Anonymous, **p. 173. Translated by Charles Perry.**

PLATE 1   *al-Sanbusak al-Hulu* (see p. 19).

PLATE 2   *Isfunj* (see p. 30).

PLATE 3 *Kunafa* (see p. 39).
PLATE 4 *Kunafa (rolled)* (see p. 43).

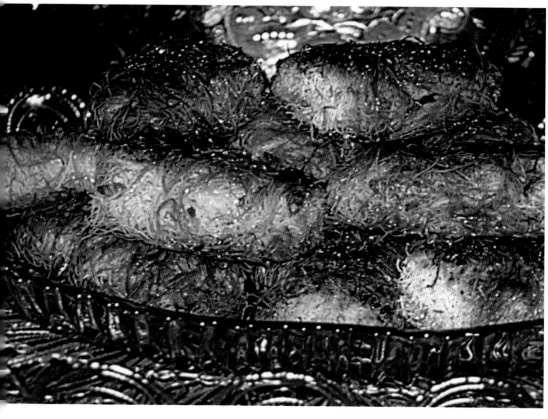

PLATE 5 *Lawzinaj* (see p. 45).

PLATE 6 *Mushash Zubayda* (see p. 52).

PLATE 7   *M'hansha* (see p. 55).
PLATE 8   *Muhajirin Cannoli* (see p. 75).

PLATE 9 *Qarmush* (see p. 76).

PLATE 10 *Qata'if Mahshi* (see p. 79).

PLATE 11   *Irnin* (see p. 107).

PLATE 12   *Klaycha* (see p. 110).

PLATE 13 *Ka'k Suri* (see p. 120).

PLATE 14 *Ka'k bi Halib* (see p. 121).

PLATE 15 *Ka'k Mahshi* (see p. 124).

PLATE 16 *Maqrud* (see p. 130).

PLATE 17   *Nuhud al-'Adhra'* (see p. 133).

PLATE 18   *Biscochitos* (see p. 135).

PLATE 19 *Faludhaj* (see p. 155).

PLATE 20 *Natif* (see p. 157).

PLATE 21 *Soplillos* (see p. 161).

PLATE 22 *Torta Imperial* (see p. 162).

PLATE 23 *Makshufa* (see p.171).

PLATE 24 *Sabuniya* (see p.173).

PLATE 25 *Arnadí de Carabassa* (see p. 191).

PLATE 26 *Basisa* (see p. 195).

PLATE 27 *Dimagh al-Mutawakkil* (see p. 199).

PLATE 28 *Balouza* (see p. 204).

PLATE 29 *Muhallabiya* (see p. 208).

PLATE 30 *Hays* (see p. 211).

PLATE 31 *Jawadhib al-Mawz* (see p. 214).

PLATE 32 *Juraydat* (see p. 220).

There are two Andalusian recipes for *Muqawwara*, a type of cake seemingly unique to *al-Maghrib*. It comes with its own edible 'cover', which is used as a scooping device.

The term *muqawwara* derives from the verb *qawwara*, meaning 'to scoop out', 'to hollow' or 'to dig out'. This cake is so named because of its hollow interior filled with layers of breadcrumbs, sugar, ground almonds and walnuts. In one recipe, the dough is prepared into patties, allowed to rise like buns, and then fried. Once cooked, they are then sliced near the top, with the lids reserved. The interior part is removed, crumbled and mixed with sugar and nuts, forming a stuffing that is then re-inserted into the buns. The lid is replaced, and the syrup is poured over them. The second recipe involves the same method but is for one large *Muqawwara*.

Although the original recipes call for the dough to be deep-fried, we chose to bake it instead. Not only is it healthier, but the dough rose better when baked. We also cut back on the 15 egg yolks called for in the original recipe, so that the dough would be lighter in texture. Frying dough and using too many eggs is a little risky for a healthy diet, and yet our adaptation otherwise is as close as possible to the original recipe.

❦ Traditional recipe ❧

Serves about 8
Preparation time: 50 minutes
Standing time: 2 hours 50 minutes
Cooking time: 35 minutes

Ingredients

½ ounce (16 g) active dry yeast
3 tablespoons plus ½ cup (100 g) granulated sugar
½ cup (125 ml) warm water
½ cup (120 ml) whole milk, scalded then cooled, but still warm
1 teaspoon salt
1 egg, beaten
5 tablespoons unsalted butter, melted
2¾–3 cups (330–360 g) plain flour
1 cup (340 g) liquid honey
½ cup (50 g) ground almonds
½ cup (50 g) ground walnuts
2 tablespoons rose water or orange blossom water
Crumbs from the *Muqawwara*
Confectioner's/icing sugar for decoration

143

Method

To prepare the *Muqawwara* dough, in a bowl, dissolve the yeast and two tablespoons of the granulated sugar in the water. Cover and let sit for ten minutes until it becomes frothy.

Stir the milk, one tablespoon of granulated sugar, the salt, egg, one tablespoon of butter and half of the flour into the yeast mixture. Mix until smooth.

Add enough remaining flour to make the dough easy to handle, adding more milk or flour if necessary. Turn the dough onto a floured surface and knead well for about ten minutes. Shape the dough into a ball about 6 inches (15 cm) in diameter, place it in a greased bowl, and cover. Allow to rise in a warm place until it doubles in size, about an hour.

Punch down, cover, and let rise again for half an hour. Shape again into a ball, and let rest for ten minutes.

Place in a greased round baking dish, 8 inches (20 cm) in diameter and 4 inches (10 cm) deep. Cover the loaf loosely with plastic wrap/cling film, then cover with a dish cloth. Allow to sit for about an hour, or until the sides reach the top of the dish. Do not let the loaf rise over the sides of the dish.

Preheat the oven to 425°F (220°C), then bake for 25–30 minutes, or until deep golden brown. Immediately remove the *Muqawwara* from the baking dish and allow to cool.

With a knife, about ½ inch (1.25 cm) from the top, carefully cut horizontally across, lifting off the top and setting it aside. Hollow out the *Muqawwara*, and set the scooped out crumbs aside too.

To make the syrup, in a small saucepan, mix the honey and the remaining butter, and bring to the boil over a medium-low heat, then keep warm over a low heat.

To make the filling, mix the almonds, walnuts, the remaining granulated sugar and the rose water or orange blossom water together.

Fill the *Muqawwara* evenly with alternate layers of the almond–walnut mixture and the crumbs, repeating until filled to the top.

Spoon half of the prepared syrup evenly over the top of the filling in the *Muqawwara*. Place the top back on the *Muqawwara* to cover it, then pour the remaining syrup over the top. Allow to cool, sprinkle with confectioner's/icing sugar, then serve, cutting into wedges.

MURAKKABA (ARRANGED TOGETHER)
A MULTI-LAYERED HONEY-DRENCHED CAKE

Moderately difficult

⋙ *Historical version* ⋘

A dish which is made in the region of Constantine and is called *kutamiyya*. Knead a well-made dough from semolina like the *Isfunj* dough with yeast, and break in it as many eggs as you can, and knead the dough with them until it is slack.

Then set up a frying pan of clay [*hantam*] on a hot fire, and when it has heated, grease it with clarified butter or oil. Put in a thin circle of the dough, and when the bread is cooked, turn over.

Take some of the dough in the hand, and smear the surface of the bread with it. Then turn the smeared surface to the pan, changing the lower part with the upper, and smear this side with dough too. Then turn it over in the pan and smear it, and keep smearing it with dough and turning it over in the tajine, and pile it up and raise it until it becomes a great, tall loaf.

Then turn it by the edges a few times in the tajine until it is done on the sides, and when it is done as it is desired, put it in a serving dish and make large holes with a stick, and pour into them melted butter and plenty of honey, so that it covers the bread, and present it.

Anonymous, pp. 35, 191. Translated by Charles Perry.

⋙ *Historical version* ⋘

Make a dough of good-quality semolina with hot water, and knead well after moistening it with water, salt and a little yeast. Continue adding water and kneading until it becomes a batter. Then add egg whites to the dough, for every *ratl* of semolina four egg whites, until the eggs are mixed in with the dough. Then place a wide clay unglazed pan over a fire. Once it is heated, wipe it with a tied-up piece of cloth that has salt in it and that has been soaked in oil or melted clarified butter. Spread out the dough in the pan. When it whitens, add more dough and turn it. Continue doing it this way until the last of the dough, and so that all the loaves appear to be one loaf. It is layered, one piece over another. Once done, it is placed in a wide vessel, and pour over it enough honey and butter to soak it. Sprinkle cinnamon over it. Eat and enjoy, God Almighty willing.

al-Tujibi, p. 78 (#26). Translated by Muna Salloum and Leila Salloum Elias.

The term *murakkaba* in Arabic means 'arranged together', and this name well describes the cake. The process involves thin pancakes placed over each other as they are fried in a pan, forming one single cake.

According to *Anonymous*, this is the version made in Constantine, a city in Algeria, where the dish is named *Kutamiya*.

The Kutama are a Berber tribe of the larger group Masmuda located in Ikjan, a mountain between Satif (Sitif) and Qastatina (Constantine) in the region of eastern Algeria. They were a prominent tribe in the tenth century, and had supported the rise of the Fatimid Dynasty in North Africa. They eventually became a powerful faction in the Fatimid army, and held a privileged position. The fertile land of eastern Algeria and western Tunisia (province of Numidia) would eventually encourage their settlement in the cultivated areas of Qastatina. The name *Kutamiya* could indicate where credit for the creation of this dish lies, or be in honour of the Kutama.

Even though thought of as a sweet, this layered-pancake pastry can also be served for breakfast. The combination of honey and semolina, and its lightweight texture, makes for a good start to the day.

The sponge (*Isfunj*) dough to which the *Anonymous* author refers is for another recipe called 'Making of elegant *Isfunja*'. The preparation for *Isfunja* is: 'You take clear and clean semolina and knead it with lukewarm water and yeast and knead again. When it has risen, turn the dough, knead fine and moisten with water, little by little, so that it becomes like tar after the second kneading, until it becomes leavened or is nearly risen' (34, 191).

In a recipe for another type of *Murakkaba* found in the same cookbook, pounded dates (date paste) can be smoothed over each cooked pancake before they are piled on top of each other on a serving platter. For the date paste, try using *Judhab al-Tamr* (see p.218).

◈ Traditional recipe ◈

Serves 6–8
Preparation time: 25 minutes
Standing time: 2 hours 10 minutes
Cooking time: 25 minutes

Ingredients

1 cup (340 g) liquid honey
¼ cup (60 g) unsalted butter
1 tablespoon granulated sugar
1¼ cups (300 ml) warm water
¼ ounce (8 g) active dry yeast
2 cups (335 g) extra-fine semolina flour
2 eggs, beaten
Light olive oil

Method

To prepare the syrup, mix the honey and butter in a saucepan and bring to the boil over a medium-low heat. Keep the syrup warm over a very low heat.

To prepare the batter, mix sugar in quarter of a cup (65 ml) of water and add the yeast. Cover, and keep in a warm place, allowing the yeast to rise for about ten minutes.

In a mixing bowl, add the semolina and make a well. Add the yeast mixture, the remaining water and the eggs, and mix well. Cover the bowl with a tea towel, and leave the batter to rise for two hours.

After the batter has risen, stir well. The consistency of the batter should be a little thinner than pancake batter. Add a little more warm water if the batter is too thick.

To prepare the *Murakkaba*, brush oil on the bottom of a 8 inch (20 cm) or 9 inch (22 cm) frying pan. Using a ladle, spoon the batter into the frying pan, making sure to spread it thinly into an approximately 7 inch (18 cm) circle. Over a medium-low heat, fry the *Murakkaba* for about two minutes, or until browned. Lift the *Murakkaba*, brush the frying pan with oil again, then flip the *Murakkaba* over in order to cook the second side. On the top part (the already-cooked side), spoon the batter in a very thin layer over the entire surface evenly, using a spatula. Once the bottom is cooked, lift the *Murakkaba*, brush the pan with oil, and flip the uncooked side onto the pan. Continue the process until all the batter is finished. Once the last side of the *Murakkaba* is cooked, turn the entire loaf on its side and roll it around the frying pan to make sure its edges are cooked.

Place the *Murakkaba* on a serving platter. Using a skewer, puncture many holes through the top into the layered *Murakkaba*, making sure not to pierce through the bottom layer. Pour the syrup several times evenly over the top to allow the *Murakkaba* to absorb the syrup.

Slice into serving pieces, and eat warm or cold.

◈ Modern recipe ◈

BINT AL-SAHN (DAUGHTER OR GIRL OF THE DISH), HONEY CAKE

Moderately difficult

Yemen has a traditional rich, sweet honey cake – now a national dish – named *Bint al-Sahn*. It is very similar to the medieval *Murakkaba*.

The name of the dish has a folkloric tradition linked to marriage. A prospective groom would be served the dish, prepared by his future bride. How she prepared it would foreshadow the type of wife she would make – thus 'girl of the dish'.

In Yemen it is usually served as an appetiser before the entrée, but it also makes an excellent dessert. On special occasions it is served as the first course of the meal, and many Yemenis enjoy it at breakfast.

The traditional Yemeni way of eating *Bint al-Sahn* is to break off pieces with the fingertips and dip the pieces into the butter and honey that remain on the serving platter. It may also be served by cutting it into wedges and spooning over the top any remaining honey–butter syrup that remains.

Although there is no actual evidence that there is a link between *Murakkaba* and *Bint al-Sahn* historically, there are similarities in the method of layering, arranging and sweetening the cake with honey.

Makes two 9 inch (22 cm) cakes
Preparation time: 35 minutes
Standing time: 1 hour 40 minutes
Cooking time: 25 minutes

Ingredients
4 cups (480 g) plain flour
½ teaspoon salt
¼ ounce (8 g) active dry yeast and 1 tablespoon granulated sugar dissolved in ½ cup (125 ml) warm water
5 eggs, beaten
2 tablespoons warm whole milk
1 cup (227 g) unsalted butter, melted
1 cup (340 g) liquid honey, warmed

Method

Thoroughly mix the flour and salt in a mixing bowl, then set aside.

Combine the yeast mixture, eggs and milk, then pour over the flour and knead into the dough, adding more milk or flour if necessary. Cover, and allow to stand in a warm place for one hour.

Divide into 12 pieces, and form into balls, then re-cover and allow to stand for half an hour.

Brush two 9 by 1¼ inch (23 by 3 cm) pie plates with melted butter.

Preheat the oven to 350°F (175°C).

Roll each ball into a circle the size of the pie plate. Place a circle in the pie plate, then brush with the butter. Repeat till all 12 circles are used, six on each plate.

Mix the remaining butter with the honey, then brush the tops with about two tablespoons of the mixture. Bake for 25 minutes, or until the top turns golden brown. Remove from the oven, then pour half of the remaining honey–butter syrup over the tops. Allow to stand for ten minutes, then serve by slicing into wedges and allowing each diner to add some of the remaining honey–butter syrup to taste.

MUSAMMANA (BUTTERED)
HONEYED PANCAKES

Easy

๕ *Historical version* ๖

MUWARRAQA MUSAMMANA

Take pure semolina or wheat flour, and knead a stiff dough without yeast. Moisten it little by little, and don't stop kneading it until it relaxes and is ready and is softened so that you can stretch a piece without severing it.

While a pan is heating, take a piece of the dough and roll it out thin on marble or a board. Smear it with melted clarified butter or fresh butter liquified over water. Then roll it up like a cloth until it becomes like a reed. Then twist it and beat it down with your palm until it becomes like a round thin bread, and if you want, fold it over again. Then roll it out and beat it down with your palm a second time until it becomes round and thin.

Then put a new frying pan on a moderate fire. Then put the dough round in a heated frying pan after you have greased the frying pan with clarified butter, and whenever the clarified butter dries out, moisten little by little. Turn the dough around until it cooks, and then take it away and cook more until you finish the amount you need.

Anonymous, pp. 39, 168. Translated by Charles Perry.

๕ *Historical version* ๖

AL-MUWARRAQA AND IT IS AL-MUSAMMANA

Knead *samidh* or white flour with water and salt and work it hard into a dough. Then melt clarified butter and roll out a piece of the dough from the kneading bowl in it as thin as is possible, then fold it after having buttered inside it. Stretch it out again and pat it down hard with one hand, and put it in the frying pan or in the *malla* over the fire, after having greased the *malla* with a little clarified butter so as not to burn it. When it is cooked, take it off the fire. Slapping it hard with both hands will cause it to separate so that it scatters about. Then put it in a bowl and cover it with a piece of linen. Do the same with the remainder of the dough, until they are done. Then satiate it with hot honey and sprinkle cinnamon and sugar over them. Use, God Almighty willing!

al-Tujibi, p. 72 (#17). Translated by Muna Salloum and Leila Salloum Elias.

Musammana is a light and buttery type of pancake. Corriente's *Dictionary of Andalusi Arabic* defines this as 'fried rolled wafers', while *Musammana, Ka'k^{un} Musamman^{un}* and *Musammanat* are defined as 'buttercake' (262).

And on the dining tables of the aristocracy, *Musammana* earned its place. Butter was a rich and valued additive in the preparation of sweets, clarified butter even more so.

Take the case of one recluse who had a clay jar of clarified butter and honey which he had saved over time. He knew its value. One day he sat studying the jar, and began to think about the fortune he would have if he were to sell the jar for ten dirhams. He would buy five goats and have them mate twice a year, and thus after two years, the number would reach 200. For every four, he would buy a cow, which he would use to plant crops. This would produce more money, so that he could take a wife who would bear him a son, whom he would name such-and-such and whom he would teach manners and politeness. However, if the son refused to listen and rebelled against him, then he would take the cane before him and hit him over the head with it. At this, the reclusive man lifted the cane above his head, as if to hit the invisible delinquent son, and struck, hitting the jar of butter and honey. The jar shattered, along with his dreams (al-Husri 184).

Musammana is also known as *Muwarraqa* ('leafy') because of its thin layers. In preparing this sweet, we have attempted to simplify the process, and have therefore diverged slightly from the original instructions found in *Anonymous* and al-Tujibi. We found that adding oil to the dough made it more pliable. It stretched better and was easier to handle.

Al-Tujibi offers two choices as to how the dough can be cooked. One is in the frying pan, the other using a *malla*, a pit of hot coal and ashes used to bake flat breads (50, 54).

⨞ Traditional recipe ⨞

Serves 8
Preparation time: 25 minutes
Standing time: 30 minutes
Cooking time: 40 minutes

Ingredients
1¼ cups (245 g) clarified butter, melted
1 cup (340 g) liquid honey
3 cups (360 g) plain flour
½ teaspoon salt
½ cup (120 ml) vegetable oil
1 cup (250 ml) warm water
Granulated sugar

Method

Place one cup (195 g) of the butter in a saucepan, and keep warm over a very low heat.

In another saucepan, to make a syrup, mix the honey and the remaining butter, and bring to the boil over a medium-low heat. Keep the honey–butter syrup warm over a low heat.

In a mixing bowl, stir together the flour and salt. Make a well in the middle, and pour in the oil and water.

Knead well to form a smooth elastic ball of dough, adding more flour or oil if necessary. Keep the dough in the bowl, and cover, then let sit for half an hour.

Divide the dough into 12 balls. Roll each ball, one at a time, into a very thin circle.

Brush the bottom of a large frying pan generously with the butter. Place a circle in the frying pan and brush the top part with the butter. Fry over a medium-low heat for two minutes. Flip the circle over, and fry for one to two minutes, making sure to brush now the cooked side with the butter. Remove from the frying pan, and place on a serving dish. Brush the top of the cooked circle with the honey–butter syrup.

Continue the process of frying and brushing the rounds with the butter, placing each cooked round on top of the other and making sure to brush the top of each with the syrup. Make sure that the frying pan is well buttered each time you are ready to fry a round of dough.

Pour any excess syrup over the top of the *Musammana* layers. Allow to cool slightly, then sprinkle with the sugar and serve.

∿ **Modern recipe** ∿

M'SEMMEN (BUTTERED), BUTTERY PANCAKES FROM MOROCCO

Easy

Musammana is another one of those sweet dishes that emigrated from al-Andalus with the Moors. The name has remained the same, but is pronounced in the Moroccan dialect as *M'semmen* – 'made of butter'.

Traditionally, *M'semmen* are heated in a mixture of butter and honey and served hot. They are generally a breakfast treat, but are also eaten as a late-day snack.

There are those who prefer them savoury. Instead of serving them with sugar and honey, they can be used as a bread base for cheese, such as feta, for olives and for fresh herbs. But, for those with a sweet tooth, a filling of ground almonds mixed with sugar can be placed into the pancake, before it is folded into a square.

Makes 15–20 pieces
Preparation time: 35 minutes
Cooking time: 20 minutes

Ingredients

4 cups (480g) plain flour
1½ teaspoons salt
1½ cups (375ml) warm water
Vegetable oil
Melted clarified butter for frying
Granulated sugar (for the topping)
Cinnamon (optional)
Liquid honey (for the topping, optional)

Method

In a bowl, mix the flour and salt. Make a well in the centre, and gradually add the water. On an oiled surface, knead into a smooth dough (it is advisable to oil your hands when kneading).

Moisten the hands with oil, and form the dough into balls the size of golf balls, and place them on an oiled tray.

Press the balls down with your hand, then, using the palm of your hand, stretch the dough out until it is very thin.

Fold in the edges of the stretched dough to form a 3½–4 inch (8.25–10cm) square.

Brush a medium-sized frying pan well with butter, and cook each square until both sides are lightly browned over a medium heat. Butter the pan each time a pancake is cooked. When the pancake is cooked, remove and place on a serving platter, then sprinkle with sugar. If preferred, dust cinnamon over the sugar. If you prefer honey, brush it on each square as soon as it is cooked.

Modern recipe

TORTA DE AMÊNDOAS (LITTLE ALMOND CAKES)

Easy

In the southern province of the Algarve – the name itself derived from the Arabic *al-gharb* (the west) – which stretches from Tavira westward to Sagres, and very close to North Africa, the cuisine is noticeably Moorish in influence, particularly the desserts. The Algarve was the last region in Portugal under the Moors to achieve its independence, and thus the impact of the Moors was to last longer.

The diffusion of new culinary ideas – along with ingredients such as sugar, egg yolks, almonds, honey and cinnamon – introduced by the Moors enriched the regional sweetmeats of Portugal – such as the Algarve's renowned marzipan. These all served as the basis for the future development of Portugal's fabulous sweets.

Between the sixteenth and eighteenth centuries in the convents of Guimarães, for example, the nuns perfected and sold the Moorish-influenced sweets based on egg yolk and sugar, making their nunneries and the sweets they produced a source of national pride.

With the defeat of the Arabs in al-Andalus, and the fervour and fanaticism of the Inquisition to erase anything non-Catholic, it is ironic that it was in these sanctified halls of Catholic worship and devotion that Moorish cuisine found a safe haven.

The Arabs delivered to Portuguese dessert-making almonds, oranges, lemons, figs, cinnamon, sugar and eggs. The sugar-cane fields of Madeira, for example, planted in the first quarter of the fifteenth century, had their origins in the sugar-cane plants of Sicily, originally planted by the Arabs. These innovations all led to Moorish-inspired Portuguese sweets such as marzipan cakes filled with egg yolk, *Doces de Ovos* (egg-based sweets), honey cakes (*Bolos de Mel*), *Fartura* (see p. 98) and *Torta de Amêndoas.*

Makes about 16 pieces
Preparation time: 15 minutes
Cooking time: 45 minutes

Ingredients

3 eggs
2 tablespoons unsalted butter
1 cup (200 g) sugar
½ cup (60 g) plain flour
1 teaspoon baking powder
1 cup (150 g) blanched whole almonds, finely ground
1 teaspoon almond extract/essence
1 teaspoon rose water

Method

Preheat the oven to 350° F (175° C).

In a food processor, place the eggs, butter and sugar, then process for a few moments until smooth.

Add the remaining ingredients, then process further until a soft batter is formed, adding a little water if necessary. Pour into medium-sized greased cupcake pans, two-thirds full, then bake for 45 minutes. Allow to cool and transfer to serving platter.

Candies

FALUDHAJ (STRAINED OR GILDED)
CHEWY HONEY ALMOND CANDY

Easy

∽ Historical version ⌘

Take good, clean honey and put it on a moderate fire in a clean boiling kettle [*tinjir*]. For each *ratl* of honey add two *uqiya*s of starch, that dilutes and mixes with the honey, and stir it continually. If you want, colour it with saffron. Stir it with a spoon so it doesn't stick.

When it is almost thickened, add for each *ratl* of honey four *uqiya*s of oil and continue to stir it. Add half an *uqiya* of good yellow wax for each *ratl* and a half of honey. When the oil begins to dribble/leak through, remove that oil with a cloth, clarifying the oil.

Then add to it peeled, chopped almonds in a sufficient amount. With the almonds, you might add some hulled sesame seeds, and stir.

Pour it over an oiled *salaya*. Make with it large or small rounds. Use them as they are or make with them whatever kind of shapes you may wish.

Anonymous, p. 197. Translated by Charles Perry.

Attesting to the popularity of *Faludhaj*, it is often mentioned anecdotally in Arabic literature, whether in its pudding form (see p.200) or, as in this case, as a type of chewy candy.

When the Caliph al-Mahdi (r. AD 775–85) asked Abu 'Abd Allah Sharik al-Nakha'i to consider taking on the position of Chief Judge of Kufa, Sharik responded that he had grown old and that his brain had changed with age. One of the suggestions the Caliph recommended was that Sharik prepare daily a *ratl* of *Faludhaj*. This would invigorate him, since the sweet could increase strength in the body and the brain, especially when made with honey. Sharik expressed his worry about becoming young again, fearing that the foolhardiness of youth would impair his judgement, but finally agreed to do so, and donned the robes of the *Qadi* (Ibn Hamdun IX 285). So high in prestige and honoured was this sweet that its nickname came to be *Abi al-'Ala'* ('father of nobility').

In one of al-Baghdadi's recipes for this sweet, the author suggests forming the *Faludhaj* into slices or melon shapes and triangles (76), as does the author of *Anonymous*.

This is a very sweet type of soft candy, and a little goes a long way.

✍ Traditional recipe ✍

Serves 8–10
Preparation time: 30 minutes
Cooking time: 20 minutes

Ingredients

2 cups (680 g) liquid honey
3 tablespoons cornstarch/cornflour
Pinch of saffron
6 tablespoons light sesame oil
1½ tablespoons comb honey mixed with 1½ tablespoons liquid honey
1¼ cups (150 g) coarsely chopped blanched almonds

Method

In a medium-sized saucepan, bring the honey to the boil over a medium-low heat. Stir in the cornstarch/cornflour until diluted in the honey, making sure there are no lumps. Stir in the saffron, and continue to stir until the mixture begins to thicken, about 15 minutes.

Stir in the oil until well blended, then add the comb honey mixture. Allow to heat through, stirring occasionally. Once heated through, lightly pat the top of the *Faludhaj* with a paper towel to remove any excess oil.

Remove from the heat, and stir in the almonds.

Spread the mixture onto a platter. Allow to cool, then cut into serving pieces.

NATIF
NOUGAT

Moderately difficult

❧ *Historical version* ❧

HARRANI NATIF

Take purified and refined honey with the froth removed and put it in
a round copper pot or in a round *tinjir* [brass or copper] pot. Pour over it a
quarter *ratl* of water and beat over the fire for an hour. Then leave it until
it cools. For every ten *ratl*s the whites of ten eggs, and put them in it. Then
beat vigorously until mixed. Then return it to the fire, then beat vigorously to
avoid the eggs burning. Continue stirring it until it whitens. When it begins
to thicken, throw in cassia, pepper, cloves and spikenard. Put in it what you
want of dried fruit, almonds, pistachios, hazelnuts, walnuts, coconut, pine
nuts, hulled sesame seeds and/or hemp seeds. If you would like to include
these, then do so. If you would like it to be plain, then do so. The amount of
time needed to beat it is three hours until it firms up, God willing.

**al-Warraq, p. 278. Translated by Muna Salloum and Leila Salloum Elias. (See also
the translation by Nawal Nasrallah: al-Warraq, *Annals of the Caliphs' Kitchen*, p. 428.)**

Natif is a form of nougat made with a mixture of egg whites and honey or sugar.
These are whisked together until white, creating a texture similar to a soft toffee.
From this, a number of sweets developed in Europe, such as Spain's Turrón and
Sicily's *Torrone*, thanks to the introduction of *Natif* by the Arabs.

Natif itself was an ingredient in some candy and cookie recipes, acting as a
meringue or as an ingredient to make candies crispy, such as in *Halwa*. According
to Abu al-Faraj al-Isfahani, *Natif* is a type of *Halwa* that is also known as *Qubbayt*
(*Al-Ima'* 1). Al-Muqaddasi also reports that during his travels through Bilad al-Sham
(Greater Syria), carob was used to make *Natif*, which the locals call *Qubbayt*, and
that in the same area anything made of sugar was called *Natif* (183–84).

Natif was popular in the souks of Iraq, Syria and Egypt. The *Natif*-sellers were
many, and the trade must have been financially viable, enough to feed and educate
family members. A good example is that of the Judge Shams al-Din al-Halawi al-
Dimashqi (b. AD 1364), whose father was a *Natif*-seller (al-'Asqalani *Inba'* VIII 445).

But not all who sold *Natif* did well. Take the case of the Judge Ibn Khazima, who
visited the Vizier al-Muhallabi (d. 963) during Ramadan on a very hot day. While
sitting in the Vizier's tent, where it was cool, they heard the voice of a man calling
out that he had *Natif* for sale. Ibn Khazima felt bad for this man, who was offering
his sweets at the worst time of day. The sun was hot, and the *Natif*-seller could
only sell his wares by walking on the hot sands. The Vizier asked that the seller be

brought to his tent. When the man entered, both Ibn Khazima and the Vizier were shocked by what they saw: a frail old man in ragged clothes wearing a cover on his head and carrying a box of *Natif*. He asked the seller his reason for choosing this time of day. The old man responded,

> I was not a seller of *Natif* in the bygone past
> But it was reasons of fate that led me to that path
> The orders from my customers, in any way I must complete
> To make my living, on burning coals my feet must withstand the heat.
>   (Yaqut al-Hamawi *Al-Arib* III 187–88)

A light and chewy candy, *Natif* is simple to make but a little tricky because of the need to work quickly with the ingredients to produce the proper results. Honey, the binding agent, makes this candy especially sweet. The importance of honey cannot be overstated and for this reason al-Warraq lists over 10 types of prepared honey that can be used in cooking (Nasrallah *Annals* 592–93).

Instead of beating by hand and pulling the candy, we decided to take advantage of the electric mixer to make *Natif*.

∽ Traditional recipe ∾

Serves 8–10
Preparation time: 30 minutes
Chilling time: 2 hours
Cooking time: 5 minutes

Ingredients

2 egg whites
3 cups (1 kg) liquid honey
¼ cup (65 ml) cold water
¼ teaspoon cassia
⅛ teaspoon ground cloves
⅛ teaspoon white pepper
⅛ teaspoon spikenard
1 tablespoon each of shredded coconut, slivered almonds, pine nuts, sesame seeds
4 tablespoons raisins, rinsed

Method

Grease an 8 inch square (20 cm) baking pan, then set aside.

Place the egg whites in a mixing bowl, and beat with an electric mixer until stiff peaks form. Set aside.

Place the honey and water in a medium-sized saucepan, then over medium-high heat stir until the honey thickens somewhat. Remove from the heat, and slowly pour about a quarter of this thickened honey into the stiff egg whites, with the mixer running constantly. Continue to beat the egg white–honey mixture until the mixture holds its shape.

With the mixer still running, gradually pour the remainder of the thickened honey into the honey–egg mixture, and continue beating until the mixture is thick and stiff. Stir in the remaining ingredients to make the *Natif.*

Spread the *Natif* evenly in the pan, then refrigerate for two hours, or until the *Natif* sets. Cut into 1 inch (2.5 cm) squares, then allow to rest at room temperature, before serving.

If it is to be kept over a longer period, store in an airtight container in the refrigerator.

⤚ Modern recipe ⤜

MODERN ARAB NOUGAT

Moderately difficult

In Syria's northern city of Aleppo, one still finds a form of *Natif.* It is a sweet marshmallow-like topping made as a dip for *Karabij* cookies (see *Irnin*, p.107). It is made from the *'irq* or *shirsh al-halawa* (root of the *Quillaja Saponaria*, or soap-bark tree) and *qatr*, beaten together to form a light white mousse. The same process is used by confectioners in Lebanon, more specifically in Tripoli, a city noted for its varieties of traditional sweets.

However, nowadays the process has changed: the trend is now for whipped marshmallow mixed with egg whites; or in some areas egg whites, tartar cream and sugar are whipped to form the new *Natif.*

Serves 8–10
Preparation time: 30 minutes
Cooking time: 10 minutes

Ingredients
2 cups (400 g) granulated sugar
1½ cups (360 ml) light corn syrup
¼ teaspoon salt
¼ cup (65 ml) cold water
2 egg whites
2 teaspoons rose water
1 cup (150 g) whole pistachios, toasted

Method

Line an 8 inch square (20 cm) baking pan with aluminum foil, and spray the foil with a non-stick cooking spray.

Place the egg whites in a mixing bowl, and beat with an electric mixer until the whites form stiff peaks.

While the whites are beating, combine the sugar, corn syrup, salt and water in a large saucepan over a medium-high heat. Stir until the sugar is dissolved, and continue to cook until the mixture reaches a hard-ball stage, at 250°F (120°C). Remove from the heat and gradually drizzle approximately quarter of the cooked mixture into the stiff egg whites, with the mixer running constantly. Continue to beat the egg whites until the mixture holds its shape.

Return the saucepan with the remaining sugar syrup to the heat, and continue to cook over a medium-high heat until the mixture reaches 300°F (150°C) (hard-crack stage). Remove from the heat and, with the mixer running, pour the saucepan contents slowly into the egg-white mixture, continuing to beat until the mixture is thick and stiff. Stir in the rose water and fold in the nuts until just combined.

Spoon the nougat into the prepared pan, and press it smoothly and evenly. Keep it in the refrigerator until the nougat is set. Take it out of the mould, and cut it into squares.

Store the nougat in an airtight container in the refrigerator, but allow it to come to room temperature before serving.

∽ Alternative modern recipe ∾

TORRONE, NOUGAT FROM ITALY

Moderately difficult

Spain and Sicily offer probably the best types of *Torrone* (in Spanish *Turrón*), and all can trace their origins to *Natif.*

Serves 8–10
Preparation time: 20 minutes
Chilling time: 3 hours
Cooking time: 35 minutes

Ingredients

1½ cups (300 g) granulated sugar
1 cup (340 g) honey
4 tablespoons unsalted butter
¼ cup (65 ml) cold water
2 egg whites
1 cup (150 g) blanched whole almonds, toasted
½ cup (75 g) whole pistachios
1½ teaspoons vanilla extract/essence
2 tablespoons lemon juice
½ cup (60 g) confectioner's/icing sugar

Method

In a medium-sized saucepan, place one cup (200 g) of the sugar, honey, butter and the water, then, stirring constantly, bring to the boil over a medium heat. Remove from the heat. Allow to cool for about three minutes.

Thoroughly beat the egg whites with the remaining sugar until stiff peaks form, then stir into the saucepan mixture. Return to the heat, and then cook over a medium heat, stirring occasionally for 30 minutes. Test by dropping a few drops of the mixture into cold water to test if it hardens. If it does not, cook further, and re-test as many times as necessary to reach the consistency of nougat.

Stir in the almonds, pistachios, vanilla and lemon juice, then pour into a well-greased baking tray to a thickness of ½ inch (1.25 cm), and allow to cool for an hour.

Cut into pieces 1 inch (2.5 cm) square. Chill in the refrigerator for an hour.

Remove the pieces from the tray, then sprinkle heavily or roll in the confectioner's/icing sugar. Serve or store in an airtight container in a cool place.

✍ Alternative modern recipe ✍

SOPLILLOS, LIGHT AND AIRY CANDY COOKIES FROM GRANADA

Easy

While in a small pastry shop in the city of Granada, one of Andalusia's throbbing centres of Arab history, we were introduced to *Soplillos*, a very light textured cookie. We asked the owner of the shop about them. He explained that these, like the Alhambra, were remnants of the Arabs legacy in his city.

According to the Granadians, this is the most recognisable sweet legacy of the Moors in Andalusia. They are easily identified as of Arab origin because of their main ingredients: egg whites, lemon peel and almonds.

Makes 20–25 pieces
Preparation time: 20 minutes
Cooking time: 1 hour

Ingredients
4 egg whites
½ teaspoon cream of tartar
½ teaspoon almond extract/essence
1½ cups (300 g) granulated sugar
3 tablespoons finely chopped lemon peel
2 cups (235 g) coarsely chopped toasted almonds

Method

Beat the egg whites until they are frothy, then gradually add the cream of tartar, almond extract/essence and sugar, then beat until stiff peaks are formed. Gently fold in the lemon peel and the almonds until all the ingredients are well blended.

Preheat the oven to 275°F (135°C).

Drop a tablespoon of mixture onto baking trays lined with parchment paper, making sure to space them, since they expand slightly when baking.

Bake for an hour. Remove from the heat, and allow to cool completely. They will be soft when they come out of the oven, but will firm up when cooled.

Place carefully on a serving dish.

TORTA IMPERIAL (IMPERIAL CAKE) AND TORTA REAL (ROYAL CAKE)
MERINGUE-BASED RECIPES DERIVED FROM THE USE
OF EGG WHITES INTRODUCED BY THE ARABS

In Andalusia, two types of cake exist whose Arab origins the Spanish proudly proclaim: the *Torta Imperial* (Imperial Cake) and *Torta Real* (Royal Cake).

✍ Modern recipe ✐

TORTA IMPERIAL (IMPERIAL CAKE)

For the experienced cook

Torta Imperial is delicious, rich and nutty in taste, but very light and crispy. It is made in three parts: meringue, praline and creamy light custard. You will need time to make this regal dessert, but in the end the preparation time is worth the effort.

Serves 8–10
Preparation time: 45 minutes
Standing time: 45 minutes
Cooking time: 1 hour

Ingredients

Parchment paper, cut into three 8 inch (20 cm) circles and brushed lightly with
   vegetable oil
½ cup (50 g) ground almonds
½ cup (50 g) ground hazelnuts
2 tablespoons cornstarch/cornflour
1 cup (225 g) caster sugar
6 egg whites
1 cup (117 g) hazelnuts, coarsely chopped
1 cup (200 g) granulated sugar
4 tablespoons liquid honey
2 tablespoons cold water
4 egg yolks, beaten
½ pound (227 g) unsalted butter, softened

Method

Place the parchment paper circles on a baking tray.

To make the meringue, in a bowl, mix together the ground almonds, ground
hazelnuts, cornstarch/cornflour and three-quarters of a cup (170 g) of the caster
sugar. With an electric mixer, beat the egg whites until they begin to stiffen, then
sprinkle in the remaining caster sugar and continue beating until stiff peaks form.
Fold in the almond–hazelnut mixture, and blend well. Spoon the meringue mixture
evenly over the parchment paper circles, spreading evenly to touch the edges of
paper. Bake in a preheated 275° F (135° C) oven for one hour. Switch the oven off,
and leave the meringue circles in the oven for half an hour, then remove and allow to
cool completely. Carefully peel off the parchment paper, and set the meringue circles
aside until ready to use.

Prepare the praline by mixing together the chopped hazelnuts and granulated sugar
in a medium-sized heavy-bottom frying pan, then cook over a medium heat, stirring
constantly until the sugar melts completely. Continue cooking, stirring constantly, for
three to four minutes, or until the melted sugar caramelises and turns golden brown.
Spread the praline mixture evenly onto a greased baking tray, and allow to cool and
harden. Break the hardened praline into very small pieces and set aside.

To prepare the filling, mix together the honey and water in a saucepan and bring
to the boil over a medium-low heat, and continue boiling, stirring occasionally, for a
further five minutes. Pour the egg yolks into the hot honey and beat until the mixture

is slightly warm. Cream the butter, then beat into the honey–egg yolk mixture. Fold in half of the praline, blending well.

Place one meringue circle on a serving platter, then spread a third of the filling onto it. Place the second meringue on top, then spread a third of the filling onto that. Add the final meringue, and spread the remaining filling on top. Sprinkle the top of the *Torta* with the remaining praline.

Refrigerate until the filling is firm, then serve, cut into slices.

～ Modern recipe ～

TORTA REAL (ROYAL CAKE)

For the experienced cook

This meringue-based cake hails from the city of Motril, in the province of Granada, its egg and almond base boasting its Arab heritage.

Serves 8–10
Preparation time: 15 minutes
Standing time: 40 minutes
Cooking time: 1 hour

Ingredients
One 8 or 9 inch (20 or 22 cm) circle of parchment paper
1 tablespoon vegetable oil
6 egg whites
1 cup (200 g) granulated sugar
3 cups (285 g) ground almonds
Peel of a whole lemon, grated finely
3 tablespoons confectioner's/icing sugar
½ teaspoon cinnamon

Method

Place the parchment paper circle on a baking tray, and brush it with the oil.

In a bowl, beat the egg whites until soft peaks form. Add the sugar, and beat into stiff peaks. Fold in the almonds and the lemon peel, and blend well.

Evenly spread the mixture on the parchment paper circle.

Bake in a preheated 275° F (135° C) oven for one hour. Switch the oven off, and leave the meringue in the oven for half an hour, then remove from the oven and allow to cool completely. Carefully peel off the parchment paper.

Sprinkle with the confectioner's/icing sugar, then with the cinnamon, and serve.

HALWA WARDIYA (ROSE-SCENTED HALWA)
DELICIOUS ROSE-SCENTED CANDY

Moderately difficult

๑ *Historical version* ๑

HALWA WARDIYA LADHIDHA

Boil roses in water until it takes on their colour, then put syrup until it takes on a consistency. Gradually moisten it with rose water. When it is almost thickened, dissolve starch in the usual way with rose water. Throw in water. Then throw in some fresh rose petals and stir with it sesame oil. Put pistachio meats in it, and flavour it with musk and rose water.

Ibn al-'Adim, p. 640. Translated by Muna Salloum and Leila Salloum Elias.

A dense sweet confection, *Halwa* is made with pistachios, poppy seeds and hazelnuts, or with dates. Some varieties are coloured with saffron or based on rose water. In some recipes, honey is used instead of sugar as the sweetener. Our choice was a rose-water-based *Halwa* recipe that is quite simple to prepare. Rose water is such a historical ingredient in Arab cuisine, and continues to be one of the most popular – in jams and jellies, preserves, syrups, juleps, beverages, and especially sweets.

The Arabs learned the techniques of rose-petal distillation from the Persians, and improved the practice as they built distillation plants throughout their empire.

The distillation of rose petals was a booming business, and the aromatic was popular. The *kharaj* tax paid by Persia to the Caliph in Baghdad included 30,000 bottles of the extract/essence of red roses (al-Tha'alibi *Thimar* II 774). People involved in the trade as a seller or maker bore the profession's name as their surname, al-Mawardi – for example the Muslim jurist Abu al-Hasan 'Ali ibn Muhammad ibn Habib al-Mawardi (AD 972–1058) of Basra.

Rose water arrived in Europe during the time of the Crusades, entering through the western regions of Sicily and southern Spain. Damascus was one of the top exporters of the product (Hayward 2–3).

Halwa Wardiya can be cut into various shapes: squares, diamonds or triangles. We tried this recipe out on various friends. Though many found it tasty, and a good after-dinner treat, others thought that it should be a little sweeter.

⤚ Traditional recipe ⤙

Serves 8–10
Preparation time: 15 minutes
Cooking time: 25 minutes

Ingredients

¾ cup (150 g) granulated sugar
1½ cups (375 ml) cold water
1 tablespoon rose water
½ cup (60 g) cornstarch/cornflour mixed with ¼ cup (65 ml) warm water (stir
   until smooth with no lumps)
2 tablespoons light sesame oil
½ cup (60 g) chopped pistachios
1 tablespoon whole pistachios

Method

In a saucepan, mix the sugar and water, and cook over a medium heat until it comes
to a gentle boil. Lower the heat to medium-low, and continue cooking for ten more
minutes, stirring occasionally.

Stir in the rose water, cornstarch/cornflour solution and the oil. Continue cooking
over a medium-low heat, stirring constantly, until the mixture thickens (after about
ten minutes) and pulls away from the side of the saucepan. Remove from the heat,
and quickly stir in the chopped pistachios. Spread evenly on a serving platter and
decorate immediately with whole pistachios, pressing down slightly.

Once the *Halwa* has cooled, cut into serving pieces.

Halwa should be kept refrigerated. It keeps well for up to three days.

HALWA' SUKKARIYA (SUGARED HALWA')
SUGARED SWEET

Easy

⤚ *Historical version* ⤙

Boil one *ratl* of sweet oil in an earthenware pot over a fire. Add to it
one *ratl* of pounded sugar and a third *ratl* of breadcrumbs made of white
and refined flour and the beaten whites of six eggs. Stir constantly over a
low fire until it thickens. Allow to cool and sprinkle on it pounded sugar
and spikenard.

al-Tujibi, p. 246. Translated by Habeeb Salloum and Muna Salloum.

In AD 1332 a wedding ceremony took place in Egypt between al-Malik Muhammad ibn al-Sultan and the daughter of the Emir Baktamur al-Saqi. The groom presented his bride with thousands of Egyptian dinars, and for the wedding over a thousand sheep, goats, camels and chickens were slaughtered. On this special day, 18,000 *qintars* (100 *ratl*s or approximately 100 pounds) of *Halwa Sukkariya* were prepared (Abu al-Fida' II/7 123).

Perhaps one reason this sugar candy was selected is that it is simple to prepare yet elegant in presentation. Considering the amount needed for the wedding festivities, it was a good choice. And to be among the food served at the royal wedding it must have been made flawlessly. The trick to perfecting it is to beat the egg whites well and vigorously, and this would have meant, in a world with no mixers and food processors, great strength.

Abu al-Husayn al-Zahid (d. AD 1153) had such strength that he became the whipping master of the souk. While at Suq al-'Arab in the Hijaz province, al-Zahid was asked by some friends to cook his famous *Halawa* for them. He agreed, and asked for a copper pot, and filled it with watermelon rinds. He lit a fire beneath it and proceeded to whip and whip them by hand until, to the amazement of those watching, they became *Halawa*, the best *Halawa*, unparalleled among sweets (al-Dhahabi 3817). Needless to say, his strength became celebrated and proverbial.

We have replaced the spikenard of the original recipe with cinnamon.

Traditional recipe

Serves 8–10
Preparation time: 15 minutes
Cooking time: 15 minutes

Ingredients

6 tablespoons (90 ml) vegetable oil
2 cups (400 g) granulated sugar
2/3 cup (80 g) dry breadcrumbs
6 egg whites, beaten to stiff peaks
2 tablespoons confectioner's/icing sugar mixed with 1/4 teaspoon cinnamon

Method

In a frying pan, combine the oil, sugar, breadcrumbs and egg whites, and mix well until smooth. Over a medium-low heat, cook the mixture, stirring constantly, for about ten minutes, or until the mixture begins to stiffen and turns lightly golden in colour. Remove from the heat, and spread quickly into a well-greased serving platter.

While still slightly warm, cut into serving pieces (squares, rectangles or triangles). When cool, sprinkle with the sugar–cinnamon mixture.

AL-LAWZINAJ AL-YABIS (DRIED ALMOND CANDY)
CANDY MADE WITH ALMONDS

Moderately difficult

⊰ *Historical version* ⊱

Take sugar and make it into syrup. It should be cooked like that of *aqras al-laymun* [that is dissolve the sugar until it reaches half of its original capacity], add rose water and musk to it, and allow it to decrease in capacity until it whitens. Add finely pounded almonds to it. Grease a tile slab with sesame oil, and spread it on it and cut into triangles. Arrange them on plates.

Kanz, p. 118 (#311). Translated by Muna Salloum and Leila Salloum Elias.

Lawzinaj is the name used for two types of almond-based sweets: one made of a very thin dough wrapped around an almond–sugar-based filling (see p. 45); or, as in this recipe, a type of marzipan popular in the medieval Arab world. The candy version is a combination of melted sugar mixed with almonds and then spread onto a surface and cut into various shapes.

The virtues of *Lawzinaj* were extolled in poetry. One poet said, 'if the eyes see it, they will never tire of looking at it.' As for taste, 'the teeth when coming upon it, will not move away' (al-Mas'udi VIII 242).

If poets versified it, others spoke of it. Al-Hasan ibn Sahl (d. AD 850/851), considered *Lawzinaj* made with *tabarzad* sugar among the foods of the kings (al-Tha'alibi *Al-Lutf* 58–59). Abu Bakr ibn Qari'a called it 'the gurgler of the throat' (*mugharghar al-halqum*) (Ibn Hamdun IX 119).

One among the many medieval recipes for *Lawzinaj* is that of the eleventh-century Ibn Jazlah. In his dietetic manual *Minhaj al-Bayan* he maintains that *Lawzinaj* is finer than *Qata'if* and more quickly digested, but less nutritious. The recipe instructions are simple: it is made with ground almonds and sugar melted with rose water until a kind of dough is formed, from which the *Lawzinaj* is made.

The simple *Lawzinaj* – filling and candy – eventually developed into the many coloured and shaped forms that we see today, and that Perry refers to as the possible ancestor of marzipan (Perry 'Cooking With' 21). In Syria and Lebanon today, marzipan is made of a paste composed of crushed almonds, sugar and orange blossom water. Besides making the paste into flowers such as daisies, poppies, roses or dandelions, some create bells to celebrate Christmas and eggs for Easter time.

In *Anonymous*, a recipe for *Jawzinaq* appears, which Perry describes as being very similar to the almond marzipan (*Lawzinaq*), both popular in al-Andalus. *Jawzinaq* is a combination of walnuts (*jawz*) and sugar syrup, made into a paste, then shaped into various forms.

Though Venice, Lübeck, Cyprus and Sicily lay claim to first creating marzipan, Baghdad is most likely the origin. The clues leading to this conclusion lie in its short and simple list of ingredients – almonds and sugar – and that the first references to it in the Arab world date back to AD 700 (Eigeland 'Arabs, Almonds' 34–35).

Almond-based sweets, such as the early form of marzipan, arrived in Iberia with the Arabs at the beginning of the eighth century. The *Mozarabes* (Christians living under Muslim rule) were by the eleventh century celebrating Christmas with marzipan on the table as the festive sweet.

The Spanish convents preserved the craft of making marzipan, continuing the tradition of the Arabs in the Iberian Peninsula. As the centuries progressed, so did the perfection of the sweet. In Spain, Toledo became, as it is now, the leading centre (Eigeland 'Arabs, Almonds' 36).

There is an interesting story told in connection with *Lawzinaj* – the candy. It is because of this version of *Lawzinaj* that, according to Maxime Rodinson, the word 'lozenge' entered the European continent, as did its culinary technique ('Ma'muniyya' 185). Perry also explains that the geometric term 'lozenge' came to displace the word 'rhombus' in England, France and other surrounding countries due to the shape of the original Arab *Lawzinaj,* which was served cut into rhomboids (Rodinson 'Venice' 210).

The making of this candy spread west across Arab-controlled North Africa, Sicily and the Iberian Peninsula. Also, Crusaders returning from the Holy Land between the eleventh and thirteenth centuries carried this sweet back with them.

The traditional recipe calls for musk as one of the aromatic ingredients. During the medieval and Renaissance periods, musk was not used only for perfumes, but also as a very strong flavouring in cooking. However, since it is virtually impossible to get now, we have replaced it with almond extract/essence – as it turns out, a good choice.

✌ Traditional recipe ☙

Serves 8–10
Preparation time: 20 minutes
Cooking time: 20 minutes

Ingredients
1 cup (250 ml) cold water
3 cups (675 g) caster sugar
1 tablespoon rose water
1 teaspoon almond extract/essence
4 cups (380 g) finely ground almonds
Confectioner's/icing sugar

Method

In a saucepan, add the sugar to the water and cook over a medium heat until the sugar dissolves, stirring constantly with a wooden spoon. Stir in the rose water and almond extract/essence, and over a medium-high heat, bring to the boil, stirring constantly until the mixture has the consistency of syrup, about seven to ten minutes. With a teaspoon, drop a little bit of the sugar mixture into a glass of cold water. If the drop hardens, the sugar mixture is ready. Remove from the heat.

Stir in the almonds until well blended, then return to the heat. Over a low heat, cook the almond–sugar mixture until the mixture stops sticking to the saucepan, about three to five minutes, stirring constantly. Remove from the heat.

Place the mixture on a baking sheet, and while still warm, using a rubber spatula or wooden spoon, lift and fold the edges of the mixture into the centre, until cool enough to handle. Begin kneading smooth by hand. If the mixture is too sticky, knead with some confectioner's/icing sugar.

The *Lawzinaj* can immediately be formed into shapes, or simply made into a log and sliced into pieces. It should be stored in an airtight container or covered with plastic wrap/cling film.

✑ Modern recipe ➢

MELINDRES DE YEPES (MARZIPAN FROM YEPES), SPAIN

Easy

One of the most indelible remnants of the Arab presence in Spain is the country's marzipan, whose colours, flavours and stuffings are characteristic of their makers. Of the hundreds of varieties available throughout the country, we chose the marzipan from Yepes, an example that is near identical to its precursor of almost a thousand years ago.

Serves 8–10
Preparation time: 30 minutes
Standing time: overnight plus 1 hour

Ingredients

4 cups (380 g) finely ground almonds
2 cups (400 g) granulated sugar
½ cup (125 ml) cold water
Confectioner's/icing sugar for sprinkling tray
2 egg whites
1 cup (115 g) confectioner's/icing sugar
2 teaspoons lemon juice

Method

Place the almonds in a food processor, and process for one minute or until they become a paste. Continue processing at high speed, and add the granulated sugar, processing for another one minute, then dribble in the water, processing until the mixture comes together as a dough.

Sprinkle confectioner's/icing sugar on a flat tray.

Break off walnut-sized pieces of dough, and shape into ½ inch (1.25 cm) patties. Place them on the tray, and allow to sit uncovered overnight to dry.

To make the glaze, beat the egg whites with an electric mixer until soft peaks form, then beat in the confectioner's/icing sugar until thickened, about three to four minutes. Add the lemon juice, and beat for five minutes more.

Dip each patty in the glaze, and place back on the tray. Allow to sit until the glaze hardens, about an hour.

MAKSHUFA (UNCOVERED)
ALMOND AND PISTACHIO CANDY

Easy

⊰ *Historical version* ⊱

Take sugar and peeled almonds, both pounded, and equal parts of honey and sesame oil. Mix the almonds with the sugar. Take enough saffron to colour it, and dissolve it in a little rose water. If you want to flavour it, let there be musk or excellent camphor with the rose water, as much as is chosen and mixed. Mix half an ounce of toasted *samid* flour with every pound of almonds. Then put sesame oil in the cauldron, which is on the fire, and when it boils and bubbles, throw the honey on it. When it boils and bubbles again, and scum appears, throw the almonds and sugar [in]. Stir continuously until it thickens as much as you want. Let the fire be quiet. If you want to put in pistachios instead of almonds, do so, and it is better.

Familiar Foods, pp. 417–18. Translated by Charles Perry.

Makshufa is the Arabic for 'uncovered'. We suspect that this candy was given the name because its ingredients are clearly visible once cooked. It is a type of candy that can be made either a little soft or hard.

Al-Baghdadi, Ibn al-'Adim and *Kanz* each include a recipe for this sweet. There are two recipes for *Makshufa* in the fourteenth-century *Familiar Foods*, one of which differs slightly from the others in its addition of flour. This recipe is reproduced below.

The only change we have made is to replace camphor and musk with mahaleb, only because camphor and musk are not easily available.

Makshufa is coloured with saffron, a colouring agent that is still used in appetisers, main dishes or desserts of the Middle East, North Africa and Spain, more so for decoration and appearance. This is not a new idea but rather a carry-forward from the medieval period, when the use of saffron for prepared dishes at a dining table represented elegance, sophistication and affluence at festive occasions such as weddings. The Caliph al-Muntasir (r. AD 861–862) apparently agreed. The Caliph provided the dowry and ordered that almonds be dyed with saffron to celebrate the marriage of two lovers who had been separated in their youth. These he had scattered upon the newlyweds in celebration of long lost love reunited. The good news is that the two stayed married a very long time, regardless, that at the end, the husband tired of his wife, and they parted their separate ways (al-Mas'udi VII 311–20). Yet, al-Jahiz would remind us that saffron serves another purpose. A wall gecko will not enter a house in which there is saffron (*Kitab al-Hayawan* IV 228).

⤮ Traditional recipe ⤶

Makes 25 pieces
Preparation time: 20 minutes
Cooking time: 15 or 20 minutes

Ingredients

½ cup (50 g) ground almonds or ground pistachios
½ cup (100 g) granulated sugar
1 tablespoon extra-fine semolina, toasted
½ teaspoon ground mahaleb
Pinch of saffron, mixed with 2 teaspoons rose water
½ cup (120 ml) light sesame oil
½ cup (170 g) liquid honey

Method

In a bowl, mix together the nuts, sugar, semolina and mahaleb. Stir in the saffron–rose water mixture, ensuring that there are no lumps.

In a saucepan, heat the oil over a medium-high heat until it begins to sizzle. Add the honey and cook, stirring constantly, until it begins to foam. Immediately add the nut mixture, then lower heat to medium-low. Stirring constantly, cook for 10 or 15 minutes (15 minutes for a harder version, 10 minutes for chewy). The mixture will thicken and turn golden.

Pour the candy mixture evenly onto a flat buttered plate, and allow to cool. When the candy is still slightly warm, cut into 25 squares, then allow to cool completely.

SABUNIYA (SMOOTH LIKE SOAP)
A SMOOTH NOUGAT

Moderately difficult

◈ *Historical version* ❧

SABUNIYYA

Dissolve sugar, then take half of it up from the cauldron and put it in another cauldron or a vessel. Then throw sesame oil into the cauldron, and when it boils, take some good starch, as much as needed, a sixth as much. If it is rice starch, better. Then stir it uninterruptedly, and when it is nearly thickened, throw the [other] half of the syrup on it bit by bit, stirring continuously. Then take two ounces of honey for every pound of sugar [and throw it in]. Then throw in some pounded peeled almonds, two ounces for every pound, and a quarter ounce of rose water, and moisten it with sesame oil and stir it continuously. When it is entirely done, spread it out and sprinkle it with pounded sugar.

Familiar Foods, p. 417. Translated by Charles Perry.

◈ *Historical version* ❧

Dissolve the sugar, then remove half of what is in the pot. Dissolve starch and throw into what remains in the pot. It should be one-sixth. If it is rice starch, it is better. Then stir, bringing it all together. When it is almost thickened, gradually add the rest of the syrup and it should be stirred with the sesame oil. Then throw one-sixth bee's honey on it. When it is done, remove it and put with every *ratl* two *uqiya*s of crushed almonds and pistachios and two *uqiya*s of rose water. Then spread it out and sprinkle sugar on it. Indeed it is extraordinary.

Kanz, p. 115 (#302). Translated by Muna Salloum and Leila Salloum Elias.

Sabuniya was among the sweets bought, placed on a platter and carried by the porter in the *Tales from the Arabian Nights* story 'The Porter and the Three Ladies of Baghdad'.

So well loved was this sweet that a few would, literally, take it with them to the grave. Take the case of the thirteenth-century al-Shaykh ibn al-Hasan, who directed that upon his death 500 dirhams-worth of *Sabuniya* be purchased for those who came to pay their final respects at his burial. History records that his instructions were carried out (al-'Ayni IV 289–90). Hasan 'Ali al-Sadr stipulated that *Sabuniya* be distributed to all who attended his funeral, and on 27 August AD 1327 rich and poor came together and ate the sweet (al-Safadi *A'yan* II 206).

This recipe seems to have been quite popular throughout the medieval period, appearing in most of the medieval Arabic culinary sources. According to Perry, the candy was so named due to its waxy texture (*A Baghdad Cookery Book* 99 n. 1).

In texture like soft nougat, *Sabuniya* can be cut into triangles or squares, or just left on the serving plate (as below) and broken into pieces, according to taste. For a different take, try spreading it between two loaves of Arabic bread. Indeed a sweet eaten like this, with bread, is like two lovers embracing each other (al-Tha'alibi *Al-Lutf* 53).

We have provided two medieval recipes, showing a clear similarity even though they are separated by almost a century.

✑ Traditional recipe ↷

Serves 8–10
Preparation time: 10 minutes
Cooking time: 35 minutes

Ingredients

2 cups (400 g) granulated sugar
¾ cup (185 ml) cold water
2 tablespoons light sesame oil
¼ cup (30 g) cornstarch/cornflour diluted in 2 tablespoons water
2 tablespoons liquid honey
¼ cup (25 g) ground almonds
1 teaspoon rose water
2 tablespoons confectioner's/icing sugar

Method

In a saucepan, mix together the sugar and water, and cook over a medium heat, stirring constantly until it boils. Lower the heat to medium-low and simmer, stirring constantly for a further ten minutes to make a syrup. Pour half of the syrup into a bowl, and keep the other half in the saucepan.

In the saucepan, add the oil to the simmering syrup and bring to the boil over a medium-low heat. Stir in the diluted cornstarch/cornflour and stir continuously, making sure there are no lumps, until it begins to thicken (about four minutes). Add the remaining syrup from the bowl, a little at a time, stirring constantly until it boils. Add the honey, almonds and rose water, and continue stirring until the mixture thickens, scraping the sides of the pot (about ten minutes). Then quickly spread the saucepan contents onto a greased serving plate. Allow to cool, then sprinkle the confectioner's/icing sugar evenly over the top.

Cut into serving pieces.

SHAWABIR (TRIANGLES)
A CRISPY HARD CANDY

Moderately difficult

✑ *Historical version* ✑

Take a round frying pan with raised sides. Put an amount of two *uqiyas* of sesame oil in it. When it boils, throw an amount of three *uqiyas* of honey in it. Then take half a *ratl* of toasted *samidh* flour and with this mix two *uqiyas* of toasted almonds, pistachios and hazelnuts, shelled and finely pounded and two *uqiyas* of finely pounded sugar. Then sprinkle it on the honey and stir until it thickens and its aroma is diffused. If it needs to be thicker, add some of the [above] described flour. Then remove until it cools and turn it over on a smooth tile slab, and cut into triangles that you dip into syrup. Then sprinkle finely pounded scented sugar over them and serve.

al-Baghdadi, p. 82. Translated by Muna Salloum and Leila Salloum Elias. (See also the translation by Charles Perry, *A Baghdad Cookery Book*, p. 106.)

Sugar production became a large-scale industry, especially during the Abbasid period (AD 750–1258), when more refineries were established across the empire. Refining sugar cane meant a crushing, extraction and crystallisation process, to which water would be added to make a paste. It was this paste that would be dried to become sugar. The outcome was a coarse and brownish-coloured sugar that would have to be finely pounded, crushed or melted in order to be used for pastry-making. In this recipe both sugar and honey are used to make this ultra-sweet sweet.

Shawabir is a very sweet crispy hard candy with a distinctive flavour, and can be compared to modern day nut brittle. The name describes the shape of the finished candy.

Shawabir appears in Ibn al-‘Adim and *Familiar Foods*, with the inclusion of saffron dissolved in rose water.

∽ Traditional recipe ⌒

Serves 8–10
Preparation time: 25 minutes
Cooking time: 5 minutes

Ingredients

Half the basic *qatr* recipe using rose water (see 'Basic recipes' section)
¼ cup (30 g) confectioner's/icing sugar
¼ teaspoon cinnamon
⅛ teaspoon ground cloves
1 cup (167 g) extra-fine semolina, lightly toasted
2 tablespoons ground almonds, toasted
2 tablespoons ground pistachios
2 tablespoons ground hazelnuts
2 tablespoons granulated sugar
2 tablespoons light sesame oil
3 tablespoons liquid honey

Method

In a bowl, mix together the confectioner's/icing sugar, cinnamon and cloves, and set aside.

In another bowl, thoroughly mix together the semolina, almonds, pistachios, hazelnuts and sugar.

In a saucepan, heat the oil over a medium heat, then stir in the honey and cook for one minute. Stir in the semolina–nut mixture, and cook over a medium-low heat for two minutes, stirring constantly, ensuring that all the ingredients are thoroughly mixed.

Remove from the heat, and quickly spread into a 9 inch square (22 cm) greased baking pan. While still warm, carefully cut into triangles with a sharp knife.

Carefully remove each triangle from the tray and dip into the cooled syrup, then dip both sides of the triangles into the spiced sugar mix. Place on a serving platter.

HALWA' YABISA (BRITTLE HALWA')
A DRY, SWEET, BRITTLE CANDY

Easy

∽ *Historical version* ⌒

The way to prepare it is to take sugar, dissolve it in water, and boil until it thickens. Then remove it from the pot and put it on a smooth tile slab until lukewarm. Then pound an iron peg with a smooth head [into the wall] and throw it on it. Continue stretching it by hand and repeat [folding it over and stretching] it on the peg in this way until it whitens. Then throw it on the tile slab and knead into it pistachios. Cut it into strips and triangles. Whoever would like to colour it, do so with saffron or cinnabar. Some of it may be kneaded with some peeled almonds or sesame seeds or poppy seeds.

al-Baghdadi, pp. 74–75. Translated by Muna Salloum and Leila Salloum Elias. (See also the translation by Charles Perry, *A Baghdad Cookery Book*, pp. 98–99.)

Halwa' can be soft and chewy, or in the form *yabisa*, literally stiff, hard or dry, similar to nut brittle. Crunchy and sweet, it is made with pistachios, almonds, sesame seeds and pine nuts, in combination or on their own. So popular was this sweet during the medieval period that Ibn al-Ukhuwa, one of the prominent *muhtasib*s of the fourteenth century, notes in his market-inspector's manual the many kinds available in the markets, including those made with starch, almonds, pistachios and poppy seeds (181).

The 'dough' or candy base would be made first, then hung over a large iron peg. The trick was to keep pulling and stretching it until it turned white, while maintaining its elasticity. The nuts would then be kneaded into the 'dough' (Nasrallah *Annals* 389 n.8). Finally, it would be cut into various shapes.

For our modern kitchens, the iron peg is not necessary. Once the sugar–water mixture has melted, it should be removed immediately and placed on a flat surface that is slightly damp or lightly oiled, then patted down flat and even with the hands. Working quickly with the mixture, and using both hands, it must be continually pulled and folded until it whitens. The next step is to place the pliable 'taffy' on a flat surface and work the nuts into it.

In whichever form, *Halwa'* was a delicacy obviously preferred during festive occasions such as Eid al-Fitr and Eid al-Adha. The Fatimid rulers were noted, for example, for hosting large feasts during these celebrations. At these events, in the Caliph's throne room a long table would be set up, decorated with fragrant flowers, the table dressed along its sides with baskets of bread weighing three pounds, made with the finest flour, and 21 magnificent large round trays: on each tray, 21 grilled lambs and a mixture of 350 hens, chickens and pigeons. More importantly, each dish would be decorated along its edges with sliced-up pieces of *Halwa' Yabisa* (al-Qalqashandi IV 265).

We did not use the 'pulling process' to make the *Halwa' Yabisa*. The method below worked just as well. The result is a brittle crunchy candy.

✍ Traditional recipe ✍

Serves 8–10
Preparation time: 20 minutes
Cooking time: 25 minutes

Ingredients

2 cups (400 g) granulated sugar
½ cup (125 ml) cold water
1½ cups (225 g) whole pistachios
½ cup (75 g) blanched whole almonds
⅛ teaspoon powdered saffron, dissolved in 1 tablespoon warm water

Method

Place the sugar and the water in a medium-sized heavy frying pan and stir constantly until the sugar dissolves, then, stirring almost constantly, cook for 20 minutes over a low heat or until the sugar syrup thickens and begins to turn slightly golden. Stir in the remaining ingredients, then cook for a further few minutes. Spread in a greased baking tray to a thickness of about ¼ inch (6 mm), and leave to harden. Break up into pieces and serve.

✍ Modern recipe ✍

SICILIAN TORRONE DI MANDORLE

Easy

Torrone recalls Sicily's Arab past and today is a part of Sicily's identity. It is made with pistachios or almonds, or both. Later versions developed over the centuries, so that now Sicily offers *Torrone* made with hazelnuts and peanuts, chocolate-covered or plain. Other versions are enhanced by orange peel. But it is the original version that remains most popular among the Sicilians.

Makes about 2 pounds (900 g)
Preparation time: 15 minutes
Standing time: 15 minutes
Cooking time: 20 minutes

Ingredients

½ pound (227 g) blanched whole almonds
½ pound (227 g) whole pistachios
2 cups (400 g) granulated sugar
½ lemon

Method

In a medium-sized heavy frying pan, heat the almonds, pistachios and sugar over a very low heat, stirring constantly for about 20 minutes. It is important to stir the mixture constantly to prevent it from burning. During the cooking process, the sugar will change colour gradually, and will crystallise around the almonds. As soon as the sugar has melted and has turned brown, the *Torrone* is ready.

Immediately turn it out onto an oiled tiled surface, and flatten it into a thin sheet, using the flat side of a half lemon. Allow to cool, then break into pieces.

✌ Alternative modern recipe ✌

CUBAITA DI GIUGGIULENA, SESAME CUBES

Easy

In Sicily, Arab culture continued for the first century and a half of Norman rule, following the Arab defeat of AD 1091. So embedded was Arab culture in the island's life that the court of the new Norman ruler, Roger I, at Palermo 'seemed more Oriental than Occidental' (Hitti 607). The Arab preference for certain sweets – such as cookies, cakes and sherbets – laid the foundation for Sicilian cooking. One example is Sicily's *Cubaita* (also spelled *Cubbaita*) *di Giuggiulena*. *Cubaita* is popular all over the island. The sweet's Arab origin is clear not only from its ingredients and method of preparation, but also from its name.

In the Sicilian dialect, *Cubaita* originates with the Arabic term *qubbayt*, meaning 'cubes'. This sweet was originally made of honey, almonds and *giuggiulena* (derived from the Arabic *juljulan*, 'sesame seeds'). There are various types of this candy – such as *Confetti* (see p.182), *Torrone* (see p.160) and the Spanish *Alajú* (see p.181) – using different ingredients, including almonds, pistachios, peanuts or toasted chickpeas. Those made with sesame seeds are called *Cubaita* in some areas of Sicily, *Giuggiulena* in others.

Simeti states that *Cubaita* is an exact replica of the *Halwa' Yabisa* of al-Baghdadi's text (see p.176). In Morocco, *Hilu di al-Juljulan* (sesame-seed sweet), a mixture of sugar or honey melted then mixed with sesame seeds and almonds, is another version of this sweet.

Serves 8–10
Preparation time: 15 minutes
Standing time: 10 minutes
Cooking time: 35 minutes

Ingredients

1 pound (454g) blanched whole almonds, halved, or a mixture of ½ pound
   (227g) blanched whole almonds, halved, and ½ pound (227g) whole
   pistachios
1 cup (155g) sesame seeds
½ cup (170g) liquid honey
2⅔ cups (470g) granulated sugar

Method

Preheat the oven to 300°F (150°C).
Toast the almonds for 15–20 minutes, stirring occasionally with a wooden spoon to
ensure all the sides are golden brown. Allow to cool.

Mix the almonds (or the mixture of almonds and pistachios), sesame seeds and
the honey together to make the nut mixture, and set aside.

In a heavy medium-sized frying pan, cook the sugar slowly over a low heat,
stirring briskly with a wooden spoon and scraping down the sides of the pan while
the sugar is cooking, for about 20 minutes, until it melts into a thick paste and has
begun to turn light brown. Stir the nut mixture into the sugar paste, and mix well,
cooking over a low heat for a further one minute until the honey dissolves.

Working quickly, turn the mixture out onto an oiled baking sheet, and spread out
evenly to a thickness of no more than ¼ inch (6mm). When the mixture has cooled
to warm, cut into small diamonds, triangles, strips or squares with an oiled knife.
Allow to cool, and serve.

✑ Alternative modern recipe ✒

TURRÓN, ALMOND NOUGAT FROM SPAIN

Easy

Further west, in Spain, *Turrón* is another reflection of the Arab heritage. A similar
candy, *Guirlache*, made of walnuts, honey or sugar and sesame, is believed to have
been brought by the ninth-century composer–musician Ziryab when he came to al-
Andalus from Baghdad (Lebling 33).

Almonds were used extensively in al-Andalus for making sweets, just as they are
today. Good examples are *Alajú* (see p.181), a paste of almonds, and *Alfajor*, a paste
of honey and almonds, both names derived directly from the Arabic. There is also
Spain's *Atalvina*, an almond dessert, the name deriving from the Arabic *al-Talbina*, a
Moorish dish made from almonds, milk and honey.

A crispy hard nougat made crunchy with almonds, *Turrón* is truly a gift from the
Arabs to Spain – and to the rest of the Latin-speaking world.

Serves 8–12
Preparation time: 20 minutes
Standing time: 2 hours
Cooking time: 35 minutes

Ingredients

1 pound (454 g) liquid honey
1¼ cups (250 g) granulated sugar
2 egg whites
1½ pounds (680 g) blanched whole almonds
1 teaspoon lemon zest
1 teaspoon almond extract/essence

Method

In a saucepan, heat the honey over a low heat until heated through, stirring constantly to avoid burning.

Stir in the sugar until it dissolves. Set aside, allowing it to cool.

In a mixing bowl, beat the egg whites until stiff peaks form. Stir them into the cooled honey–sugar mixture, and continue stirring for 12 minutes.

Return the saucepan to a low heat, and continue stirring constantly until the saucepan contents begin to caramelise, after about ten minutes.

Add the almonds, zest and extract/essence, and stir well together. Remove from the heat, and allow to cool for three minutes.

Using a lightly buttered spatula, transfer the saucepan contents to a well-greased 9 by 9 by 2 inch (22 by 22 by 5 cm) baking pan, and pat down to make it level. Set aside to cool for two hours.

When the *Turrón* has cooled, cut into 1 inch (3.75 cm) squares.

Serve, or store in an airtight container.

◅ Alternative modern recipe ▻

ALAJÚ, ALMOND CANDY

Moderately difficult

Alajú, more commonly known in Spain as 'Arabic honey slice' has not changed since the Arabs introduced it into al-Andalus.

The Arab medieval sweets *Makshufa* (see p.171), *Shawabir* (see p.175) and *Basisa* (see p.195) are basically made of the same ingredients as the filling for the *Alajú*. Spanish and Arabic etymological works generally state that the Spanish term *alajú* comes directly from the name of an Arab sweet paste, *al-hashu*, made of toasted bread, honey, sesame seeds and spices, and stuffed into *qursa*s (patties).

Today, in Spain, *Alajú* is made either with or without breadcrumbs, just as it was in medieval times.

For this recipe, you will need to toast the almonds. Place the sliced almonds in a pan in a preheated 300°F (150°C) oven for 15–20 minutes, shaking the pan occasionally to ensure the almonds are toasted on all sides.

Makes one 8 or 9 inch (20 or 23 cm) round
Preparation time: 20 minutes
Cooking time: 10 minutes

Ingredients

1 cup (340 g) liquid honey
Grated peel of 1 orange or grated peel of ½ lemon
½ cup (46 g) toasted sliced almonds
¼ cup (40 g) walnut halves
¾ cup (90 g) dry fine breadcrumbs
½ teaspoon orange blossom water
2 sheets rice paper, 8 inches (20 cm) or 9 inches (23 cm)

Method

In a medium-sized heavy saucepan, add the honey and stir in the peel. Cook over a medium heat for two minutes, then lower the heat and cook for a further two minutes, stirring constantly.

Remove from the heat, then stir in the almonds and walnuts. Add the breadcrumbs. Return to a medium heat and stir constantly for five minutes or until the mixture begins to become a heavy paste.

Remove from the heat, and stir in the orange blossom water.

Turn the mixture onto a sheet of rice paper, and pat it evenly into a round disc almost reaching the edges of the paper. Cover with the second piece of rice paper, and press down gently. Allow to cool.

Store in an airtight container, and slice into pieces as needed.

∾ Alternative modern recipe ∾

CONFETTI, ALMOND CANDY FROM SICILY

Easy

Following in the tradition of the Sicilian *Cubaita* (see p.179) and *Torrone* (see p.160), *Confetti* is another form of *Halwa' Yabisa* (see p.176) which the Sicilian kitchen offers.

Serves 8–10
Preparation time: 10 minutes
Cooking time: 15 minutes

Ingredients

1 cup (150 g) blanched whole almonds
4 tablespoons unsalted butter
¾ cup (170 g) granulated sugar
1 teaspoon vanilla extract/essence

Method

In a medium-sized heavy frying pan, place the almonds, butter and sugar, then, stirring constantly over a medium heat, cook for about 15 minutes, or until the sugar becomes candy-like. Test for this by dropping quarter of a teaspoon of this mixture into a glass of cold water. It should form into a soft round ball. If it does not, continue to cook, and test again after one minute. Continue to test until the round-ball stage is reached.

Stir in the vanilla, then spread on a well-greased tray, pressing to a thickness of ¼ inch (6 mm). Allow to cool, then break into pieces and serve, or store in an airtight container.

SHAKARINAJ (SUGARED)
SUGAR CANDY

Easy

⊱ *Historical version* ⊰

Take one and half *ratl*s of skinned almonds, and finely pound them. Take two *ratl*s of *tabarzad* sugar, pound and sift. Then take a shallow earthenware saucepan [*tajin*], and put into it a quarter *ratl* of almond oil. Throw onto it a weight of one and a half dirhams of saffron. Light a gentle fire beneath it until the oil heats. Then throw into it the almonds. Then throw onto it the pounded sugar and stir it well. Then add honey and an *uqiya* of rose water, and stir until it thickens and it becomes one [piece]. Then throw it on a tile slab or a flat table and spread it with a *sawlaj* [short and hooked pole] to a medium thickness. Cut into equal-sized pieces resembling *luqum* [bite-sized pieces]. Put them into a serving vessel and serve.

Kanz, pp. 119–20. Translated by Muna Salloum and Leila Salloum Elias.

The Fatimid Caliph al-'Aziz bi-Allah (AD 975–996) built Dar al-Fitra near his palace in Fustat to prepare, supply and distribute the large quantities of pastries for the celebration of Eid al-Fitr. He was known for his lavish and splendid public celebrations, and for his distribution of sweetstuffs during religious ceremonies, and Dar al-Fitra housed the ingredients needed to prepare those sweets made of honey and sugar, saffron, aromatics and flour. Al-Maqrizi records that distributed among the sweets to the soldiers, courtiers and other officials were *Khushkananaj, Ka'b al-Ghazal* and pistachios (al-Maqrizi *Al-Mawa'iz* II 401–2). With the variety of sweet ingredients housed at Dar al-Fitra, a sugar-based candy such as *Shakarinaj*, could also have been made there.

Most probably, this candy is of Persian origin. The word for 'sugar' in Persian is *shakarin*, and there is a sugar-based confection known in Persian as *Shakarina*.

Bite-sized pieces are recommended in *Kanz*, most likely due to its sweetness.

৯ Traditional recipe ৶

Serves 6
Preparation time: 15 minutes
Cooking time: 15 minutes

Ingredients

½ cup (120 ml) almond oil
Pinch of saffron
1½ cups (145 g) finely ground almonds
2 cups (230 g) confectioner's/icing sugar
½ cup (170 g) liquid honey
1 tablespoon rose water

Method

In a heavy medium-sized saucepan, add the oil and the saffron, and heat through over a low heat. Stir in the almonds and the confectioner's/icing sugar, blending well. Add the remaining ingredients, and stir continually until the *Shakarinaj* thickens and comes together, after about 12 minutes. Remove from the heat and immediately spread on a flat serving plate. Cut into 1 inch (2.5 cm) square pieces.

Puddings
and other sweet delights

AL-KAHIN
EGG-WHITE PUFFS

Easy

✥ *Historical version* ❧

Mill starch fine and sieve it, and take for every dirham of it an egg white and beat it well. Then take a nice quantity of it with a spoon and throw it in sesame oil and put it in syrup. It comes out excellently.

Familiar Foods, p. 422. Translated by Charles Perry.

Even though this recipe is untitled in *Familiar Foods*, it is without doubt the same fried puff found in *Kanz* and in the text of Ibn al-'Adim, named *al-Kahin*.

These are egg-white puffs fried then dipped in syrup. They should be eaten immediately because if they sit too long they become soft and limp.

As for oil versus butter, both are good agents for frying. We tried both, and found that butter created a lighter taste, not as heavy as with oil. We also found that buttering the serving platter prevented the puffs from sticking to it.

❧ Traditional recipe ❧

Makes 15–20 pieces
Preparation time: 20 minutes
Cooking time: 25 minutes

Ingredients

Half the basic *qatr* recipe using rose water (see 'Basic recipes' section)
3 egg whites
1½ teaspoons cornstarch/cornflour
¼ teaspoon rose water
1 cup (240 ml) light sesame oil or 1½ cups (340 g) butter, melted

Method

In a bowl, mix together the egg whites, cornstarch/cornflour and rose water. Stir well until there are no lumps. Beat the mixture with an electric beater until stiff peaks form.

In a saucepan, heat the oil or butter over a medium-low heat. Drop a teaspoonful of the egg-white mixture into the oil or butter, and fry the puffs until they begin to turn a slightly golden colour, turning over once. Remove with a slotted spoon and immediately dip the puffs into the *qatr*, then place on a well-greased serving platter.

Serve immediately.

ARUZZ HULU (SWEET RICE)
SWEET RICE PUDDING

Easy

❧ *Historical version* ❧

RIZZ HULU

Put rice in boiling water until it swells and is nearly done. Then put a sweet ingredient with it until it thickens, and sprinkle it with ginger and take it off the fire.

Ibn al-Mabrad, p. 472. Translated by Charles Perry.

According to the physician Ibn Jazlah, rice keeps the face youthful, makes the body fertile, and induces good dreams. Also, when rice is cooked with milk and mixed with sugar, it is filled with nutrients (al-Warraq 32).

Whether Ibn Jazlah's words were taken to heart, or whether for the simple reason that rice tastes good, in the Arab world today, especially in the east, the importance of rice cannot be overstated. It is a staple. Main dishes such as stews or stuffings are bare without it. Even in desserts rice is not to be left out.

But when did this love affair with rice begin? A couple of Arab historians may have given us an insight into this.

When the Caliph 'Umar ibn al-Khattab received word in AD 635 that the Persian army was receiving reinforcements and food supplies from the city of al-Ubulla, he decided that the city must be taken, and named 'Utba ibn Ghazwan as commander of the Arab army for the task. As reported by Nafi' ibn al-Harith, when the troops approached the city, 'Utba, realising that his troops were hungry, ordered them to find something to eat. They entered the thicket of reeds, where they found two abandoned baskets, in one dates, in the other rice in its husks. They ate only the dates. They did not touch the contents of the other basket because they were unfamiliar with these grains. 'Utba presumed the grains were poison and that the enemy had left the basket on purpose. His troops were ordered not to go near it.

One of the army's untethered horses wandered off, approached the basket of grains, and began to eat from it. Discovering it, the troops considered killing it. They did not want the horse to suffer a slow death from the poison. However, its owner said that he would watch it during the night. If he felt that it would die, he would put it out of its misery.

The next morning, the horse was fine. Nafi''s sister recalled what their father had taught them – that when poison is cooked, it loses its harmful effects. The grains were cooked until their husks separated, leaving white grains. The rice was put into a large dish, and 'Utba announced that all should mention God's name and eat from it. They found it to be delicious (Yaqut al-Hamawi *Mu'jam al-Buldan* II 194–95) al-'Askari *Jamharat* II 215–16). This was the Meccans' first encounter with rice.

It grew to become their love affair.

⮜ Traditional recipe ⮞

Serves 8
Preparation time: 15 minutes
Cooking time: 30 minutes

Ingredients
4 cups (1 litre) cold water
1 cup (200 g) uncooked long-grain white rice, rinsed
½ cup (170 g) liquid honey
½ teaspoon ground ginger

Method

Place the water in a medium-sized saucepan and bring to the boil, then stir in the rice. Cover and cook over medium-low heat for 15 minutes. Stir in the honey and cook for a further ten minutes or until the mixture thickens.

Spoon into serving cups, sprinkle with pistachios, then allow to cool. Cover each cup with plastic wrap/cling film and refrigerate until ready to serve, at least an hour.

When ready to serve, sprinkle with the ginger.

⸙ Modern recipe ⸙

*RIZZ BI-HALIB (RICE WITH MILK), RICE PUDDING
FROM THE EASTERN ARAB WORLD*

Easy

A comparison with the medieval recipes for sweetened rice shows that Arab rice pudding has remained basically the same, although along the way there have been various additions, such as cinnamon in one region or raisins or pine nuts in another.

Serves 6–8
Preparation time: 10 minutes
Standing time: 20 minutes
Cooking time: 20 minutes

Ingredients

1 cup (250 ml) cold water
¼ cup (50 g) uncooked long-grain white rice, rinsed
1 cup (240 ml) 10% cream/light cream/single cream
1 cup (240 ml) whole milk
¼ cup (40 g) seedless raisins, washed
¼ cup (50 g) granulated sugar
1 tablespoon cornstarch/cornflour
1 teaspoon orange blossom water
2 tablespoons chopped pistachios

Place the water and rice in a medium-sized saucepan, bring to the boil, then cook over a medium heat for ten minutes. Add the remaining ingredients, except the pistachios, then bring to the boil. Cook for a further ten minutes over a medium heat, stirring constantly, then remove from the heat. Immediately spoon into serving cups, sprinkle with pistachios, then allow to cool and refrigerate covered with plastic wrap/cling film until ready to use.

◖ Alternative modern recipe ◗

ARROZ CON LECHE (RICE WITH MILK), RICE PUDDING FROM SPAIN

Easy

The Arab occupation of Iberia and Sicily introduced great gains in irrigation systems and the introduction of numerous new crops, such as rice and sugar cane. The increase in rice production and *riziculture* very early on in Spain eventually led to it being exported from Sicily in the tenth century. Valencia, one of the most important regions for rice plantations established by the Arabs, continues today to hold its water tribunal meetings on Thursdays, just as it did during Arab rule.

With the Arab introduction of rice to the peninsula, and their seven-hundred-year rule, the crop remained an important ingredient in Spanish cooking. *Arroz con Leche*, is a classic Arab-inspired sweet rice pudding with cinnamon.

It may be served either warm or cold.

Serves 6
Preparation time: 20 minutes
Cooking time: 20 minutes

Ingredients
2 cups (480 ml) whole milk
1 cinnamon stick
1 tablespoon lemon zest
Pinch of salt
½ cup (105 g) uncooked short-grain white rice, rinsed
3 egg yolks, beaten
⅓ cup (70 g) granulated sugar
4 tablespoons unsalted butter, melted
1 teaspoon ground nutmeg

Method

In a medium-sized saucepan, add the milk, cinnamon stick, zest and salt, and bring to the boil over a medium heat. Remove the cinnamon stick, then stir in the rice and the egg yolks. Reduce the heat to low, and allow the rice to simmer for about 15 minutes, stirring constantly. Remove from the heat.

Add the sugar and butter, and combine well. Pour the mixture into a serving dish, then sprinkle with nutmeg. Serve warm or once it has cooled.

KHABIS AL-YAQTIN (CONDENSED GOURD PUDDING)
BUTTERNUT SQUASH PUDDING

Moderately difficult

⊸ *Historical version* ⊷

That is that you take gourds and peel them and boil them, then you strain them of all water and pound them and squeeze them. Then throw them in the tray after they have been sweetened with sugar. Throw in almonds with a little starch, and the almonds and starch are coloured. Then whip it with sugar and sesame oil. When it comes out of cooking, spread it out in vessels and put sugar over and under it.

Familiar Foods, p. 415. Translated by Charles Perry.

The medieval Arabs used gourds for main dishes, in desserts, and for making jams and candied fruit. We find a recipe for sweet *Khabis* and a *Faludhaj* made with gourds as the basic ingredient (al-Tujibi 226).

Khabis is a type of thick condensed pudding which came to be associated with 'fine dining'. Beginning as a simple combination of dates, flour and butter, over time new ingredients replaced the old. Carrots, bread, almonds and gourds brought *Khabis* to a new level.

We learn from al-Warraq that caliphs enjoyed it. Take, for example, the Caliph al-Muktafi, who is credited with two recipes for the almond type of *Khabis*, one sprinkled with rose water and powdered sugar, the other having the option of using saffron as a colouring (256).

⊸ Traditional recipe ⊷

Serves 6–8
Preparation time: 25 minutes
Cooking time: 35 minutes

Ingredients

1 butternut squash, about 2 pounds (900 g), peeled and chopped into large pieces
1 cup (200 g) granulated sugar
1 cup (150 g) blanched whole almonds
Pinch of saffron diluted in 2 tablespoons of warm water, then mixed with 1 tablespoon cornstarch/cornflour
2 tablespoons light sesame oil

Method

Place the squash in a saucepan, and cover with water. Bring to the boil, then cover and cook over a medium heat for 25 minutes, or until the squash is well cooked. Drain, then place in a strainer. Press down the squash with the palm of the hand to squeeze out excess water. Transfer to a bowl, and mash. Stir in half a cup (100g) of the sugar. Then stir in the almonds, starch mixture and sesame oil. Place the mixture in a saucepan, and heat over a medium heat for five minutes, stirring constantly.

Divide the remaining sugar in half. Sprinkle half of the sugar over the bottom of six to eight dessert cups. Spoon the *Khabis* into each cup, then sprinkle the remaining sugar evenly over the top of the *Khabis*.

Serve immediately.

⤷ Modern recipe ⤶

ARNADÍ DE CARABASSA, PUMPKIN-CAKE-LIKE PUDDING FROM VALENCIA

Moderately difficult

This pudding-like cake, according to Roden, is of Arab origin, and is common throughout the region of Valencia in Spain (Roden *Mediterranean* 196). The Valencians themselves acknowledge its connection to the Arabs.

Arnadí de Carabassa can either be classified as a cake or as a pudding. Delicious, moist and spicy, it exudes Arab influences with its ingredients: pumpkin (replacing the gourd), cinnamon, nutmeg, cloves, almonds; other versions have pine nuts and citrus rind.

According to Spanish etymological sources, *Arnadí* is derived from the Arabic name of the city of Granada, Gharnati, most likely referring to the dish's original home, or to a variety of pumpkin or gourd cultivated there. The term *carabassa*, meaning 'gourd', is derived, according to *Webster's* Second and Third Editions *International Dictionary* and Klein's *A Comprehensive Etymological Dictionary of the English Language,* from the Arabic *qar'a* or *qar'* ('gourd') and *yabisa* ('dry'). We can conclude that the gourd was the original ingredient for this dessert, and was eventually replaced by the pumpkin.

Serves 4–6
Preparation time: 25 minutes
Cooking time: 1 hour

Ingredients

1 large egg
Peel of half a lemon, finely chopped
1/8 teaspoon ground cloves
1/8 teaspoon ground nutmeg
3/4 teaspoon cinnamon
1/2 cup (100 g) granulated sugar
1/2 cup (50 g) finely ground almonds
1 16 ounce (454 g) can, mashed pure pumpkin, drained
20 blanched whole almonds
1 tablespoon confectioner's/icing sugar

Method

In a mixing bowl, beat together the egg, lemon peel, cloves, nutmeg, half a teaspoon of the cinnamon and the sugar, forming a smooth lightly golden-coloured paste. Stir in the ground almonds, then add the pumpkin, mixing well.

Preheat the oven to 375°F (190°C).

Pour the pumpkin mixture into a well-greased 8 by 1½ inch (20 by 4 cm) or 9 by 1½ inch (23 by 4 cm) round oven dish and bake for one hour.

Firmly press the whole almonds evenly on top of the *Arnadí de Carabassa*, then sprinkle the confectioner's/icing sugar and the remaining cinnamon over the top.

Serve cold.

⤷ Alternative modern recipe ⤶

PASTEL CORDOBÉS, CORDOVAN PUFF-PASTRY PIE

For the experienced cook

This pie, according to food historians and Andalusian chefs, is of Arab origin (Eigeland 'The Cuisine of al-Andalus' 34). Although the Arabic source recipe is a pudding, the connection to the *Pastel Cordobés* is the use of a type of gourd to make this tart with a sweet filling.

Serves 8–10
Preparation time: 40 minutes
Cooking time: 45 minutes

Ingredients

1 16 ounce (454 g) can mashed pure pumpkin
2 tablespoons and 2 cups (240 g) plain flour
¾ cup (150 g) granulated sugar
½ teaspoon salt
¼ cup (60 ml) light olive oil
2 teaspoons white vinegar
⅓ cup (80 ml) cold water
½ cup (227 g) unsalted butter, melted and divided into six parts
1 egg, beaten
Confectioner's/icing sugar
Cinnamon

Method

In a mixing bowl, stir together the pumpkin, the two tablespoons of flour and the sugar, and set aside.

In another mixing bowl, mix the remaining two cups (240 g) of flour and the salt. Make a well, and add the oil and the vinegar. Mix by hand until crumbly, then slowly add the water, kneading into a soft dough.

Roll the dough out, then spread one of the one-sixth portions of butter evenly over the dough. Fold the dough over, then roll the dough again. Repeat the procedure another five times, adding a little more flour if the dough is too soft to handle. You will know that the dough is too soft if it sticks to the fingers.

Preheat the oven to 400°F (200°C).

Divide the dough into two equal-sized parts, and roll them out into two circles (to fit into a 8 by 1¼ inch (20 by 3 cm) or 9 by 1¼ inch (23 by 3 cm) greased pie pan). Place one round in the pie pan, and lift the dough up the sides evenly. Spread the pumpkin mixture over the layer of dough, then place the second round of dough evenly on top. Pinch the edges to seal the two rounds together, then brush the egg lightly along the edges.

Bake for 45 minutes, broil/grill until the top is evenly golden, then remove from the oven.

Once the *Pastel* has cooled, sprinkle the top with confectioner's/icing sugar and cinnamon.

Cut into wedges, and serve hot or cold.

AL-MARIS (SOAKED DATES)
DATE PUDDING

Easy

৯ *Historical version* ৯

Remove the pits from the dates. Take the pith of *kamaj* [a white unleavened bread], put through a sieve. Then take sesame oil, or fresh butter, or clarified butter, or sheep tail fat, in the amount one wants, and put it in a frying pan. Throw on it the dates [and cook] until they soften. Then throw the pith in it and stir well. Sprinkle sugar on it, enough to sweeten it. Then throw crushed, roasted pistachios on it. Ladle it into dishes.

Ibn al-'Adim, pp. 623–24. Translated by Muna Salloum and Leila Salloum Elias.

Since the Arabic verb *marasa* means 'to dilute and mash', *maris* is applied to dates soaked in water or milk, and thus dates mashed with the same liquids are given the name of this sweet pudding (Ibn Durayd II 721). Also, in Baghdad the name given to thin, flat breads kneaded with butter and dates was also *Maris* (Ibn Khallikan I 278).

Ancient Mari's *Mersu*, a stirred-up mixture with a base of dates, butter and pistachios, was 'the meal of a king' (Bottéro *Oldest Cuisine* 23), so it seems natural that over two thousand years later *al-Maris*, a date pudding with pistachios, would come to grace the tables of nobility in thirteenth-century Aleppo.

Among the Arabs, the date was the original sweet, and almost synonymous with life itself.

Al-Hajjaj ibn Yusuf (d. AD 714), Governor of Iraq, took a poll among those sitting with him one evening, asking each one to write down on a piece of paper his favourite food. When he collected the papers, he found that each had written dates and butter (Ibn Qutayba III 197).

Al-Maris is a rich dessert, and should not be served after a full meal. It is a small meal in itself.

৯ Traditional recipe ৯

Serves 8
Preparation time: 20 minutes
Cooking time: 15 minutes

Ingredients

2 pounds (900 g) pitted dried dates
4 tablespoons clarified butter
1 cup (115 g) dry fine breadcrumbs
4 tablespoons granulated sugar
3 tablespoons ground roasted pistachios

Method

Chop the dates, then set aside.

Melt the butter in a saucepan over a low heat. Add the dates to the saucepan, and continue stirring over a low heat until the dates have softened and take on a consistency of a thick paste. Stir in the breadcrumbs until they are completely absorbed into the dates. Stir in the sugar, then mix well. Remove from the heat. Spoon the date mixture into eight serving dishes, then sprinkle with the pistachios and serve.

BASISA (MADE OF CRUMBS)
CRUMBLED BREAD DESSERT

Easy

✍ *Historical version* ✍

A BASISA WHICH IS CALLED LUBABIYYA

It is made in several varieties, and the best that is made is that you take crumb bread, which has been baked the day before. Then take its crumb out and mix it with oil; that is, crumble it by hand and rub it with sesame oil until it becomes like poppy seeds. For every pound of it, let there be an ounce of sesame oil boiled on the fire. Rub it vigorously with it and sprinkle an ounce of finely pounded sugar on it, and the amount of a third of an ounce of poppy seeds with a bit of toasted sesame seed which you mix with it. Then pour two ounces of syrup thinned with rose water on it. If you want, put honey instead. Mix it with it and put it in a plate or tray and sprinkle half an ounce of sugar on its surface, and pistachio meats, and take it up.

Familiar Foods, p. 436. Translated by Charles Perry.

Basisa derives its name from the Arabic verb *bassa*, meaning 'to spread butter and honey on bread'. In North Africa, *Basisa*, a dish popular among the working classes and the poor, was made with raw barley flour mixed with water, oil and lemon juice. The thin, flat cake-forms were made with the pulp of dried dates, mixed and kneaded with wheat, a good packing food for caravans as they travelled. Another form included aniseed and fenugreek (Dozy 82).

Among the Bedouin of Egypt, dried *nabq* (the fruit of the lote tree) were ground, together with their stone, and preserved. The Bedouin referred to this as *Basisa*, and stored it in leather skins. According to Burckhardt, it was an excellent food for travelling in the desert because all that was needed to complete the dish was buttermilk. It was a nourishing, tasty and refreshing meal (732).

Ibn Khallikan notes that in Baghdad the name *'maris* is given to flat, thin breads soaked with clarified butter and dates while, in Egypt, the people there make the same kind but replace the dates with honey and call it *Basisa'* (I 278). Ibn al-'Adim's *Basisa* recipe is of the type from Basra.

The short-reigning Caliph Ibrahim ibn al-Mahdi's recipe for *Basisa* is two parts dough, each rolled out to the size of the frying pan to be used. One portion is to be placed in the pan, with the sides of the dough pressed up to line its sides, then honey and clarified butter is added, and then this is topped with the other portion of the dough. This pie of bread is baked in the slow heat of the *tannur*, or in a brick oven (*furn*), or at the community bakery. Once baked, it is cooled, crumbled and sprinkled with pounded sugar (al-Warraq 260).

During Hulagu's siege of the citadel city of Mayyafariqin in Syria in AD 1259, the basic ingredients of butter, bread and honey rose to such an exorbitant price that bread was being sold for 700 dirhams a *ratl*, 2 *uqiyas* of honey for 600 dirhams, and 2 *uqiyas* of butter for 600 dirhams, making a total cost of 1900 dirhams for the one dish of *Basisa* ordered by the city's Prince al-Kamil Muhammad (Ibn Shaddad III/2 508).

It is interesting to note that Edward William Lane, during his travels in nineteenth-century Egypt, described a dish of *Libabeh* as one of the dishes served to guests after the birth of a child. It is prepared by the women of the house, and the family is of middle or wealthy class. Lane describes the dish as being made of broken or crumbled bread, honey, clarified butter and a little rose water. The butter is first melted, then the bread and the honey are added (510).

ᵔᔐ Traditional recipe ᔐᵔ

Serves 6–8
Preparation time: 15 minutes
Cooking time: 5 minutes

Ingredients
2 cups (230 g) dry breadcrumbs
3 tablespoons light sesame oil
1 tablespoon confectioner's/icing sugar
1 teaspoon poppy seeds
1 tablespoon toasted sesame seeds
3 tablespoons honey mixed with 1 teaspoon rose water
2 teaspoons granulated sugar
1 tablespoon ground pistachios

Method

Mix the breadcrumbs with two tablespoons of the oil until the breadcrumbs are well coated.

In a frying pan, heat the remaining tablespoon of sesame oil over a medium-low heat. Add the breadcrumbs and stir constantly until they begin to turn light brown. Stir in the confectioner's/icing sugar, poppy seeds and sesame seeds, then stir-fry for a further minute. Remove from the heat, and stir in the honey–rose water mixture, mixing well.

Place the *Basisa* in a serving plate, then sprinkle with sugar and pistachios.

A SWEET OF DATES AND HONEY

Easy

∽ *Historical version* ∾

Take *shaddakh* dates. Clean them of their pits and fibres, and pound a *ratl* of them in a mortar. Then mix them with water in a *tinjir* on a gentle fire. Add an equal amount of skimmed honey. Stir it until it binds together.

Throw in a good amount of peeled almonds and walnuts. Put in some oil so it doesn't burn, and to bind firmly.

Pour it over a greased *salaya*. With it you make small round or square candies. Cut it with a knife in big or little pieces.

Anonymous, p. 198. Translated by Charles Perry.

Dates make any sweet delicious, quite apart from their nutritional value, because of the way they taste, especially mixed with nuts and spices. Dates have been the mainstay of the Arabs for millennia. For the Arab of the desert, the fresh date was like a fresh slice of meat, while the dried date was considered *al-qadid* ('dried meat') (al-'Askari *Diwan* I 282).

Since ancient times, the date palm has been a source of food for urbanites and Bedouin alike in the Arabian Peninsula, Mesopotamia and the Greater Syria region. Its branches and leaves served as protection against the elements. Ropes and mats can be woven from the branches of the tree, and the bark used as a building material. The date stone, once soaked, dried and powdered, is used as cattle feed. The fruit itself and the juice from the palm tree are used as ingredients in baking and cooking.

Although dates formed part of the usual Bedouin fare, they were not forgotten when city life replaced that of the desert. The medieval Arabic culinary texts attest to this, as dates earned their place on the dining tables of caliphs and kings. They were so valuable that they were considered as 'precious stones or rubies that set coal on fire' (al-Asbahani *Al-Aghani* 2555).

The date palm, mentioned more than any other fruit-bearing plant in the Qur'an, is a symbol often associated with Islam and Muslims. The date is referred to as *tuhfat Maryam* (precious gift to Mary, Mother of Jesus), as it was this fruit that nurtured her during childbirth (al-Tha'alibi *Thimar* I 106). Despite its popularity throughout the month of Ramadan, when fasting is broken at sunset with dates, this most important fruit of the Arabs retains a secular role. There are no religious boundaries when it comes to enjoying them.

The Arabs of pre-Islamic times cherished their dates and their honey, and the Prophet Muhammad is also known to have favoured both. The tradition has continued, dates forming the basis of many Arab dishes and being enjoyed on their own, while honey has been the luxurious sweetener of so many desserts.

This dish is a mixture of dates, honey, nuts and spices, and we chose to serve them in the form of patties.

∽ Traditional recipe ≈

Makes about 36 pieces
Preparation time: 15 minutes
Cooking time: 20 minutes
Chilling time: 15 minutes

Ingredients

1 pound (454 g) chopped dates
¹/₃ cup (80 ml) cold water
1 tablespoon light olive oil
4 tablespoons liquid honey
¾ cup (113 g) blanched whole almonds
¾ cup (90 g) coarsely chopped walnuts

Method

In a medium-sized saucepan, mix together the dates, water and oil, and cook over a medium heat, stirring constantly until the dates become a thick paste. Stir in the honey, and continue cooking for ten minutes, still stirring constantly. Remove from the heat.

Add the almonds and walnuts, mixing thoroughly.

Spread the mixture evenly into a buttered 8 by 8 by 2 inch (20 by 20 by 5 cm) dish, and pat down smooth.

Refrigerate for about 15 minutes. Cut into 1 inch (2.5 cm) squares. Form the squares into patties, and place on waxed paper.

Refrigerate or keep in a cool place until ready to serve.

DIMAGH AL-MUTAWAKKIL (THE BRAIN OF AL-MUTAWAKKIL)
A SWEET NUTTY PUDDING

Moderately difficult

✥ *Historical version* ✥

Take four *ratl*s of liquid honey and cook in a pot over a fire, then add to it spikenard, crushed mastic gum, half a dirham of each; then add cornstarch/cornflour, being half the amount of the honey, bit by bit to the honey while constantly stirring. Continue stirring until it thickens and coagulates. Then add to the mixture a quarter measure of peeled sesame and two *uqiya*s of peeled almonds and oil and cook until it becomes the consistency of *Faludhaj*. Remove from the fire and place in a glass or earthenware vessel until it is time to use it. And if desired, before use, sprinkle with powdered sugar and ground almonds or walnuts.

al-Tujibi, p. 253. Translated by Habeeb Salloum and Muna Salloum.

Chaotic times can bring on strange names for dishes, and so was the case of the *Dimagh al-Mutawakkil*.

The ninth-century Caliph al-Mutawakkil was noted for supporting magnificent building projects such as cities, canals and mosques, and for his many reforms. Upon his succession to the caliphate, he commissioned the construction of the Great Mosque of Samarra, and it was from Samarra that he ruled, keeping Baghdad as the capital. He was deeply involved in religious debates, antagonised the Muslim Shiites, Christians and Jews, and has come down in history as a man with a cruel and vindictive nature.

Though al-Mutawakkil's seat of power was Baghdad in the eastern Arab world, this dessert is found only in al-Tujibi's cookbook in the section 'Of the Eastern Types'. On the other hand, in many of the eastern Arabic source manuals there is another dish named after the Caliph: *Mutawakkiliya*, a thick stew of meat, taro, caraway, pepper, cinnamon, coriander, onions and garlic which does not appear in the Andalusian cookbooks.

Two of the original ingredients cited in the source cookbook, spikenard and mastic gum, are not easily available in grocery outlets. We therefore substituted them with rose or orange blossom water and mahaleb, respectively. As noted in the original recipe, confectioner's/icing sugar can be sprinkled on top of the *Dimagh* for decoration, but we found that the dessert is sweet enough on its own.

ᵯ Traditional recipe ᕚ

Serves 6
Preparation time: 10 minutes
Cooking time: 25 minutes

Ingredients

1 cup (340 g) liquid honey
1 teaspoon rose water or orange blossom water
¼ teaspoon mahaleb
½ cup (60 g) cornstarch/cornflour
¼ cup (30 g) slivered almonds
¼ cup (40 g) sesame seeds
2 tablespoons light sesame oil
2 tablespoons confectioner's/icing sugar (optional)
2 tablespoons ground almonds or walnuts (optional)

Method

Heat the honey over a medium-low heat for five minutes or until thinned. Stir in the rose water or orange blossom water and mahaleb, mixing well. Slowly and constantly stir in the cornstarch/cornflour until well blended. Stir in the almonds, sesame seeds and sesame oil. Continue stirring until the mixture thickens and pulls away from the side of the saucepan. Pour onto a flat serving dish, and allow to cool.

If desired, sprinkle with the confectioner's/icing sugar and ground almonds or walnuts.

Dimagh can be eaten directly from the serving dish with spoons.

FALUDHAJ (STRAINED AND GILDED)
HONEY-ALMOND PUDDING

Easy

ᵯ *Historical version* ᕚ

A FALUDHAJ OF THE CALIPHS

Take as much as you wish of a good quality white honey and pour it into a large pot [with a rounded bottom]. Light a gentle fire beneath it. Skim its froth and strain it using a *rawuq* [a type of utensil used for straining]. Return it to the pot after having put fresh, good quality sesame oil into it [the pot], the equivalent of half of the amount of the honey. Add starch in a bowl in the amount of one-fifth or one-sixth of that of the honey, with cold water, rose water and camphor, [the three equalling] the weight of the starch. Once the honey in the sesame oil boils, pour the starch over it and continue to stir until it thickens and its oil separates (rises). Continue to stir with the *istam* [iron spatula] in order that it does not stick. It is necessary to taste the starch in case it has soured. If you wish, take saffron in the amount you want and add it to the starch before using it. Take what you like of toasted and peeled almonds, or crush them and throw them on it. Once it thickens and its oil separates, remove from the fire. Spread it onto a sturdy serving platter that has been greased with pistachio or almond oil. Take some refined sugar and crush it with musk and sprinkle over it. Serve, God willing.

al-Warraq, p. 242. Translated by Muna Salloum and Leila Salloum Elias (See also the translation by Nawal Nasrallah: al-Warraq, *Annals of the Caliphs' Kitchen*, pp. 382–83.)

In AD 837, 'Abd Allah, brother of the rebel Babak, chief of the Khurrami sect, was captured by Abbasid forces. Before his execution, his last request was for his final meal on earth to include *Faludhaj* (al-Tabari XXXV 54–55).

One of the most referenced and revered sweets, not only in medieval Arabic culinary texts but in classical and medieval Arabic literature, *Faludhaj* is a pudding introduced to the Arabs by the Persians. The name is actually an Arabisation of the Pahlavi term *palude* and the Persian *paluda*, meaning 'strained' or 'refined'.

Credit for bringing it into the Arab sphere is given to one of the leading members of the Quraysh tribe in the seventh century, 'Abd Allah ibn Jud'an, who returned to Mecca after having eaten *Faludhaj* at the court of the Sassanid King (al-Isfahani *Kitab al-Aghani* VIII 331–32). It would eventually reach the tables of the caliphs and the elite, so that al-Warraq would include our source recipe as well as two recipes that the Caliph al-Amin prepared (244). Associated with luxury and prosperity at its best, *Faludhaj* spread throughout the Arab East as an elaborate must-serve for any festive event.

Faludhaj on any dining table was a mirror to the extravagance of a host. There is a story of one man who hosted a very large wedding party. The guests arrived in anticipation of a great dinner feast. However, the only item served for dinner was a huge dish of *Faludhaj*. The shock was not that this was the only dish served and the enormous size of it, but rather that it was such an expensive dish to prepare. Apparently the host had put up with such an expense to keep the women in his family from nagging him about his miserly ways (al-Jahiz *Al-Bukhala'* 155).

One name given to *Faludhaj* was *al-Siritrat*, or *al-Surrayt* (from the verbal root *srt*, 'to swallow', 'to gulp'), as it is swallowed or gulped with ease, according to Ibn 'Abd Rabbih (AD 860–940) (VI 291–92).

And gulp the *Faludhaj* they did. Take the case of the Umayyad singer Ahmad al-Nasbi, who died, some say, in his mad rush to satisfy his lust for the sweet.

Though fully aware that table etiquette dictated that piping hot foods should not be swallowed quickly (al-Warraq 332), 'including hot *Faludhaj*', his greedy appetite could not stand the wait (al-Asbahani 636). So tempting was the pudding that when the Caliph Yazid ibn al-Walid (r. AD 744) served a dish of *Faludhaj*, his guest, al-Ghadiri, began to eat it quickly. Yazid advised him to calm down, to take his time, warning him that eating too much could kill him. Al-Ghadari replied, 'My life is on the path to the cemetery and I have never seen a funeral in which the one who died, died from eating *Faludhaj*' (al-Raghib al-Asbahani II 620–21). Finally, nothing would stop one Bedouin from eating the sweet. When the Governor of Iraq, al-Hajjaj, saw that his Bedouin guest was ready to take a bite of the *Faludhaj*, the Governor announced that anyone who ate *Faludhaj* would have his head struck off. But the *Faludhaj* was too tempting. The Bedouin turned to the Governor and said, 'Well then, I trust you to care for my children!' (Ibn Hamdun IX 382).

The pudding is very sweet, and knowing now the story of al-Nasbi, it is recommended to let the pudding cool before eating it.

∽ Traditional recipe ↣

Serves 4
Preparation time: 15 minutes
Cooking time: 20 minutes
Chilling time: 2 hours

Ingredients

2 tablespoons cornstarch/cornflour dissolved in ½ cup (125 ml) cold water with pinch of saffron
½ cup (100 g) granulated sugar
½ cup (170 g) liquid honey
1 tablespoon almond or light sesame oil
4 tablespoons toasted ground almonds

Method

Place the cornstarch/cornflour mixture in a saucepan. Over a medium-low heat, bring to the boil, stirring constantly. Remove from the heat and stir in the sugar and honey. Return to low heat, and constantly stir until the mixture thickens, similar to a very thick pudding, after about 12–15 minutes. Stir in the oil and blend well, then remove from the heat. Stir in the almonds.

Place the *Faludhaj* on a serving plate, and refrigerate two hours before serving.

ঔ৯ Modern recipe ৯ঔ

ALMASIYA (LIKE A DIAMOND), SHIMMERING JELLIED PUDDING

Moderately difficult

If one was to choose a modern-day *Faludhaj*, the Syrian *Almasiya* might be the best choice. Although honey is not an ingredient, *qatr* replaces it.

Almasiya is Arabic for 'diamond-like', and the jelly-like pudding is light and refreshing – a great dessert after a heavy meal.

Our Grandmother Nabiha and our Grandmother Shams both made *Almasiya* on special occasions. They would surprise us by presenting it in various shapes and sizes, at times making it with milk instead of water. Both grandmothers took pride in the fact, as they constantly reminded us, that this pudding was as old as time, and that it was important to learn how to make it as part of our 'old country' tradition.

Serves 6–8
Preparation time: 15 minutes
Cooking time: 35 minutes
Chilling time: overnight

Ingredients
½ cup (60 g) cornstarch/cornflour
4½ cups (1.125 litres) cold water
¾ cup (150 g) granulated sugar
1½ tablespoons rose water
2 tablespoons ground pistachios
Half the basic *qatr* recipe using rose water (see 'Basic recipes' section)

Method

In a mixing bowl, mix together cornstarch/cornflour and one cup (250 ml) of the water. Stir well, diluting the cornstarch/cornflour, making sure there are no lumps.

In a deep saucepan, over a medium-high heat, bring the remaining water to the boil. Stir in the cornstarch/cornflour mixture, stirring constantly until the mixture comes to the boil, then lower the heat to medium-low, constantly stirring and allowing to simmer for 30 minutes, until it thickens. Stir in the sugar until dissolved, then stir in the rose water. Remove from heat.

Prepare the mould into which the *Almasiya* will be placed by moistening it slightly with water. Sprinkle one tablespoon of the pistachios around the inside of the mould, then pour the hot *Almasiya* into the mould. Refrigerate overnight.

When ready to serve the *Almasiya*, invert the mould onto a serving platter, and sprinkle with the remaining pistachios. Slice the *Almasiya* into individual serving dishes, then pour the *qatr* over each piece according to taste.

ᏺ Alternative modern recipe ᏽ

*BALOUZA ('CHOICE' PUDDING), CREAMY MILK
PUDDING TOPPED WITH APRICOT PASTE*

Moderately difficult

Balouza takes its name from the Persian term *paluda,* just as *Faludhaj* does, and is another version of that long-established dish (Mardam-Bey 152 n. 2). It is prepared in almost the same way as *Almasiya* but creamier due to its milk base. However, as a milk-based pudding, we are more inclined to consider it as an offspring of the medieval *Muhallabiya* (see page 208).

Tunisians claim this pudding as a traditional national sweet, Algerians likewise, but refer to it as *Palouza,* although Berthoud, travelling through the country in the mid-nineteenth century, maintained that it was a type of rice pudding (II 141). The Syrian *Balouza* is milk based and topped with a delicious orange sauce.

Serves 6
Preparation time: 25 minutes
Cooking time: 45 minutes
Chilling time: 2 hours

Ingredients

6 tablespoons (50 g) cornstarch/cornflour
2 cups (480 ml) whole milk
½ cup (100 g) plus 2 tablespoons granulated sugar
½ teaspoon rose water
1 tablespoon orange blossom water
2 tablespoons toasted ground almonds
2 tablespoons ground pistachios
½ cup (125 ml) water
4 tablespoons finely chopped dried apricots
1 tablespoon unsalted butter
2 tablespoons fresh orange juice or 2 tablespoons water mixed with small pinch of saffron
Whipped cream (optional)
Pistachios, coarsely ground (optional)

Method

Mix four tablespoons of the cornstarch/cornflour with one cup (240 g) of the milk in a saucepan. Stir in the remaining milk, half a cup (100 g) of the sugar, the rose water and orange blossom water, making sure all the ingredients are dissolved and blended well.

Over a medium heat, cook the mixture, constantly stirring until it thickens, similar to a smooth pudding. Remove from the heat and stir in the almonds and the pistachios. Evenly spoon the mixture into six serving cups, and chill in the refrigerator for an hour.

In a saucepan, add quarter of a cup (65 ml) of the water, the apricots and the butter. Cook over a medium-low heat, stirring constantly until the apricots are dissolved, making sure there are no lumps. Remove from the heat, and stir in the remaining two tablespoons of sugar and the orange juice or water mixed with saffron.

Mix together the remaining water and the remaining two tablespoons of cornstarch/cornflour, then stir into the apricot paste. Return the paste to a medium-low heat, and stir constantly until the mixture thickens, after about ten minutes. Remove from the heat.

Evenly spoon the apricot paste over the chilled pudding, then return to the refrigerator for another hour.

Once the *Balouza* is chilled, serve immediately, or top with whipped cream sprinkled with ground pistachios.

FALUDHAJ (MELON)
PUDDING MADE WITH MELON

Moderately difficult

∿ *Historical version* ∾

MELON FALUDHAJ

Take five very sweet melons and cut them into pieces. Then throw away the rind and whatever else is not needed. Then mash by hand and squeeze through a wide-sieve of [animal] hair into a wide bowl. This is done with the melon until its pulp goes through it and its waste is removed. Then take half a *ratl* of starch and throw half a dirham of crushed saffron over it. Mix them with two *uqiya*s of water. Take two *ratl*s of honey in a big pot [with a rounded bottom] and strain into it the starch [mixture]. Pour the melon over it. Light a gentle fire beneath it until it thickens. Then moisten it with fat. When it is cooked and its fat has separated, remove it from the fire and put it in a serving vessel. If you like it to be sweeter, sweeten the melon with a little sugar. Then serve, God willing.

al-Warraq, p. 245. Translated by Muna Salloum and Leila Salloum Elias. (See also the translation by Nawal Nasrallah: al-Warraq, *Annals of the Caliphs' Kitchen,* **p. 387.)**

For this recipe we chose watermelon over cantaloupe because of its higher water content, making it juicier and easier to puree, therefore more suitable for preparing a pudding.

If it appears that there is an ambiguity with the translation of the term *bittikh*, this is because the Arabic term can refer to either, in its generic form, melon or watermelon. Added to this are the varieties of both, some designated by colour such as *bittikh akhdar* (literally 'green melon') meaning watermelon; others by place of origin such as *bittikh Khurasani*, a type of melon from Khorasan (Ibn al-Wardi 142), others by simple description, such as the Hijazi *habhab* ('too-many-seeds watermelon') (Nasrallah *Annals* 625). There were numerous varieties, too many to be counted, as noted by the ninth/tenth century figure Ibn Wahshiya (Watson 59).

Khawarizm's melons were so much considered the best and most delicious that the Caliph al-Ma'mun and the Caliph al-Wathiq would have them imported in leaden containers filled with snow at a price of 700 dirhams for each (al-Nuwayri I 368). In the twelfth century, the Andalusian traveller Ibn Jubayr was impressed with the extraordinary melons of Mecca because of their wonderful perfumed aroma and exquisite taste, as if one was eating melted sugar (97–98). It is little wonder, then, that sweets would be created to complement the fruit.

If *Faludhaj* came to represent prosperity and luxury, being among the most magnificent and exquisite of sweet dishes, this particular *Faludhaj* was proof positive.

∽ Traditional recipe ∾

Serves 6–8
Preparation time: 30 minutes
Cooking time: 45 minutes

Ingredients

1 medium seedless watermelon
1 cup (120 g) cornstarch/cornflour mixed with ⅛ teaspoon saffron
3 tablespoons warm water
4 cups (1.4 kg) liquid honey
½ cup (115 g) unsalted butter
4 tablespoons granulated sugar (optional)

Method

Peel the watermelon, then chop and place enough pieces in a blender to make four cups (1 litre) of pureed watermelon, then set aside.

In a large saucepan, stir together the starch–saffron mixture and the water until thoroughly dissolved. Stir in the honey, and mix well. Stir in the watermelon, then place on a medium-low heat and cook, stirring often until the *Faludhaj* thickens, after about 40 minutes. Add the butter and continue to stir until the butter melts completely. Remove from the heat and place in a serving bowl.

If desired sprinkle with the sugar and serve.

⤷ Modern recipe ⤶

GELO DI MELONE, JELLIED WATERMELON PUDDING FROM SICILY

Moderately difficult

The Sicilians are noted for a sweet jellied pudding inherited from the Arabs. The medieval *Faludhaj* made with melon was more than likely the inspiration for *Gelo di Melone*. Commonly served in the summer, this pudding oozes with the indelible Arab influences on Sicilian cuisine, with its ingredients of watermelon, pistachios, candied fruit, cinnamon and rose water.

Even though the watermelon originated in subtropical Africa as a bitter fruit, it is better known in its sweet variety, which made its journey westward from India. It moved first to Afghanistan, then Iran, then Mesopotamia, travelling west through the Greater Syria region across to North Africa, Sicily and the Iberian Peninsula. It carried the name 'Indian melon' in Iraq and Syria, 'Palestinian melon' in Egypt and 'Algiers melon' in Spain, denoting in each case the country which had introduced it (Watson 59).

The watermelon reached the west during the ninth century. However, it was some time during the thirteenth and fourteenth centuries that it took hold as a popular fruit, so that Arab fruit and vegetable souks were known as *dar al-battikh* (The House of Watermelons). Up to the fourteenth century, the melon called *bittikh* in Arabic became *batèque* and later *pastèque* in French, in Spanish, *albudeca* and in Portuguese, *albudieca* and *pateca*.

Serves 6
Preparation time: 15 minutes
Cooking time: 20 minutes
Chilling time: overnight

Ingredients

1½ pounds (680 g) seedless watermelon pulp, cut into small pieces
5 tablespoons (40 g) cornstarch/cornflour
1 cup (200 g) granulated sugar
1 teaspoon rose water
⅛ teaspoon cinnamon
½ cup (112 g) candied fruit, finely chopped
2 tablespoons chopped pistachios

Method

In a blender, place the watermelon pieces and liquefy, making a juice.

In a saucepan, add the cornstarch/cornflour, then stir in ¾ cup (185 ml) of the watermelon juice to dilute the cornstarch/cornflour, making sure there are no lumps.

Stir in the remaining watermelon juice and the sugar, and cook over a low heat, stirring constantly until the sugar is dissolved. Stir in the rose water and cinnamon. Raise the heat to medium, and stir constantly until the mixture thickens and turns glossy.

Remove the saucepan from the heat and allow the contents to cool for five minutes, stirring occasionally. Stir in the candied fruits. Pour the mixture into six pudding cups, cover with plastic wrap/cling film, then refrigerate overnight. When ready to serve, decorate with the pistachios.

MUHALLABIYA (THAT OF AL-MUHALLAB)
A RICH MILK PUDDING

Easy

✒ *Historical version* ✒

Take one *ratl* of walnuts and almonds and finely pound them. Then take 30 eggs and break them open over a wide bowl and throw over them two *ratls* of pounded refined sugar. Then throw in after this the pounded walnuts and almonds, and beat them together until they are well blended. Then take a clean pot and pour into it 10 *ratls* of milk that is still warm from being freshly milked. Then ignite a fire beneath it and boil it until it boils down to 5 *ratls*. Then pour over it the eggs and the almonds. Stir quickly and continuously until it thickens. When it thickens, if you would like to pour in honey, then do not stop stirring it until it thickens, and remove it from the fire.

al-Warraq, p. 262. Translated by Muna Salloum and Leila Salloum Elias. (See also the translation by Nawal Nasrallah: al-Warraq, *Annals of the Caliphs' Kitchen*, p. 407.)

It is said that this dish was named after al-Muhallab ibn Abi Sufra, an Umayyad General and Governor who served under the first Umayyad Caliph, Mu'awiya ibn Abi Sufyan (r. 661–80). It was so named because he enjoyed it (al-Ghazali 31). However, according to *Anonymous*, its origin goes back to the same al-Muhallab, but only after it had been prepared by a Persian cook seeking the Governor's favour. He enjoyed it so much that the cook named his creation after al-Muhallab. Al-Ghazuli, on the other hand, states that its origins lie with the Banu al-Muhallab tribe, which first adopted it (367).

Muhallabiya is in the tradition of dishes named after their creators or supporters, such as *Haruniya* (a sumac meat stew), named after or for the Caliph Harun al-Rashid, *al-Ma'muniya* (a rice or semolina pudding, see p. 225, and also a meat dish), after the Caliph al-Ma'mun, and *al-Mutawakkiliya* (a spicy meat stew), for the Caliph al-Mutawakkil.

Muhallabiya was essentially a sweet pudding made with chicken, rice, milk and sugar, or prepared without the meat. There is also another *Muhallabiya* made with dry noodles (*itriya*) instead of rice. Without doubt, the dish, in its various forms, was a favourite in the ruling court, being associated by name in two instances with the Caliphs al-Ma'mun and al-Wathiq (al-Warraq 262–63).

If it is made with milk, it can be classified as a pudding, if made with eggs it is more of a custard. In both cases, it has a rich flavour and smooth texture.

⋐ Traditional recipe ⋑

Serves 6–8
Preparation time: 15 minutes
Standing time: 15 minutes
Cooking time: 35 minutes
Chilling time: 2 hours

Ingredients

½ cup (50 g) ground walnuts
½ cup (50 g) ground almonds
6 eggs, beaten
1 cup (200 g) granulated sugar
5 cups (1.2 litres) whole milk
4 tablespoons liquid honey (optional)

Method

Place the walnuts, almonds, eggs and sugar in a food processor, and process into a smooth paste.

In a medium-sized saucepan, pour in the milk, then bring to the boil over a medium heat, stirring constantly. Lower the heat to medium-low, bringing the milk to a soft boil, continuing the process uncovered for about 30 minutes or until the milk boils down to approximately half. Stir in the food processor contents, stirring quickly and continuously until the *Muhallabiya* thickens. If a sweeter dish is desired, stir in the honey. Remove from the heat.

Spoon the *Muhallabiya* into serving cups, and allow to sit at room temperature for 15 minutes. Cover each cup with plastic wrap/cling film, and refrigerate for two hours, then serve.

✧ Modern recipe ☙

MIHALLABIYA, CORNSTARCH/CORNFLOUR MILK PUDDING

Easy

A popular dessert in the Middle East and in North Africa, *Mihallabiya* (as it is pronounced in the colloquial) is one of those desserts that has really not changed since its medieval birth. Simple to prepare, and with its creamy texture and silky taste, it is no wonder that it retains its status as one of the more elegant offerings on the dessert table.

Serves 8
Preparation time: 15 minutes
Standing time: 15 minutes
Cooking time: 35 minutes
Chilling time: 2 hours

Ingredients
½ cup (60 g) cornstarch/cornflour
5 cups (1.2 litres) whole milk
6 tablespoons raisins
½ cup (100 g) granulated sugar
1 teaspoon vanilla extract/essence
¼ teaspoon ground cardamom
1 teaspoon cinnamon
2 tablespoons finely chopped pistachios

Method

In a bowl, dissolve the cornstarch/cornflour in one cup (240 ml) of the milk, then set aside.

Place the remaining milk, the raisins and sugar in a saucepan; then bring to the boil over a medium heat, stirring until the sugar dissolves. Reduce the heat to low, then add the dissolved cornstarch/cornflour and, stirring constantly with a wooden spoon, simmer for about 15 minutes or until the mixture is thick enough to coat the spoon heavily. Stir in the vanilla, cardamom and half a teaspoon of the cinnamon. Remove from the heat.

Pour the mixture into small individual dessert bowls. Sprinkle with the remaining cinnamon, and then scatter the pistachios decoratively on top. Allow to sit at room temperature for 15 minutes. Cover each bowl or goblet with plastic wrap/cling film, then refrigerate for at least two hours before serving.

HAYS (A MIXTURE OF DATES, CURD AND BUTTER)
DATE BALLS

Easy

✎ *Historical version* ✎

Take good-quality dry bread or *Ka'k* [dried hard loaves] and pound well. There should be a *ratl* of this and three quarters of a *ratl* of *azadh* [a type of high-quality dates] or *al-maktum* dates [another top-quality variety] that should have their pits removed, and three *uqiyas* of pounded almond and pistachio meats. Knead all of them together very well by hand. Then refine two *uqiyas* of sesame oil and pour this over it. Continue to rub by hand until it is mixed in. Make into kebabs, and sprinkle with finely pounded sugar. If one wants, in place of the sesame oil, put clarified butter. This is beneficial to those who are travelling.

al-Baghdadi, pp. 81–82. Translated by Muna Salloum and Leila Salloum Elias. (See also the translation by Charles Perry, *A Baghdad Cookery Book*, p. 105.)

Hays was a popular sweet among the Bedouin. In its earliest form, it was made with dates, dried curd and clarified butter kneaded or rubbed vigorously, and pressed by hand to force the date stones out.

As the Arab empire expanded, foreign contacts were made, trade and a thriving economy brought new ingredients and new ideas into the traditional realm. *Hays* is an example of the effects of these changes. A simple dessert in its origins, these date morsels evolved into a luxury for the tables of the medieval Arab elite.

Rich additions, such as pistachios and almonds, along with sugar became the new basic ingredients. So rooted was *Hays* to the Arabs and their culture, we find a snippet of advice on how to eat it. *Hays* should be eaten with one hand, this rule applying equally to the pudding style and the balls variant (al-Jahiz *Kitab al-Hayawan* VI 424).

✎ Traditional recipe ✎

Makes 35 pieces
Preparation time: 30 minutes

Ingredients
¾ pound (340 g) fresh, soft pitted dates, chopped
2 cups (230 g) finely ground dry breadcrumbs
1 cup (95 g) ground almonds
1 cup (117 g) chopped pistachios
9 tablespoons (135 ml) light sesame oil
Confectioner's/icing sugar or caster sugar

Method

Place the dates, breadcrumbs, almonds and pistachios in a food processor, and process for two minutes. Pour the sesame oil evenly over the mixture, and process for three to four minutes or until the mixture binds well. Test the mixture by pressing a small amount in the palm of the hand to make sure it sticks together. If it does not, process the mixture further until it begins to bind.

Form the mixture into balls about the size of a walnut.

Roll the balls into the confectioner's/icing sugar or caster sugar, and place on a serving plate.

✍ Modern recipe ↩

BOLAS DE FIGO E AMÊNDOAS, FIG AND ALMOND BALLS

Easy

Old Portuguese cookbooks, such as the seventeenth-century *Arte de Cozinha* by Domingos Rodrigues, contain many Moorish recipes such as 'Moorish lamb', 'Moorish sausage', 'Moorish hen', 'Moorish fish', 'Moorish broth'. The Arab fondness for confections also passed to the Portuguese. Candied fruits and pastries using almonds, egg yolks, honey–almond paste, figs, dates and rose water are of pure Moorish origin, and are found predominantly in the Algarve region.

Hays is most likely the antecedent of Portugal's *Bolas de Figo e Almêndoas*. Instead of dates, figs are used, and the sesame-seed oil is replaced by honey. The following recipe is by Habeeb, who developed it after visiting Portugal and experiencing this crunchy and rich natural sweet.

Makes about 36 pieces
Preparation time: 45 minutes

Ingredients

1 cup (150 g) blanched whole almonds, toasted and pulverised
½ pound (227 g) dried figs, with stock ends removed
Orange peel of half an orange, finely chopped
4 tablespoons creamed honey
1 teaspoon rose water
1 teaspoon cinnamon
¼ cup (30 g) confectioner's/icing sugar

Method

In a food processor, place the almonds, figs and orange peel, then process until the ingredients are finely ground. Add the honey, rose water and cinnamon, then process until a dough is formed. Form into 36 balls, then set aside.

Place the confectioner's/icing sugar on a platter, then roll the balls in the confectioner's/icing sugar. Place on a serving tray, then sprinkle with any leftover confectioner's/icing sugar, and serve.

ISNAN AL-'AJUZ (TEETH OF THE OLD PERSON)
HONEY–NUT CRUNCHY DESSERT

Moderately difficult

✎ Modern recipe ✎

Many times, oral tradition offers tidbits of tradition. Because the Arabic medieval culinary texts that have survived are limited, it is fair to include recipes that our great-grandmothers, grandmothers and mothers have inherited as cultural heirlooms.

Though many recipes recorded in medieval cookbooks continue to this day, there are still many that have been orally passed down generation after generation.

One such example is this recipe which hails from Damascus, the oldest continuously inhabited city in the world. Supposedly resembling an aged person's teeth, the name does not do it justice. Crunchy, delicious and light, it is no wonder this sweet has passed the test of time.

Samira, one of our close friends from Damascus, offered this recipe, explaining that it is as old as her family's history. She remembers her grandmother telling the story of how her own mother gave her the recipe as part of her bridal trousseau. This was her family tradition.

As to the origin of this dish, there is a thirteenth-century sweet named *Barad* ('hail') (al-Baghdadi 77) that may be the origin of *Isnan*. *Barad* involves the preparation of a batter which is dripped through a sieve into hot oil, forming tiny balls of 'hail' that are then mixed with a thick honey syrup that binds the balls together. *Isnan* follows the concept of preparing tiny balls, but these are shaped by hand, then deep-fried, then mixed with almonds and hazelnuts, and finally hot honey is poured in and everything is mixed well.

We found the name intriguing, and once this sweet is placed on a serving platter, one cannot help but envision *Isnan al-'Ajuz*. As the saying goes, 'don't judge a book by its cover' – this candied treat must be judged by its content and taste, not by its appearance and name.

Serves 12–14
Preparation time: 1 hour 10 minutes
Cooking time: 25 minutes

Ingredients

5 eggs
1 teaspoon vanilla extract/essence
1 teaspoon baking powder
3 ¼ cups (780 g) plain flour
Vegetable oil for deep-frying
1½ cups (162 g) slivered almonds, toasted
1½ cups (225 g) whole hazelnuts, toasted
1 cup (340 g) liquid honey
1 cup (200 g) granulated sugar

Method

In a mixing bowl, beat the eggs, then stir in the vanilla and the baking powder until smooth. Stir in the flour. Knead into a sticky dough, adding more flour if necessary. Pinch off a piece of dough the size of a walnut, and roll on a flat surface into a thin rope, approximately ½ inch (1.25 cm) in diameter, then cut into pea-sized pieces. Cover the pieces with a tea towel as you continue the process, until all the dough has been formed into balls.

Heat the oil over a medium heat. Deep-fry the pieces until light golden brown. Remove with a slotted spoon, and drain on paper towels, then place in a large mixing bowl. Add the almonds and the hazelnuts, and mix well.

In a medium-sized saucepan, add the honey and stir in the sugar until all the sugar is absorbed by the honey. Cook over a medium heat, stirring constantly, until the honey begins to boil. Continue cooking until the honey froths and rises about three-quarters of the way up the side of the saucepan. Remove from the heat, and stir to bring down the froth. Immediately pour the honey, while hot, into the fried dough–nut mixture, and stir to coat all the pieces. Pour the mixture into a buttered large serving platter, and pat down evenly.

Allow to cool, then cut into serving pieces. Alternatively, break off into bite-sized pieces.

JAWADHIB AL-MAWZ (VARIETY OF BANANA PUDDING)
FRIED BATTER-COATED BANANAS

Moderately difficult

ᔐ *Historical version* ᔐ

Sugar complements it. Take good fresh bananas in which there is some firmness and which are not fully ripe. Peel and cut up and cover [*yukhammar*] with batter of semolina flour which has been kneaded in the form [*hai'a*] of *khubz al-qata'if* [the consistency of batter]. Then take them out. Put them down for a moment [*lahza*] on something woven [*shai' mushabbak*], then boil sesame oil in a *tinjir* and fry them in it. Take them out and throw them in syrup and take them [*yushal*] from it and throw in sifted pounded sugar crystals. Then load in the *judhab* tray [*judhabdana*] with thin bread [*ruqaq*] over and under [the bananas], and hang a fat chicken over it [in the tandoor].

Ibn Jazlah. Translated by Charles Perry.

Bananas are believed to be one of the earliest cultivated fruits. Their history is closely woven with legends and mythology. In the medieval world, many believed that the serpent that tempted Eve hid in a bunch of bananas, hence the label 'fruit of Paradise'. In Hindu lore, bananas were the favoured food of the gurus, giving us its scientific name *Musa sapietum* ('fruit of the wise men').

By the ninth century, bananas were a well-known commodity in the eastern Arab world and Egypt (Watson 51, 54). From Egypt bananas were taken across to North Africa and into al-Andalus, where they were cultivated especially along the coastal plains of the peninsula. And it was from the east coast of Africa that the Arabs took banana cultivation right across Africa to the Atlantic coast (54).

The name by which they are known in English is probably derived from the Arabic *banan* ('fingers'), the name that the early Arab traders gave to the smaller sized variety of bananas that they found in Africa and Asia. In later centuries, the Portuguese carried them to the Canary Islands, from where the Spaniards introduced them into the New World.

So well loved was the fruit among the Arabs, that it was announced that 'there is nothing in the world that resembles what is in paradise, except for the banana' (al-Suyuti II 433).

In the early ninth century, the Caliph al-Ma'mun's physician Mikha'il ibn Masawayh's prescriptions did not include bananas, just as the medical books of earlier physicians had not mentioned them (Ibn Abi Usayba'a 256). By the tenth century, however, medical advice encouraged people who complained of a dry stomach to eat soft fruits such as bananas, dates and figs, followed by eating something slightly sour (al-Warraq 66). A hundred years later, Ibn Jazlah explains that his *Jawadhib* recipe contains the humoral qualities of hot and moist, increases semen, stimulates the flow of urine, eases digestion, and benefits roughness in the chest.

The fruit was popular, and its good taste led to its increasing use in cooking for the simple reason that bananas were easy to peel, rich in colour and a natural delicacy. In one story, we learn of the Judge Ibn Fariqa who one day went to visit the Emir 'Izz al-Dawla al-Buwayhi. As he entered, the Judge found the Emir seated with a large platter of bananas before him. Seeking the Emir's blessings for prosperity and success, the Judge assumed that he would be offered the bananas. However, the Emir responded, 'You can eat these only if you describe them.' And thus the Judge began, 'That which I describe is the silken sheath. In it are golden bars, as if stuffed with butter and honey, or grainy pudding [*Khabis*]; the most delicious of fruit as if being the pith of the tree; easy to peel; can gently be broken open; a sweet food in taste; it glides down the throat.' He then reached out his hand, took a banana and ate it (al-Suyuti II 433).

There are various types of *Jawadhib* (sing. *Judhaba*) included in medieval Arabic cookbooks. Generally, they can be described as sweet puddings made up of various ingredients and placed under meat that is being roasted in a *tannur*, so that the meat's drippings fall onto the pudding. However, this source recipe differs from the standard *Judhaba* in that pieces of bananas are dipped into a batter, then fried.

∽ Traditional recipe ≥

Makes 36 pieces
Preparation time: 30 minutes
Standing time: 1 hour 15 minutes
Cooking time: 35 minutes

Ingredients
Half the basic *qatr* recipe using rose water (see 'Basic recipes' section)
1 tablespoon granulated sugar
¼ cup (65 ml) warm water
¼ ounce (8 g) active dry yeast
¼ cup (30 g) plain flour
¼ cup (40 g) extra-fine semolina
1 egg, beaten
¼ cup (50 g) shortening
1 cup (250 ml) cold water
6 firm bananas
Light sesame oil for deep-frying
Confectioner's/icing sugar

Method

Dissolve the sugar in the quarter cup (65 ml) of warm water, then stir in the yeast. Cover and let sit for ten minutes, or until it rises and is frothy.

In a large mixing bowl, stir together the flour and semolina. Form a well, then add the egg, the shortening and the cold water. Beat well until smooth. Cover and let the batter sit for an hour.

Peel the bananas and cut each into three equal pieces, then slice in half lengthways. Put all the slices in the batter, being sure to cover them well.

In a large saucepan, heat the sesame oil over a medium heat. When ready to deep-fry the bananas, remove them from the batter, shaking off any excess batter.

Fry the bananas until a deep golden colour, turning over once. Remove with tongs, and dip immediately into the *qatr*, being sure to coat the entire banana slice. Place on a serving dish in one layer.

Allow to cool, then sprinkle with confectioner's/icing sugar.

ANOTHER VERSION OF JAWADHIB AL-MAWZ: JUDHABA AL-MAWZ LI-IBN AL-MAHDI (MADE FOR OR BY THE CALIPH IBRAHIM IBN AL-MAHDI)
A LAYERED BANANA CASSEROLE

Moderately difficult

❧ *Historical version* ❧

IBN AL-MAHDI'S JUDHABA OF BANANAS

Take bananas, peel them and put aside. Then take a pot [a special pan with sides used for making *judhaba*] and spread out a thin round of bread in it and arrange the bananas over it. Then sprinkle pure sugar over it. Then take another thin round of bread and put it over it. Then put again more bananas and sugar over it until it is full. Drench it in rose water and above it hang an excellent type of chicken, God willing.

al-Warraq, p. 236. Translated by Muna Salloum and Leila Salloum Elias. (See also the translation by Nawal Nasrallah: al-Warraq, *Annals of the Caliphs' Kitchen*, p. 375.)

This source recipe is included as a reminder that some caliphs and princes, such as Ibrahim ibn al-Mahdi, although active with their political duties, found the time to set aside business and create their own dishes. Ibrahim, half-brother of Harun al-Rashid, was also the author of the cookbook *Cooked Food*, and ruled for two years after the death of the Caliph al-Amin. There is a strong chance that Ibrahim was motivated to cook through the influence of his servant-girl Bid'a, who had the reputation of being an expert cook (al-Warraq 133).

Whether it was Ibrahim or Bid'a who created the following *Judhaba*, credit is due to al-Warraq for preserving it.

We have used butter to take the place of the chicken dripping. Even though the rose water alone gave a good flavour, we preferred *qatr* made with rose water to give the sweet a richer taste.

The recipe calls for a thin bread. We chose the very thin flat Arab bread *marquq*, which can be folded and rolled. It can be purchased in most Middle Eastern groceries or bakeries.

⋐ Traditional recipe ⋑

Serves 10–12
Preparation time: 25 minutes
Cooking time: 20 minutes

Ingredients

Basic *qatr* recipe using rose water (see 'Basic recipes' section)
12 large ripe but firm bananas, peeled
6 loaves thin, flat Arab bread (*marquq*)
1½ cups (340 g) unsalted butter, melted
¾ cup (150 g) granulated sugar

Method

Cut the bananas in half, then slice lengthwise. Divide the slices into five equal portions, and set aside.

Preheat the oven to 375°F (190°C).

Butter a large round baking pan with sides, and spread one sheet of the bread evenly over the bottom. Brush with butter. Place one portion of the bananas evenly over the top of the bread, and sprinkle with two tablespoons of the sugar. Continue the same process four more times, buttering each sheet of bread, layering each sheet with one portion of the remaining bananas, sprinkling each layer of bananas with two tablespoons of sugar. Cover with the remaining sheet of bread, and sprinkle the remaining two tablespoons of sugar evenly over the top. Carefully slice into 12 wedges, and pour the remaining butter evenly over the top.

Bake for 20 minutes, or until the bread begins to brown.

Remove from the oven, and pour the *qatr* evenly over the top.

Serve immediately.

JUDHAB AL-TAMR (DATE PUDDING)
A THICK DATE PUDDING

Easy

⋐ *Historical version* ⋑

Take four *ratl*s of dried dates (and ten *ratl*s of water) and put them in a pot. [Keep] the fire lit beneath it until they are cooked. Then macerate by hand vigorously and strain through a sieve. Then return it to the pot and put over it half a *ratl* of sugar, quarter of a *ratl* of honey, half a dirham of saffron, one *ratl* of crumbled bread pith, one *ratl* of sesame oil and quarter of a *ratl* of shelled walnuts. Stir until almost cooked. Fill between two thin loaves of bread. When decorated with almonds, it is *'Asida al-Tamr*. It can be made without sugar and honey.

al-Baghdadi, pp. 71–72. Translated by Muna Salloum and Leila Salloum Elias. (See also the translation by Charles Perry, *A Baghdad Cookery Book*, p. 94.)

Generally, the dish called *Judhab* or *Judhaba* was prepared with morsels of bread soaked in water, then sweetened with honey or sugar or a combination of both. To this was added fruit such as dates, mulberries, melons or apricots, along with some spices. The mixture was then placed in a *Judhabadan*, a specific cooking tray used for *Judhab*. In some cases ground almonds flavoured with rose water would be mixed with the bread along with butter.

There is also an interesting recipe for a more complicated *Judhab* that involves a three-way process of baking a certain type of bread with a specific type of flour, then preparing a meat mixture to which milk, honey and spices are added. It is then cooked, the meat stuffed into the bread, over which milk, butter and eggs are poured (al-Warraq 237). The tray would then be put into the bottom centre part of the *tannur* (domed clay oven), over which a plump chicken or the fatty side of ribs would be hung for a slow-cooking process, allowing the fat from the meat to drip onto the *Judhab*. Once the meat is cooked, it would be sliced and served with the tray contents.

Al-Warraq lists 18 varieties of the dish, *Kanz* only a few, and al-Baghdadi a total of eight. What might today be considered a doctor's nightmare, *Judhab*'s popularity is evident in the number of recipes in the culinary sources. Simply put, people liked it.

Such is the case with Yahya ibn Aktham. He was passionate about *Judhab*. At his house one day, one of his visitors unexpectedly talked about its drawbacks. Yahya, taken aback, concluded that the visitor must be weak in perception and deficient in common sense. Hearing what Yahya said, the guest grew nervous, and remained on guard, worried about the day he would next see him.

And he did. At this encounter, Yahya asked him, 'What do you say about *Judhab*?' Either out of fear, or simply through a change of attitude, the man expounded on its virtues, describing it as the most honourable and perfect of food, easy to swallow, delicious and nourishing, and causing no harm to the stomach. 'Right!' Yahya responded, 'This is how I want you to be!' (Abu Hayyan al-Tawhidi 3/76).

In contrast to the about-turn made by Yahya's guest, Abu al-Hasan ibn al-'Allaf took no convincing to consume 80 types of *Judhab* at one sitting, licking the trays clean afterwards (al-Abi II 249–50).

The famous party-crashers, the *tufaylis*, who used to invite themselves under cover as guests to large private parties and feasts, nicknamed certain dishes in their coded language. *Judhab* was one of these, referred to as *Umm al-Husan*, 'mother of beauty' (al-Abi II 256).

(Tip: we discovered that another good way to enjoy *Judhab al-Tamr* is to spread it generously on split loaves of Arab bread.)

❧ Traditional recipe ❧

Makes one serving platter of *Judhab*
Preparation time: 15 minutes
Cooking time: 15 minutes

Ingredients

2 cups (350 g) chopped pitted dates
½ cup (125 ml) water
¼ cup (50 g) granulated sugar
1 tablespoon liquid honey
1 tablespoon water mixed with pinch of crushed saffron
¼ cup (30 g) dry breadcrumbs
¼ cup (60 ml) light sesame oil
1 tablespoon chopped walnuts
2 loaves large Arab bread, split (optional)

Method

Place the dates and water in a medium-sized saucepan, and cook over a medium-low heat, stirring occasionally, until the dates are soft, similar to a thick paste, about ten minutes. Remove from the heat.

Stir in the remaining ingredients except for the Arab bread, and cook over a medium heat for five minutes. Remove from the heat and spread on a serving platter, or if using the bread, spread over the four pieces.

JURAYDAT (SMALL LOCUSTS)
HONEY-SPICED CANDY BALLS

Moderately difficult

❧ *Historical version* ❧

Take bread from white semolina, take it outside and put it in the sun until it dries. Grind it and sieve it, soak it in oil and leave it a day and a night. Throw on thickened honey, after cleaning it, and knead it with pepper and enough spices. Make it into round hazelnuts [small balls], God willing.

Anonymous, p. 199. Translated by Charles Perry.

These sweet-spiced cookies are formed in the shape of little balls. Perry attributes the name, 'small locusts', to the appearance of the sweet: little lumps of breadcrumbs mixed with honey and spices. There is no other explanation for the name, since

Juraydat, based upon the sources used for this study, only appears in the one Andalusian cooking manual.

Juraydat are best described as candied cookies, crispy and sweet. The original recipe calls for pepper as an ingredient in addition to 'enough spices'. What we have added, instead, is a mixture of typical North African spices commonly used in the preparation of sweets in Morocco and Tunisia.

❦ Traditional recipe ❧

Makes about 40 small or 30 medium pieces
Preparation time: 1 hour
Standing time: 1 hour
Cooking time: 5 minutes

Ingredients
2 cups (230 g) finely ground dry breadcrumbs
4 tablespoons light olive oil
½ cup (170 g) liquid honey
1 teaspoon cinnamon
¼ teaspoon ground cloves
½ teaspoon nutmeg
½ teaspoon ground aniseed

Method

Preheat the oven to 325° F (160° C).

Place the breadcrumbs on a baking tray, then sprinkle the oil over the crumbs. Mix together by hand, working the oil evenly into the crumbs. Spread the crumbs evenly on the tray, then place in the oven for five minutes. Remove the tray, allow the crumbs to cool, then place them in a mixing bowl.

In another mixing bowl, add the honey and stir in the cinnamon, cloves, nutmeg and aniseed, mixing well.

Pour the honey–spice mixture into the crumbs and mix together well by hand, then form into balls either the size of hazelnuts or a little larger, the size of meatballs. Place the balls on a tray or large plate covered with waxed paper.

Refrigerate or keep in a cool place until ready to serve. Once cooled, place the *Juraydat* on a serving plate.

KHABISA (A SWEET MADE WITH CRUSHED FRUITS)
BALLS OF CONDENSED PUDDING MADE WITH POMEGRANATE SYRUP

Easy

❧ *Historical version* ❧

Take half a *ratl* of sugar and put it in a metal or earthenware pot, and pour in three *ratl*s of juice of sweet table pomegranates and half an *uqiya* of rose water, with a penetrating smell.

Boil it gently, and after two boilings, add half a *mudd* of semolina and boil it until the semolina is cooked. Throw in the weight of a quarter dirham of ground and sifted saffron, and three *uqiya*s of almonds.

Put it in a dish and sprinkle over it the like of pounded sugar, and serve as balls the size of hazelnuts.

Anonymous, p. 201. Translated by Charles Perry.

Many varieties of *Khabis* or *Khabisa* are found in the source culinary texts in the form of a jellied pudding or sweetmeat. The recipe offered here, however, hailing from Andalusia, uniquely calls for the formation of balls and the use of pomegranate juice.

This genre of sweet derives its name from *khabasa*, 'to mix', the sweet itself a type of condensed pudding mixed with various fruit or nut ingredients. It has reportedly been known from the time of the Prophet Muhammad.

Khabis was such a temptation for Sufyan al-Thawri, a guest of Abu Ishaq al-Farzali, that when presented with a bowl of the sweet he ended up breaking his fast. In Sufyan's defence, he initially refused. It was only after al-Farzali told him that Sufyan's brother Ibrahim had eaten the sweet earlier that day. Although Ibrahim was also fasting, as a good and polite guest he had eaten the *Khabis* to keep his host happy. So it was that Sufyan put his hand in the bowl of *Khabis* and began eating, having learned the good manners of his brother (al-Dhahabi 1360).

But perhaps Sufyan was simply being logical. After all, Arab history reports that 'It is most certain that the rational person every forty days eats *Khabisa* as it preserves his strength' (al-Raghib al-Asbahani II 620). Better news yet, eating *Khabis*, according to one Rabi'a ibn Abi 'Abd Rahman, increases the strength of the brain (Ibn 'Abd Rabbih VI 293).

Seemingly as old as time, *Khabis* was enjoyed by all strata of society, with a choice of ingredients dependent upon financial circumstances and personal tastes.

When it came to the aristocratic taste of the Caliph al-Ma'mun, his preference, it seems, was for *Khabis* prepared like *Bazmaward*, a type of sandwich wrap sliced into rounds (al-Warraq 247, 256).

Different varieties of vegetables, such as gourds and carrots, or fruits, such as dates, apples and quince, were used to make different types of *Khabis*. Al-Warraq's tenth-century cooking manual devotes four chapters to this sweet, giving, for example, two recipes for *Khabis* cooked with apples, specifying his preference for the *Shami* apple variety, which should be peeled, cut, seeded, dried in the sun on a piece of cloth or on a woven date-palm mat, then ground and mixed with flour. The combination is then cooked with butter, to which honey, almond oil, pistachios and rose water are added. Once cooked, this *Khabis* should be cooled, then sprinkled with sugar (253–54).

The popularity and importance of *Khabis* inspired cookbook authors even to stipulate the shape and type of pot in which to prepare it, the type of cooking utensil needed, including, for the cooked variety, the degree of heat necessary when constantly stirring it. Al-Warraq recommends that a *tinjir* (round-bottomed pot) of white lead be used, with an iron ladle (12).

This *Khabis* is chewy, slightly sweet, slightly tart, thanks to the addition of the pomegranate syrup, which in Arabic is called *dibs rumman*. This can be bought in any grocery or supermarket that specialises in Mediterranean groceries.

⋘ Traditional recipe ⋙

Makes about 30 pieces
Preparation time: 25 minutes
Standing time: 5 minutes
Cooking time: 15 minutes

Ingredients
1 cup (200 g) granulated sugar
2 tablespoons pomegranate syrup (*dibs rumman*)
1½ cups (375 ml) cold water
2 tablespoons rose water
¾ pound (350 g) extra-fine semolina
1 cup (95 g) ground almonds
1 teaspoon cinnamon
Pinch of saffron
Confectioner's/icing sugar

Method

Place the sugar, pomegranate syrup, water and rose water in a large saucepan, stir, and then bring to the boil. Turn the heat to medium, and cook until the syrup thickens (about ten minutes), stirring constantly.

Add the semolina and stir over a medium heat for two minutes, stirring constantly. Remove from the heat.

Stir the almonds, cinnamon and saffron into the semolina mixture, then allow to cool slightly, but warm enough that the dough can be handled.

Working quickly with the dough while it is still warm, form into balls about the size of a walnut.

Roll the balls in the confectioner's/icing sugar to coat them, and place on a serving platter.

⤚ Modern recipe ⤙

KHABIS FROM THE ARABIAN GULF

Easy

In Kuwait, in the United Arab Emirates and in Oman, *Khabis* is usually served as a dessert, as a breakfast dish and also during Ramadan when the fast is broken in the evening. It is a pudding-like sweet enhanced with butter and thickened with cornstarch/cornflour. The pine nuts, pistachios and almonds used for the garnish recall the history of *Khabis* as a luxury food of the medieval period.

Serves 4–6
Preparation time: 15 minutes
Cooking time: 20 minutes

Ingredients

¾ cup (90 g) cornstarch/cornflour, dissolved in ¾ cup (190 ml) warm water
½ cup (100 g) granulated sugar
4 tablespoons clarified butter
Few threads saffron, dissolved in 1 tablespoon rose water
½ teaspoon ground cardamom
2 tablespoons toasted pine nuts
2 tablespoons chopped pistachios
2 tablespoons toasted chopped almonds

Method

In a small bowl, thoroughly mix the dissolved cornstarch/cornflour and the sugar, and set aside.

In a small saucepan, melt the butter, then add the starch–sugar mixture and stir constantly over a medium-low heat until the mixture thickens. Reduce the heat to very low, then sprinkle with the saffron–rose water and the cardamom. Cook and continue to stir for two minutes, then spread on a serving platter.

Decorate with the nuts, then serve warm.

MA'MUNIYA ('OF MA'MUN')
RICE-FLOUR PUDDING

Easy

✒ *Historical version* ✒

Take a part of sheep's tail fat and boil it in water until it is cooked and falls apart. Drain the water from it and squeeze out the fat by letting it drip from a sieve into a bowl. Wash rice, pound it and sift it in a fine sieve. Add to it Egyptian sugar. Mix it with the fat in a pot. Cook over a gentle fire until it cooks and thickens. Spread into a dish and throw in it the hearts of whole, blanched and peeled pistachios.

Ibn al-'Adim, pp. 619–20. Translated by Habeeb Salloum and Muna Salloum.

In his book on dream interpretations, fifteenth-century Ibn Shahin renders *Ma'muniya* as a good sign, denoting blessings and goodness, beneficial because it is the food of kings (572). According to al-Ghazali, the Caliph al-Ma'mun (d. AD 833) liked it (31).

Ma'muniya is a slightly stiff pudding made of rice flour, sugar and fat, and falls into the category of *Muhallabiya* (see p.208). There is, however, the variety in which shredded chicken is added, yet it remains a sweet pudding. Its name is derived from Ma'mun, the Abbasid Caliph by whom or for whom it was first prepared.

One of the oldest medieval cookbooks in Europe, the Latin *Liber de Coquina*, includes *Mamonia*, a dish prepared with pounded capon meat, almond milk, honey, rice and spices. While the *Liber* was written in the early fourteenth century, the dish and name most likely originated from the Arabic. Later, English recipe texts would include variations of the name, it first appearing in the English language as 'Mauemene' in AD 1381, with instructions on how to prepare the capon variety by pounding the chicken in a mortar (see 'Mawmenny' in the *Oxford English Dictionary*).

Three recipes for *Ma'muniya* appear in Ibn al-'Adim's work, the second rated better than the first, the third better than both of the others.

Ma'muniya certainly was among the most sophisticated and best of regal sweets. It also proved to be the saving grace for a certain *shaykh* in Egypt. It saved him from being arrested. Al-Shaykh al-Salih al-Majdhub al-Misri (d. AD 1509) was the subject of malicious talk in Egypt. People said he ate *hashish*. One day, while sitting and eating, he was confronted by a soldier, who pulled out his weapon to arrest him. He admonished him, asking how someone such as he, a man of God, could be eating *hashish*. Denying it was the drug, he gave some to the soldier, who was no doubt relieved to discover it to be only a hot dish of *Ma'muniya* (Ghazzi I 167). One could say that no *hashish* was needed here to bring both the *shaykh* and the soldier to a state of euphoria!

We have replaced the fat found in the original medieval recipe with butter. This fat (*al-liya*) is the fat from the tail of a certain breed of sheep in the Middle East known as the Damara or Karakul. These sheep possess fat-tails that were and still are a valued source of cooking fat.

✑ Traditional recipe ✑

Serves 8
Preparation time: 15 minutes
Cooking time: 15 minutes

Ingredients
4 tablespoons unsalted butter
1 cup (160 g) rice flour
1 cup (250 ml) cold water
1 cup (200 g) granulated sugar
4 tablespoons whole pistachios

Method

In a saucepan, melt the butter over a low heat. Stir in the rice flour and the water, mixing well until smooth. Stir in the sugar, and continue cooking until the mixture thickens into a soft paste, after about ten minutes. Spoon into a serving bowl or onto a platter. Sprinkle with the pistachios. Serve either warm or cold.

✑ Modern recipe ✑

SEMOLINA PUDDING

Easy

A speciality of Aleppo, the modern *Ma'muniya* pudding is a direct descendant of the medieval version. Semolina now replaces the original rice flour, with whipped cream as a topping in this modernised adaptation.

The Syrians today use *qashta* (see 'Basic recipes' section) to spread over top of this semolina pudding. However, whipped cream is catching on as the replacement for homemade *qashta*.

Serves 8
Preparation time: 15 minutes
Cooking time: 20 minutes

Ingredients

4 tablespoons unsalted butter
1 cup (167 g) extra-fine semolina
1 cup (240 ml) whole milk
1 cup (200 g) granulated sugar
½ teaspoon almond extract/essence or orange blossom water
¼ cup (65 ml) cold water
1 cup (115 g) whipped cream
4 tablespoons crushed pistachio nuts

Method

Melt the butter in a saucepan, then add and stir-fry the semolina over a medium heat until it turns light brown. Stir in the milk, sugar and the almond extract/essence or orange blossom water, then stir over a low heat, adding a little water at a time, for ten minutes or until the semolina is cooked into a soft paste. Place on a platter, and then spread the cream evenly over the top. Sprinkle with the pistachio nuts, then serve warm.

AL-MUKHANNAQA (THAT WHICH IS SMOTHERED)
SHREDDED FILO PASTRY DRENCHED IN SYRUP

For the experienced cook

⋧ *Historical version* ↺

Take one *ratl* of *Kunafa*, one *ratl* of sugar, one and a half *ratl*s of bee's honey, four *uqiya*s of sesame oil, four *uqiya*s of pistachios. Dissolve half of the sugar with water [to make] the syrup, and pound the other half. Then boil the honey with the sugar syrup. Then add the *Kunafa* to it, and moisten with the sesame oil. Stir until well mixed. Remove from the heat. Pound the pistachios and add them to the pounded half of sugar then sprinkle over [the *Kunafa* mixture], then stir them in. Flavour with musk and rose water.

Ibn al-'Adim, pp. 636–37. Translated by Habeeb Salloum and Muna Salloum.

⋧ *Historical version* ↺

Take two *ratl*s of *Kunafa* and one *ratl* and a half of bee's honey, four *uqiya*s of sesame oil and four *uqiya*s of nut meats. Dissolve half of the sugar with water [to make] the syrup and pound half of it. Then throw the honey over the fire and throw the *Kunafa* over it and feed them with sesame oil, turning them over until it is mixed. Then remove them from the fire. Pound pistachios and add to them the half of the pounded sugar. Sprinkle them over it as you stir, and moisten it with sesame oil. Flavour with musk and rose water. Then place in dishes.

Kanz, pp. 113–14 (#297). Translated by Muna Salloum and Leila Salloum Elias.

Al-Mukhannaqa is shredded filo pastry drenched in a very sweet syrup. *Kataifi*, as it is known today, is very similar to the medieval Arab *Kunafa* pastry (see p.39). Of the many varieties of sweets in the medieval Arabic culinary manuals, this is perhaps among the sweetest. The sweet is smothered with three sweeteners – sugar, *qatr* and honey and possibly, because of this, its name is derived from the Arabic root *khanaqa*: to smother.

Sweets, called *Halwa* in Arabic, relaxed the mind and body, and epitomised that which was good as the finale to any meal. Sweets were part of the meal system and were held with high esteem – no meal could be complete without them. Through poetry they were lauded as the poet would extol the virtues of a beloved. In fact, the Arabic root *hlw* is the same as the root for the description of a pretty woman or handsome man: *al-hilwa* and *al-hilu*.

It seems everyone enjoyed sweets. We know that the ninth-century Vizier Isma'il ibn Bulbul had a very large appetite, and according to one historian ate daily 100 *ratls* of sweets (al-Dhahabi 2115).

The taste for a sweet delicacy after a meal was natural for the elite at the dining table. When the Caliph al-Muqtadir (r. AD 908–932) was invited for lunch by a group of sailors, he naturally assumed that the meal would end with his favourite prepared desserts. However, to his surprise, the host, Ja'far, and his comrades had no idea what these desserts were. He explained that the only desserts of which they knew were dates and oil cake. 'I never knew that there were people in the world who did not eat sweets after a meal!' declared the Caliph (al-Baghdadi VII 215).

The first time we tried this recipe, it turned out much too sweet. We therefore cut back slightly on the sugar.

⤠ Traditional recipe ⤥

Serves 8–12
Preparation time: 30 minutes
Cooking time: 20 minutes

Ingredients

Half the basic *qatr* recipe using rose water (see 'Basic recipes' section)
1 pound (454 g) *kataifi* pastry (shredded filo pastry), thawed according to package directions
1 cup (340 g) liquid honey
2 tablespoons light sesame oil
¼ cup (55 g) caster sugar
½ cup (60 g) chopped pistachios

Method

Remove the *kataifi* from its package and, over a large flat tray, separate the strands of the dough, letting them drop onto the tray. Fluff them up, separating the strands, and cover with a slightly dampened tea towel until ready to use.

In a large saucepan, add the *qatr* then stir in the honey. Over a medium heat, bring the *qatr*–honey mixture to the boil. Lower the heat to medium-low, then stir in the sesame oil.

Stir in the *kataifi*, mixing it well but quickly with the saucepan contents. Once well mixed, remove from the heat and stir in the caster sugar and quarter of a cup (25 g) of the pistachios. Spread the mixture evenly on a flat serving platter, then sprinkle with the remaining pistachios. Once cooled, cut the *Mukhannaqa* into serving pieces.

✎ Modern recipe ✎

> *RUMMIEN FI IL-MAZAHAR, POMEGRANATES WITH*
> *ORANGE BLOSSOM WATER FROM MALTA*
>
> *Easy*

This recipe is another of the many Maltese foods which derives its name from Arabic, in this case *rumman fi ma' al-zahr*, 'pomegranates in orange blossom water'. Simple to prepare, it is crunchy, juicy and, for lack of a better term, 'exotic'.

Pomegranates are believed to have originated in the Middle East over four thousand years ago. It may have been the Phoenicians (Canaanites) who introduced pomegranates to Malta in the second millennium BC, when they settled in parts of the island.

We have found no written evidence that this dish was specifically created by the Arabs. However, the name and its ingredients reveal a strong connection with the Arab presence in Malta and the profound impact of Arab cooking in the Maltese kitchen.

Serves 4
Preparation time: 20 minutes
Standing time: 1 hour

Ingredients

Seeds of 4 medium pomegranates
3 tablespoons granulated sugar
1 tablespoon lemon juice
1 tablespoon orange blossom water

Method

Combine all ingredients in a serving bowl, then chill for an hour. Toss and serve.

RUTAB MU'ASSAL
HONEYED DATES

Easy

❧ *Historical version* ❧

Take freshly plucked ripe, tender dates and spread in the shade and air for two days. Then remove their pits with a large needle or a sharp stick. In place of each pit, put a peeled almond, of the sweet and superior type. Take for every ten *ratl*s one *ratl* of refined bee's honey dissolved with one *uqiya* of rose water and boil over the fire. Skim off its froth and colour with half a dirham of saffron. Throw the dates in it. When it boils, stir gently until they soak up the honey. Then remove from the fire and spread it out on a wooden tray (made from the wood of the heath tree). Once it is lukewarm, sprinkle some scented finely pounded sugar on it. Whoever wants it warm, put musk, spikenard and some spices. Whoever wants it cool, flavour it with camphor and poppy. Place it in glass vessels, and it is not used except when it is cold and in the season of the *rutab* ['soft, moist dates'].

Kanz, p. 129 (#340). Translated by Muna Salloum and Leila Salloum Elias.

When dates reach the stage of ripe and fresh, this is the stage of *rutab*. They are moist and tender, the *rutban janniyan*, according to the Qur'an, that Mary was directed to eat before giving birth to Jesus to ease the pains of childbirth (19:23–25).

Cultivation of dates in the Middle East goes back at least five thousand years. Considered one of the world's most nutritionally complete foods, for the Bedouin of the desert, living and life go hand in hand with the date. Dates are a natural sweet, a gift of God to humankind.

When the Caliph al-Mutawakkil posed the question which was tastier, sweets or *rutab*, the response was 'That which God's hands have produced' (al-Raghib al-Asbahani II 621).

Rutab Mu'assal appears in al-Baghdadi and Ibn al-'Adim's cookbooks as well as in *Kanz*, and differ only slightly in the scents used with the sugar. *Kanz* offers some added advice: for those who prefer it warm, it should be scented with musk and spikenard, for those who want to eat it cold, camphor and poppy should be added (129).

✍ Traditional recipe ✍

Serves 8–10
Preparation time: 35 minutes
Cooking time: 15 minutes

Ingredients

1 pound (454 g) whole ripe dates (packaged or loose), Deglet Nour or Medjool
The same number of blanched whole almonds as dates
¼ cup (85 g) honey
Pinch of saffron diluted in 1 teaspoon rose water
¼ cup (30 g) confectioner's/icing sugar
¼ teaspoon cinnamon
⅛ teaspoon ground ginger
1 teaspoon poppy seeds

Method

Slit carefully each date, and remove the pits.

Gently place in the slit of each date an almond, then carefully squeeze the slit closed to cover the almond.

In a heavy bottomed frying pan, add the honey and saffron–rose water mixture, and mix well. Cook over a medium heat, stirring often, until the honey mixture comes to a soft boil. Bring the heat to medium-low, and carefully add the dates. Cover and simmer for five minutes.

Remove the pan from the heat. Gently roll the dates in the honey mixture in the frying pan and allow to cool in the pan.

Mix the confectioner's/icing sugar, cinnamon, ginger and poppy seeds together, then sprinkle the mixture over each date, or dip each date carefully into the sugar mixture and shake gently, placing the dates on a serving dish.

✍ Modern recipe ✍

DATES STUFFED WITH ALMOND PASTE FROM MOROCCO

Moderately difficult

The Arabs' love for dates seems to be born with them. Whether freshly plucked *balah* (unripe dates) from the date palm tree, or cooked in the tajines of North Africa, they are even more cherished as part of the Arab dessert table. There are the elaborate pastries such as *Ka'k* or *Ma'mul* stuffed with dates or the basics such as date syrup, the breakfast spread *Tamriya* (dates cooked with clarified butter) and date jams. In the Arab Gulf states, an undressed date stuffed with a toasted almond, candied orange or walnut serves as partner to a good cup of bitter cardamom Arab coffee. But it is the stuffed date that is still the favourite healthy sweet across the Arab world, and in this nothing appears to have changed since medieval times.

We were fortunate on one of our trips to Morocco to be there during Ramadan, when we had the opportunity to participate one evening in breaking the day's fast. That night, we were introduced to dates stuffed with an almond paste, something so elegant and yet so simple. And just when we thought that this was the ultimate, the following night our friends broke the fast with dates this time stuffed with a rich pistachio paste. Accompanied by hot sweet mint tea, we had experienced the ultimate in date sophistication.

Makes 20–25 pieces
Preparation time: 40 minutes

Ingredients
1 cup (150 g) blanched whole almonds
¼ cup (50 g) granulated sugar
¼ teaspoon cinnamon
1 tablespoon clarified butter, melted
1½ tablespoons orange blossom water
1 pound (454 g) Deglet Nour or Medjool dates
Confectioner's/icing sugar

Method

Process the almonds, sugar and cinnamon in a food processor until the almonds are powdery. Add the butter and orange blossom water, and continue processing until a smooth paste forms.

Remove the paste, and roll into small cylinders, the number of cylinders the same as the number of dates. The cylinders should be almost the same length as the dates and narrower in diameter.

Make a vertical slit in each date, deep enough to remove the pits but not cutting the dates in half.

Insert a cylinder of almond paste in each date, and press the sides of the date firmly around the paste, leaving a portion of paste exposed. Place on a serving plate and sprinkle with confectioner's/icing sugar.

ᡃ Alternative modern recipe ᡅ

DATES STUFFED WITH PISTACHIO PASTE FROM MOROCCO

Moderately difficult

Makes 20–25 pieces
Preparation time: 40 minutes

Ingredients

1 cup (150 g) whole pistachios
½ cup (113 g) caster sugar
2 teaspoons clarified butter, melted
2 tablespoons rose water
1 pound (454 g) Medjool dates

Method

Process the pistachios and sugar until finely ground, about one minute.

Add the butter and rose water, and process until a stiff paste forms, about one minute.

Remove the paste and set aside.

Make a short vertical slit in each date, deep enough to remove the pits but not cutting the dates in half.

Form the paste into balls, the number of balls equivalent to the number of dates. Mould each ball into an oval shape and place a pistachio ball in each date. They should protrude slightly above the slit.

Place on a serving platter.

RUTAB FI GHAYR AWANIH (SOFT AND MOIST DATES OUT OF SEASON)
DATES SOAKED IN WATERMELON

Easy

ᡃ *Historical version* ᡅ

RUTAB

Take large *qasb* dates, the dates that still have their stems, in the amount needed. Soak in hot water for an hour or so, then wash and spread them out until they dry. Take a watermelon and hollow out the top of it as far as the hand can go down. Remove the pulp from inside of it and soak the dates in it, and cover it. Leave it for a day, and keep checking until they are done. Remove them and put them over a latticed tray. Then arrange them and sprinkle sugar, rose water and fresh sesame oil over them.

Ibn al-ʿAdim, p. 653 (#51). Translated by Muna Salloum and Leila Salloum Elias.

The combination of dates and melon may have had its origin with Abu Hurayra (AD 603–681), a companion of the Prophet Muhammad and a narrator of the Hadith, when he related that the Prophet enjoyed eating fresh ripe dates with a piece of watermelon on top (Ibn Manzur *'Mukhtasar* 3328). This precedent, the abundant supply of various types of melon all over the eastern Arab world and beyond, and their thirst quenching qualities, fostered creative ways to enjoy them.

The recipe calls for the *qasb* date, which is a dried date so dry 'it crumbles in the mouth' (*Taj al-'Arus* 854). The recipe is for dates out of season, and these must be the dates dried and stored for future use. By preparing them this way, the dates are restored to their soft and moist state.

Be aware that in this recipe the process begins 24 hours before they are ready to eat.

❧ Traditional recipe ❧

Serves 8–10
Preparation time: 30 minutes
Standing time: 24 hours plus 2 hours

Ingredients

1 small green seedless watermelon, about 3–4 pounds (1½–1¾kg)
1 pound (454g) whole dried dates, soaked for an hour in hot water then drained and allowed to dry
4 tablespoons granulated sugar
1 tablespoon rose water
4 tablespoons light sesame oil

Method

Cut off the top of the watermelon, then scoop out the pulp. Reserve both the top and the pulp.

Place the dates inside the watermelon and cover with the reserved pulp, then replace the top. Let stand for 24 hours in the refrigerator, turning the melon contents over often.

Remove the dates and place on a rack that sits over a baking tray. Allow to sit for one hour.

Place the dates on a serving platter and sprinkle with the sugar, rose water and sesame oil.

❧ Modern recipe ❧

FIGOS CHEIOS, STUFFED FIGS FROM PORTUGAL

Moderately difficult

In Iberia, the Arabs introduced the cultivation of a variety of figs and almonds on a large scale. This was to influence southern Portugal's confectionery recipes heavily. The Algarve became noted for its superior quality of dried figs. Thanks to this heritage and to Portuguese convents, the country has inherited a rich legacy of sweets and desserts.

These new varieties of figs were planted in the Iberian Peninsula in the eighth century, and by the tenth century Malaga had become a leading exporter of large varieties of them. In the Algarve, where the climate was ideal, figs were cultivated on a large scale then exported, eventually dominating the western European and English markets. Figs were an exportable commodity due to their high sugar content, allowing them to be preserved by sun-drying and thus transportable to other regions of the then known world.

In the Arab East, figs were served after desserts, along with grapes and dates. One variety, the *Wazirà*, was a type of superior fig with very small seeds, sweeter than any other. Its outside skin was the most tender, and 'neither the figs of Syria nor the figs of Arrajan or Hulwan are comparable to them' (al-Mas'udi VII 121).

These Portuguese stuffed figs would pass the inspection of Ibn Jazlah, who recommends that dried figs be eaten with almonds or walnuts.

Makes about 40 pieces
Preparation time: 45 minutes
Cooking time: 15 minutes

Ingredients
¾ cup (75 g) finely ground almonds
6 tablespoons (85 g) caster sugar
2 tablespoons shaved semi-sweet chocolate
¼ teaspoon cinnamon
⅛ teaspoon ground aniseed
½ lemon peel, very finely chopped
2 tablespoons unsalted butter, melted
2 pounds (900 g) whole soft dried figs

Method

Thoroughly combine the almonds, sugar, chocolate, cinnamon, aniseed, lemon peel and butter to make a filling, then set aside.

Preheat the oven to 350°F (175°C).

Stem the figs, then with the forefinger press inside the fig to form a cavity. Stuff, then pinch the top to close, and place on a greased baking tray.

Bake for 15 minutes.

Remove, and serve either hot or cold.

Bibliography

PRIMARY SOURCES

al-Abi, Sa'd Mansur ibn al-Husayn. *Nathr al-Durr*. Ed. Muhammad 'Ali Qurna. 7 vols. Cairo: al-Hay'a al-Misriya al-'Amma li al-Kitab, v. 1981. Print.

Abu al-Fida', 'Imad al-Din Isma'il. *Kitab al-Mukhtasir fi Akhbar al-Bashar*. 2 vols, 7 sections. Beirut: Dar al-Fikr, 1956. Print.

Abu Hayyan al-Tawhidi, 'Ali ibn Muhammad. *Al-Imta' wa-al-Mu'anasa*. 3 sections. Beirut: Dar Maktabat al-Hayaa, 1966. Print.

al-Asbahani, Abu al-Faraj. 'Al-Aghani'. *al-Warraq*. Electronic Village in Abu Dhabi. 2000–9. Web. 25 June 2010: 17, 467, 636, 2555, www.alwaraq.net.

al-'Askari, Abu Hilal. *Diwan al-Ma'ani*. Vol. I. Beirut: Dar al-Kutub al-'Ilmiya, 1994. Print.

— *Jamharat al-Amthal*. 2 vols. Beirut: Dar al-Kutub al-'Ilmiya, 1988. Print.

al-'Asqalani, (Ibn Hajar) Shihab al-Din Ahmad ibn 'Ali ibn Muhammad. *Inba' al-Ghumr bi-Anba' al-'Umr*. Ed. Hasan Habashi. 9 vols. Cairo: n.p., 1969. Print.

— *Raf' al-Isr 'an Qudaa Misr*. Ed. 'Ali Muhammad 'Umar. Cairo: Maktabat al-Khanji, 1998. Print.

al-'Ayni, Badr al-Din Mahmud. *'Iqd al-Juman fi Tarikh Ahl al-Zaman*. 4 vols. Ed. Muhammad Muhammad Amin. Cairo: al-Hay'a al-Misriya al-'Amma li-al-Kitab, 1987–92. Print.

al-Azdi, 'Ali Ibn Zafir. *Ghara'ib al-Tanbihat 'alà 'Aja'ib al-Tashbihat*. Cairo: Dar al-Ma'arif bi Misr, 1971. Print.

al-Baghdadi, Muhammad ibn al-Hasan ibn Muhammad ibn al-Karim al-Katib. *Kitab al-Tabikh*. Beirut: Dar al-Kitab al-Jadid, 1963. Print.

al-Dhahabi, Muhammad ibn Ahmad ibn 'Uthman. 'Tarikh al-Islam al-Kabir'. *al-Warraq*. Electronic Village in Abu Dhabi. 2000–9. Web. 25 June 2010: 1360, 2115, 3817, www.alwaraq.net.

al-Ghazali, Abu Hamid. *Sirr al-'Alamayn wa Kashaf ma fi al-Darin*. Damascus: al-Hikma, 1995. Print.

al-Ghazuli, 'Ala' al-Din 'Ali ibn 'Abd Allah al-Baha'i. *Matali' al-Budur wa Manazil al-Surur*. Port Said: Maktabat al-Thaqafa al-Diniya, 2000. Print.

Ghazzi, Najm al-Din Muhammad ibn Muhammad. *Al-Kawakib al-Sa'ira bi A'yan al-Mi'a al-'Ashira*. Ed. Jibra'il Sulayman Jabbur. 3 vols. Beirut: Al-Matba'a al-Amrikaniya, 1949–59. Print.

al-Husri, Abi Ishaq Ibrahim ibn 'Ali (al-Qayrawani). *Jam' al-Jawahir fi al-Mulah wa al-Nawadir*. Ed. 'Ali Muhammad al-Bajawi. Cairo: Dar Ihya' al-Kutub al-'Arabiya, 1953. Print.

Ibn 'Abd Rabbih, Abi 'Umar Ahmad ibn Muhammad Ibn 'Abd Rabbih al-Andalusi. *Al-'Iqd al-Farid*. 7 vols. Cairo: Lijnat al-Ta'lif wa al-Tarjima wa al-Nashr, 1948–73. Print.

Ibn Abi Usayba'a. *'Uyun al-Anba' fi Tabaqat al-Atiba'*. Ed. Nizar Rida. Beirut: Dar Maktabat al-Hayaa, 1965. Print.

Ibn al-'Adim, Kamal al-Din 'Umar ibn Ahmad. *Kitab al-Wusla ilà al-Habib fi Wasf al-Tayyibat wa al-Tib*. Eds Sulayman Mahjub and Durriya al-Khatib. 2 vols. Aleppo: University of Aleppo, 1988. Print.

Ibn Battuta, Abu 'Abd Allah Muhammad ibn 'Abd Allah al-Lawati al-Tanji. *Rihlat ibn Battuta*. Beirut: Dar Sadir, 1964. Print.

Ibn al-Baytar, 'Abd Allah ibn Ahmad al-Andalus. *Al-Jami' li-Mufradat al-Adwiya wa al-Aghdhiya*. Baghdad: Maktabat al-Muthannà, 1970. Print.

Ibn Durayd, Abu Bakr Muhammad ibn al-Hasan. *Jamhara al-Lugha*. 3 vols. Ed. Ramzi Munir Ba'albaki. Beirut: Dar al-'Ilm li-al-Malayin, 1987–88. Print.

Ibn Hamdun, Muhammad ibn al-Hasan ibn Muhammad ibn 'Ali. *Al-Tadhkira al-Hamduniya*. 9 vols. Beirut: Dar Sadir, 1996. Print.

Ibn al-Jawzi, Abu al-Faraj 'Abd al-Rahman ibn 'Ali ibn Muhammad. *Al-Muntazam fi Tarikh al-Muluk wa al-Umam*. 18 vols. Eds Muhammad 'Abd al-Qadir 'Ata, Mustafà 'Abd al-Qadir 'Ata and Na'im Zarzur. Beirut: Dar al-Kutub al-'Ilmiya, 1992. Print.

Ibn Jubayr, Abu al-Husayn Muhammad ibn Ahmad. *Rihlat ibn Jubayr*. Beirut: Dar Sadir, 1964. Print.

Ibn Kathir, Isma'il ibn 'Umar. *Al-Bidaya wa al-Nihaya*. 14 vols. Beirut: Maktabat al-Ma'arif; Riyadh: Maktabat al-Nasir, 1966. Print.

Ibn al-Kattani, Abu 'Abd Allah Muhammad. *Kitab al-Tashbihat min Ash'ar Ahl al-Andalus*. Ed. Ihsan 'Abbas. Beirut and Cairo: Dar al-Sharuq, 1981. Print.

Ibn Khallikan. *Wafayat al-A'yan*. Ed. Ihsan 'Abbas. 8 vols. Beirut: Dar al-Thaqafa, 1968. Print.

Ibn Manzur, Muhammad ibn Mukarram. *Lisan al-'Arab*. 15 vols. Beirut: Dar Sadir li-al-Tiba'a wa-al-Nashr; Dar Bayrut li-al-Tiba'a wa-al-Nashr, 1955–56. Print.

— '*Mukhtasar Tarikh Dimashq*'. al-Warraq. Electronic Village in Abu Dhabi. 2000–9. Web. 25 June 2010: 3328, www.alwaraq.net.

Ibn Qutayba al-Dinawari, Abu Muhammad 'Abd Allah ibn Muslim. *'Uyun al-Akhbar*. 4 vols. Cairo: Al-Mu'assasa al-Misriya al-'Ama Li-al-Ta'lif wa al-Tiba'a wa al-Nashr,1964. Print.

Ibn Sa'id, 'Ali ibn Musa al-Maghribi. *Kitab al-Mughrib fi Hula al-Mughrib*. 2 vols. Ed. Shawqi Dayf. Cairo: Dar al-Ma'arif, 1953. Print.

Ibn Shaddad, 'Izz al-Din. *Al-A'laq al-Khatira fi Dhikr Umara' al-Sham wa al-Jazira*. Ed. Yahya 'Abbara. Vol. 3, Part 2. Damascus: Wizara al-Thaqafa wa al-Irshad al-Qawmi, 1978. Print.

Ibn Shahin al-Zahiri, Ghars al-Din Khalil. *Al-Isharat fi 'Ilm al-'Ibarat*. Ed. Sayyid Kasrawi Hasan. Beirut: Dar al-Kutub al-'Ilmiya, 1993. Print.

Ibn al-Tiqtaqà, Muhammad ibn 'Ali ibn Tabataba. *Al-Fakhri fi al-Adab al-Sultaniya wa al-Duwal al-Islamiya*. Ed. Mamduh Hasan Muhammad. Cairo: Maktabat al-Thaqafa al-Diniya, 1999. Print.

Ibn al-Ukhuwa, Diya' al-Din Muhammad ibn Muhammad al-Qurayshi al-Shafi'i. *Kitab Ma'alim al-Qurbà fi Ahkam al-Hisba*. Eds Muhammad Mahmud Sha'ban and Siddiq Ahmad 'Isa al-Muti'i. Cairo: Al-Hay'aa al-Misriya al-'Amma li al-Kitab, 1976. Print.

Ibn al-Wardi, Siraj al-Din Abi Hafs. *Kharida al-'Aja'ib wa Farida al-Ghara'ib*. Cairo: 'Abdul Hamid Ahmad Hainafi, 1950. Print.

al-Isfahani, Abu al-Faraj. *Al-Ima' al-Shawa'ir*. Ed. Jalil al-'Atiya. Beirut: Dar al-Nidal, 1984. Print.

— *Kitab al-Aghani*. 25 vols. Beirut: Dar al-Thaqafa, 1983. Print.

al-Jahiz, Abu 'Uthman 'Amr ibn Bahr. *Al-Bukhala'*. Beirut: Dar Sadir, 1957. Print.

— *Kitab al-Hayawan*. 7 vols. Cairo: Maktabat Mustafà, 1938–58. Print.

Kanz al-Fawa'id fi Tanwi' al-Mawa'id. Eds Manuela Marín and David Waines. Beirut: Franz Steiner Verlag Stuttgart, 1993. Print.

al-Khatib al-Baghdadi, Abu Bakr Ahmad ibn 'Ali. *Tarikh Baghdad*. 14 vols. Beirut: Dar al-Kitab, 1931–. Print.

Kitab Wasf al-At'ima al-Mu'tada. See *Book of the Description of Familiar Foods*.

Manoscritto Lucano. Ed. Michael Süthold. Geneva: Librairie Drozs, 1994. Print.

al-Maqrizi, Taqi al-Din Ahmad ibn 'Ali ibn 'Abd al-Qadir ibn Muhammad. *Al-Mawa'iz wa al-I'tibar bi Dhikr al-Khitat wa al-Athar*. 4 vols. Ed. Ayman Fu'ad Sayyid. London: Al-Furqa Islamic Heritage Foundation, 2002. Print.

— *Kitab al-Suluk li-Ma'rifat Duwal al-Muluk*. 4 vols. Ed. Muhammad Mustafà Ziyada. Cairo: Matba'at al-Janna al-Ta'lif wa al-Tarjama wa al-Nashr, 1956–73. Print.

al-Mas'udi, Abu al-Husayn 'Ali ibn al-Husayn. *Muruj al-Dhahab wa Ma'adin al-Jawhar. (Prairies d'Or)*. 9 vols. Trans. C. Barbier de Meynard. Paris: L'Imprimerie Nationale, 1861–77. Print.

al-Muqaddasi, Shams al-Din Abu 'Abd Allah Muhammad ibn Ahmad ibn Abi Bakr. *Ahsan al-Taqasim fi Ma'rifat al-Aqalim*. Ed. M.J. de Goethe. Leiden: E.J. Brill, 1906. Print.

al-Nabulsi, 'Abd al-Ghani. *Ta'tir al-Anam fi Ta'bir al-Manam*. Beirut: Dar al-Kutub al-'Ilmiya, 2004. Print.

al-Nuwayri, Shihab al-Din Ahmad Ibn 'Abd al-Wahhab. *Nihayat al-Arab fi Funun al-Adab*. 5 vols. Cairo: al-Mu'assasat al-Misriya al-'Amma li- al-Ta'lif wa al-Tarjama wa al-Tiba'a wa al-Nashr, 1964. Print.

al-Qadi 'Ayyad. *Tartib al-Madarik wa Taqrib al-Masalik*. 4 vols. Ed. Ahmad Bakir Muhammad. Beirut: Dar Maktabat al-Hayyaa, 1967. Print.

al-Qalqashandi, Ahmad ibn 'Ali ibn Ahmad al-Fazari. *Min Subh al-A'shà fi Kitab al-Ansha*. 5 vols. Damascus: Wizarat al-Thaqafa, 1981–83. Print.

al-Raghib al-Asbahani, Abi al-Qasim Husayn ibn Muhammad. *Muhadarat al-'Udaba' wa Muhawarat al-Shu'ara' wa al-Balagha'*. 4 vols. Beirut: Dar Maktabat al-Hayaa, 1961. Print.

al-Safadi, Salah al-Din Khalil ibn Aybak. *A'yan al-'Asr wa A'wan al-Nasr*. 6 vols. Eds 'Ali Abu Zayd, Nabil Abu 'Amsha, Muhammad al-Maw'id and Mahmud Salim Muhammad. Beirut: Dar al-Fikr al-Mu'asir; Damascus: Dar al-Fikr, 1998. Print.

— *Tashih al-Tashif wa Tahrir al-Tahrif*. Cairo: Maktabat al-Khanji, 1987. Print.

al-Saghani al-Hasan ibn Muhammad ibn al-Hasan. *Kitab al-Shawarid*. Ed. Mustafà Hijazi. Cairo: Majma' al-Lughgha al-'Arabiya, al-Idara al-'Amma li al-Mu'jamat wa-ihya' al-Turath, 1983. Print.

al-Suyuti, Jalal al-Din 'Abd al-Rahman. *Husn al-Muhadara fi Tarikh Misr wa al-Qahira*. 2 vols. Ed. Muhammad Abu Fadil Ibrahim. Cairo: 'Isà al-Babi al-Halabi & Co., 1967–68. Print.

al-Tanukhi, al-Muhassin ibn 'Ali. *Nishwar al-Muhadara*. 8 vols. Beirut, 1971. Print.

al-Tha'alibi, 'Abd al-Malik ibn Muhammad. *Al-Lutf wa al-Lata'if*. Ed. 'Umar al-As'ad. Beirut: Dar al-Masira, 1980. Print.

— *Thimar al-Qulub fi al-Mudaf wa al-Mansub*. 2 vols. Damascus: Dar al-Basha'ir, 1994. Print.

— *Yatima al-Dahr*. 4 vols. Beirut: Dar al-Fikr, 1973. Print.

al-Tujibi, Ibn Razin. *Fadala al-Khiwan fi Tayyibat al-Ta'am wa al-Alwan*. Ed. Muhammad Benchekroun. Beirut: Dar al-Gharb al-Islami, 1984. Print.

al-'Umari, Yasin ibn Khayr Allah. *Al-Rawda al-Fayha' fi Tawarikh al-Nisa'*. Beirut: Al-Dar al-'Arabiya li-al-Mawsu'at, 1987. Print.

al-Warraq, Abu Muhammad al-Muzaffar ibn Nasr ibn Sayyar. *Kitab al-Tabikh fi Islah al-Aghdhiya al-Ma'kulat wa Tayyib al-At'ima al-Masnu'at*. Eds Kaj Öhrnberg and Sahban Mroueh. Helsinki: The Finnish Oriental Society, 1987. Print.

Yaqut al-Hamawi, Shihab al-Din ibn 'Abd Allah al-Rumi. *Al-Arib ilà Ma'rifat al-Adib*. 7 vols. Ed. D.S. Margoliouth. Egypt: Matba'a Hindiya bi al-Muski, 1907; Leyden: E.J. Brill; London: Luzac & Co., 1910. Print.

— *Mu'jam al-Buldan*. 10 vols. Ed. Muhammad Amin al-Khanaji. Egypt: Maktabat al-'Arab, 1906. Print.

SECONDARY SOURCES

Abedi, Asmehan. 'Tunisians' Craze for Sweets'. *North Africa Times*. 9–15 December 2007: 30. Print.

Adamson, Melitta. Ed. *Regional Cuisines of Medieval Europe: A Book of Essays*. New York: Routledge, 2002. Print.

Anonymous Andalusian Cookbook (*Kitab al-Tabikh fi al-Maghrib wa al-Andalus fi 'Asr al-Muwahhidin, li-mu'allif majhul* (*The Book of Cooking in Maghreb and Andalus in the Era of Almohads*)), by an unknown author. Trans. Charles Perry. Web. 25 June 2010. http://italophiles.com/andalusian_cookbook.pdf.

Berthoud, Samuel Henry. *El-Ihoudi*. 2 vols. Paris: L. De Poiter, 1847.

Book of the Description of Familiar Foods (*Kitab Wasf al-At'ima al-Mu'tada*). Trans. Charles Perry. *Medieval Arab Cookery: Essays and Translations*. Maxime Rodinson, A.J. Arberry and Charles Perry. Devon: Prospect Books, 2001: 273–465. Print.

Bottéro, Jean. 'The Cuisine of Ancient Mesopotamia'. *The Biblical Archaeologist* 48/1 (March 1985): 36–47. Print.

— *The Oldest Cuisine in the World: Cooking in Mesopotamia*. Chicago: University of Chicago Press, 2004.

— *Textes Culinaires Mésopotamiens* (*Mesopotamian Culinary Texts*). Winona Lake, IN: Eisenbrauns, 1995. Print.

Burckhardt, John Lewis. *Travels in Syria and the Holy Land*. London: Association for Promoting the Discovery of the Interior Parts of Africa, 1822. Print.

Casas, Penelope. *The Foods and Wines of Spain*. New York: Knopf, 1982. Print.

Constable, Olivia Remie. Ed. *Medieval Iberia: Readings from Christian, Muslim, and Jewish Sources*. Philadelphia: University of Pennsylvania Press, 1997. Print.

Corriente, Federico. *A Dictionary of Andalusi Arabic*. Leiden: Brill, 1997. Print.

Davidson, Alan. *Oxford Companion to Food*. Oxford: Oxford University Press, 1999. Print.

Diaz Garcia, Amador. *Un Tratado Nazar sobre Alimentos: al-Kalam 'ala l-Agdiya de al-Arbuli*. Edición, traducción y estudio con glossarios. Almería: Arráez Editores, 2000, Print.

Dozy, Reinhart. *Supplément aux Dictionnaires Arabes*. 2 vols. Beirut: Librairie du Liban, 1991. Print.

Eigeland, Tor. 'Arabs, Almonds, Sugar and Toledo'. *Saudi Aramco World* 47/3 (May–June 1996): 32–39. Print.

— 'The Cuisine of Al-Andalus'. *Saudi Aramco World* 40/5 (September–October 1989): 28–35. Print.

Freedman, Paul H. Ed. *Food: The History of Taste*. Berkeley: University of California Press, 2007. Print.

Garbutt, Nina, 'Ibn Jazlah: The Forgotten 'Abbasid Gastronome'. *JESHO* 39/1 (1996): 42–44. Print.

van Gelder, Geert Jon. *God's Banquet: Food in Classical Arabic Literature*. New York: Columbia University Press, 2000. Print.

— *Of Dishes and Discourse: Classical Arabic Literary Representations of Food*. Richmond: Curzon, 2000. Print.

al-Hamadhani, Badi' al-Zaman. *The Maqamat of Badi' al-Zaman al-Hamadhani*. Trans. W.J Prendergast. London: Luzac & Co., 1915. Print.

Hassan, Fayza. 'The Sweet and the Savoury'. *Al-Ahram Weekly* 559 (November 2001): 8–14. Web. 25 June 2010. http://weekly.ahram.org.eg.

Hayward, Michael. 'The Roses of Taif'. *Saudi Aramco World* 2/6 (November/December 1997): 2–9. Web. 25 June 2010. http://www.saudiaramcoworld.com.

Herbst, Sharon Tyler. *Food Lover's Companion*. 3rd edition. New York: Barron, 2001. Print.

Hitti, Philip. *History of the Arabs: From the Earliest Times to the Present*. London: Macmillan & Co. Ltd, 1953. Print.

Ibn 'Abdun. *Séville Musulmane au Début du XXIIe Siècle: le traité d'Ibn 'Abdun sur la vie urbaine et les corps de métiers*. Trans. E. Levi-Provençal. Paris: Maisonneuve & Larose, 2001. Print.

Ibn Jazlah. *Minhaj al-Bayan fi ma Yasta'miluhu al-Insan* (*A Systematic Exposition of What is Used by Man*). Trans. Charles Perry (based upon the copy of the *Minhaj al-Bayan* manuscript located in the British Library). Unpublished manuscript, 2003. Print.

Ibn al-Mabrad (or Ibn al-Mubarrad). *Kitab al-Tibakha: A Fifteenth-Century Cookbook*. Trans. Charles Perry. *Medieval Arab Cookery: Essays and Translations*. Maxime Rodinson, A.J. Arberry and Charles Perry. Devon: Prospect Books, 2001: 467–75. Print.

Kitab al-Tabikh fi al-Maghrib wa al-Andalus fi 'Asr al-Muwahhidin, li-mu'allif majhul. See *Anonymous Andalusian Cookbook*.

Lane, Edward William. *The Manners & Customs of the Modern Egyptians*. J.M. Dent & Company, 1908.

Lebling, Robert W., Jr. 'Flight of the Blackbird'. *Saudi Aramco World* 54/4 (July/August 2003): 24–33. Print.

Limet, Henri. 'The Cuisine of Ancient Sumer'. *Biblical Archeologist* 50 (September 1987): 132–47. Print.

Littré, E. *Dictionnaire de la Langue Française: Supplément*. Paris: Librairie Hachette et C., 1877. Print.

Luard, Elisabeth. *The Flavours of Andalucia*. London: Collins & Brown Ltd, 1991. Print.

Mardam-Bey, Farouk. *Ziryab, Authentic Arab Cuisine*. Woodbury, CT: Ici La Press, 2002. Print.

Marín, Manuela. 'Beyond taste: the complements of colour and smell in the medieval Arab culinary tradition'. *Culinary Cultures of the Middle East*. Eds S. Zubaida and R. Tapper. London: I.B.Tauris, 1994. Print.

Marlowe, Jack. 'Zalabia and the First Ice-Cream Cone'. *Saudi Aramco World* 54/4 (July/August 2003): 2–5. Print.

Mendel, Janet. *My Kitchen in Spain*. New York: HarperCollins, 2002. Print.

Miranda, Ambrosio Huici. *Traduccion Española de un Manuscrito Anónimo del Siglo XIII Sobre la Cocina Hispano-Magribi*. Unpublished Master's thesis. Madrid: n.p., 1966. Print.

Nasrallah, Nawal. *Annals of the Caliphs' Kitchens: Ibn Sayyar al-Warraq's Tenth-Century Baghdadi Cookbook*. English Translation with Introduction and Glossary. Leiden: Brill, 2007. Print.

— *Delights from the Garden of Eden: A Cookbook and a History of the Iraqi Cuisine*. Bloomington, IN: 1st Books Library, 2003. Print.

Nur, 'Adli Tahir. *Kalimat 'Arabiya fi al-Lughat al-Isbaniya*. Cairo: Egyptian Universities Publishing House, 1971. Print.

Perry, Charles. (Trans.) *A Baghdad Cookery Book: The Book of Dishes (Kitab al-Tabikh* by al-Baghdadi). Blackawton, Totnes: Prospect Books, 2005.

— 'A thousand and one "fritters": the food of the Arabian Nights'. *Medieval Arab Cookery: Essays and Translations*. Maxime Rodinson, A.J. Arberry and Charles Perry. Devon: Prospect Books, 2001: 487–96. Print.

— 'Cooking with the Caliphs'. *Saudi Aramco World* 57/4. Print. (July/August 2006): 14–23.

— 'Notes on Persian pasta'. *Medieval Arab Cookery: Essays and Translations*. Maxime Rodinson, A.J. Arberry and Charles Perry. Devon: Prospect Books, 2001: 251–55. Print.

— 'Romania and other Arabic words in Italian'. *Medieval Arab Cookery: Essays and Translations*. Maxime Rodinson, A.J. Arberry and Charles Perry. Devon: Prospect Books, 2001: 165–82. Print.

— 'What to order in ninth-century Baghdad'. *Medieval Arab Cookery: Essays and Translations*. Maxime Rodinson, A.J. Arberry and Charles Perry. Devon: Prospect Books, 2001: 217–23. Print.

Roden, Claudia. *A Book of Middle Eastern Food*. London: Penguin, n.d. Print.

— *Mediterranean Cookery*. London: BBC Books, 1989. Print.

Rodinson, Maxime. 'Studies in Arabic manuscripts relating to cookery'. Trans. Barbara Inskip. *Medieval Arab Cookery: Essays and Translations*. Maxime Rodinson, A.J. Arberry and Charles Perry. Devon: Prospect Books, 2001: 91–164. Print.

— 'Ma'muniyya East and West'. Trans. Barbara Inskip. *Medieval Arab Cookery: Essays and Translations*. Maxime Rodinson, A.J. Arberry and Charles Perry. Devon: Prospect Books, 2001: 183–97. Print.

— 'Venice, the spice trade and Eastern influences on European cooking'. Trans. Paul James. *Medieval Arab Cookery: Essays and Translations*. Maxime Rodinson, A.J. Arberry and Charles Perry. Devon: Prospect Books, 2001: 199–215. Print.

Rodinson, Maxime, A.J. Arberry and Charles Perry. *Medieval Arab Cookery: Essays and Translations*. Devon: Prospect Books, 2001. Print.

Salloum, Habeeb. *Classic Vegetarian Cooking from the Middle East and North Africa*. Brooklyn: Interlink Publishing Group, Inc., 2000. Print.

— 'Medieval and Renaissance Italy: Sicily'. *Regional Cuisines of Medieval Europe: A Book of Essays*. Ed. Melitta W. Adamson. New York: Routledge, 2002: 113–23. Print.

Salloum, Habeeb and James Peters. *Arabic Contributions to the English Vocabulary*. Beirut: Librairie du Liban, 1996. Print.

— *From the Lands of Figs and Olives*. New York: Interlink Books, 1995. Print.

Simeti, Mary Taylor. *Pomp and Sustenance*. New York: Alfred A. Knopf, 1990. Print.

al-Tabari, Abu Ja'far Muhammad ibn Jarir. *The History of al-Tabari* (*Tarikh al-Rusul wa al-Muluk*): *The Reign of al-Mu'tasim (838–842)*. Vol. XXXV. Trans. Elma Marin. New Haven, CT: American Oriental Society, 1951. Print.

Tales from the Arabian Nights, Selected from the Book of A Thousand Nights and a Night. Trans. Sir Richard F. Burton. London: Bestseller Publications Ltd, 1985. Print.

Toussaint-Samat, Maguelonne. *History of Food*. Trans. Anthea Bell. New York: Barnes & Noble Books, 1992. Print.

Waines, David. *In a Caliph's Kitchen*. London: Riad El-Rayyes Books, 1989. Print.

— 'The Culinary Culture of al-Andalus'. *The Legacy of Muslim Spain*. 2 vols. Ed. Salma K. Jayyusi. Leiden: E.J. Brill, 1994: 725–38. Print.

Watson, Andrew M. *Agricultural Innovation in the Early Islamic World*. Cambridge: Cambridge University Press, 1983. Print.

Weekley, Ernest. *An Etymological Dictionary of Modern English*. 2 vols. Toronto: Dover Publications, Inc., 1967. Print.

Wright, Clifford A., *A Mediterranean Feast*. New York: William Morrow, 1999. Print.

Zayyat, Habib. 'Kitab al-Hisba'. *Al-Mashriq* 35 (1937): 384–90. Print.

WEBSITES

A Critique of Charles Perry's Translation of *A Baghdad Cookery Book* (published as issue number 79 of Petits Propos Culinaires) and 'His Response' (March 2008): 1–53. Web. 20 February 2013. https://prospectbooks.co.uk/samples/Baghdad-critique.pdf.

Del Rio, Mariano. 'Las Torrijas'. *Group Gastronmómico Gaditano* Año XIII/3. Web. 25 June 2010. http://grupogastronomicogaditano/Articulos/LasTorrijas.htm.

Malzone, Carol. 'Delicious Italy: Sicily dishes: dessert – Sicilian style'. *Delicious Italy*. N.p. n.d. Web. 25 June 2010, www.deliciousitaly.com/Siciliadishes10.htm.

Plouvier, Liliane. 'L'Europe se met à table'. Project paper for DG Education et Culture, Initiative Connect lancée par la Commission européenne et le Parlement européen: Brussels: N.p. 2000. Web. 25 June 2010. http://pagesperso-orange. fr/Noiredenlignelth38/noiredenligneith38/Dos%20licence/liliane%20plouvier%20 historique.pdf.

Serbe, Diana. 'Sicilian cooking: the history and development of Sicilian cooking'. N.p. n.d. Web. 25 June 2010. http://www.inmamaskitchen.com/FOOD_IS_ART/ sicilian_food_cooking.html.

Sobral, José Manuel. 'Culinária e História' ('Culinary Tradition and History'). *Área Metropolitana de Lisboa* (July 2004): 69–85. Ed. João Ferrão. Trans. Richard Wall and Rui Correia. Web. 25 June 2010. http://www.aml.pt/webstatic/publicacoes/ nperiodicas/_html/docs/AMLgentesPaisagensLugares.pdf.

Taj al-'Arus. al-Warraq. Electronic Village in Abu Dhabi. 2000–9. Web. 25 June 2010, www.alwaraq.net.

Wright, Clifford. 'Zeppole di San Giuseppe'. N.p. n.d. Web. 25 June 2010, http:// www.cliffordawright.com/caw/food/entries/display.php/topic_id/4/is/124.

Index